Produce & Conserve
Share & Play Square

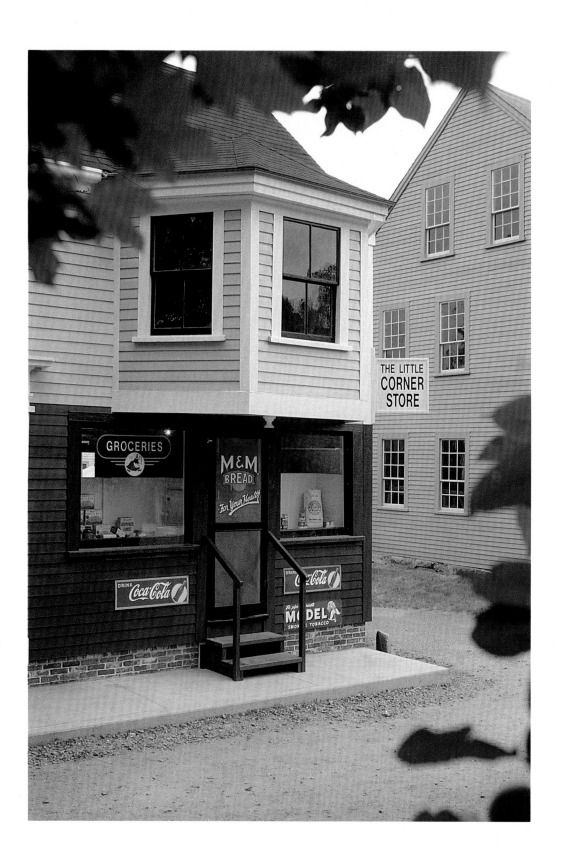

Produce and Conserve, Share and Play Square

EDITED BY

Barbara McLean Ward

WITH CONTRIBUTIONS BY

Tracey E. Adkins

Gregory C. Colati

Karin E. Cullity

Mary Drake McFeely

Ryan H. Madden

Roland Marchand

Sharon V. L. Mullen

Rodney D. Rowland

Carolyn Parsons Roy

Harvard Sitkoff

Barbara McLean Ward

Gerald W. R. Ward

The Grocer and the Consumer on the Home-Front Battlefield during World War II

Strawbery Banke Museum : Portsmouth : New Hampshire

Distributed by University Press of New England

Hanover and London

FRONT COVER: "Keep the Home Front Pledge," 1942 (cat. 1).

BACK COVER: "Save Waste Fats for Explosives," 1943 (cat. 2).

FRONTISPIECE: "The Little Corner Store," Strawbery Banke Museum, as restored to its 1943–45 appearance.

ISBN 0–87451–655–2

Unless otherwise noted, all objects are in the collection of the Strawbery Banke Museum, and all photographs are the work of Bruce Alexander Photography, Chester, New Hampshire.

This publication was funded by a grant from the National Endowment for the Humanities, a federal agency.

Typeset, printed, and bound by The Stinehour Press, Lunenburg, Vermont.

Book design by Christopher Kuntze.

DEDICATED TO

Charles E. Burden

AND THE MEMORY OF

Leslie Clough

PLATE 1. *View of the back section of the "Little Corner Store," looking southwest from the main counter, as restored to its 1943–45 appearance.*

Contents

Foreword   9
Dennis A. O'Toole

Preface and Acknowledgments   11

List of Donors   17

Introduction: Crossroads of a Neighborhood in Change,   20
the Abbotts' "Little Corner Store"
Barbara McLean Ward

Part I   The American Home Front   36
Harvard Sitkoff

Victory Begins at Home: Portsmouth and Puddle Dock   57
during World War II
Gregory C. Colati and Ryan H. Madden

A Fair Share at a Fair Price: Rationing, Resource Management,   79
and Price Controls during World War II
Barbara McLean Ward

The War in the Kitchen   104
Mary Drake McFeely

Suspended in Time: Mom-and-Pop Groceries, Chain Stores,   117
and National Advertising during the World War II Interlude
Roland Marchand

From Corner Store to Convenience Mart: A Footnote   140
Gerald W. R. Ward

Part II   Restocking the Shelves: Strawbery Banke Museum and   144
the Restoration of the Abbotts' "Little Corner Store"
Karin E. Cullity

Preparing the Collection for Display   159
Rodney D. Rowland

Selected Catalogue   171
Tracey E. Adkins, Gregory C. Colati, Karin E. Cullity,
Sharon V. L. Mullen, Rodney D. Rowland, Carolyn Parsons Roy,
Barbara McLean Ward, and Gerald W. R. Ward

Index   238

Foreword

STRAWBERY BANKE, INC., was organized in 1958 and opened to the public as an outdoor history museum in 1965. Its founding resulted from the successful effort by a group of preservation-minded local residents to restore rather than demolish a Portsmouth neighborhood that had been earmarked for urban renewal. Urban renewal became historic preservation, thanks to the efforts of these visionaries.

At first, the founders of the museum planned to create, at the ten-acre site, an idealized representation of Portsmouth during the colonial period. However, over the past 20 years, Strawbery Banke has come to recognize that its urban neighborhood, continuously occupied for more than 300 years, is a unique asset. Because many houses on the ten-acre site are modest dwellings, the museum has the ability to portray the lives of people at all points along the socioeconomic spectrum, from the wealthy occupants of the Chase House and Goodwin Mansion, to the blue-collar residents of the Drisco House 1954 apartment. Today the museum's mission is to interpret more than three centuries of life in an urban waterfront neighborhood and, through it, of other American communities.

Interpretation of 20th-century sites is central to this mission. The first exhibition of a 20th-century space at Strawbery Banke, the Drisco House 1954 apartment, opened to the public in 1988. The "Little Corner Store" restoration in Marden House portrays the neighborhood during World War II; the Dr. Jackson House restoration, planned for 1996, will present the house as it appeared in the 1920s, when it was the home of Abraham Shapiro, a Jewish immigrant, and his family.

These sites all help to further Strawbery Banke's overall intent to portray continuity amidst change, and to help visitors discover the growth and development of the city of Portsmouth and its place in the broader spectrum of American and world history.

By bringing our interpretation firmly into the 20th century, we also hope to build bridges back to the people who built this remarkable neighborhood, and who gave Puddle Dock, named after the shallow tidal waterway that once flowed through its center, its distinctive character. We hope that they will see that their story helps us to understand ourselves as part of history, and that by sharing their history, as well as by exploring the more distant past, we increase our understanding of the world we live in and learn to be better caretakers of its legacy. Our challenge is to draw visitors into more than a simple nostalgic view of the past. As they explore the structures and landscapes that surround Puddle Dock and hear its human stories, they gain an understanding of how the waterway and the activities around it changed with the ebb and flow of the fortunes of the city of Portsmouth, and of the world.

Dennis A. O'Toole
EXECUTIVE DIRECTOR
STRAWBERY BANKE MUSEUM

Preface and Acknowledgments

THIS BOOK focuses on the objects that were sold, and the human interactions that took place, in and around a small urban grocery store. The essays printed here, and the exhibitions they accompany, tell the story of the "Little Corner Store," its proprietors, its neighbors, and its town, during the years of the Second World War, and illuminate the process by which their experiences have been brought to life in Strawbery Banke Museum's restoration of this home and business.

Although Walter and Bertha Abbott founded the Little Corner Store in 1919, the museum has chosen to focus on a later period in the store's history—1941–45—to call attention to the role of the grocer and the consumer on the home front during World War II. All of the aspects of managing a store are discussed—from dealing with wholesale distributors whose supplies had been cut by wartime measures, to computing ration points and posting ceiling prices for customers. The store itself, the family kitchen, and the exhibition that accompanies them all have been installed to reflect a diversity of wartime experiences, and to demonstrate the impact of the war on people in a working-class urban neighborhood. We tell the story of the grocer and the consumer on the home-front battlefield through the people of Portsmouth, New Hampshire, but their experiences resonate far beyond the confines of this small city. We hope that our research and our presentation will make a significant contribution to the history of America during the war years.

In addition to seven introductory essays, this book includes two essays that describe the process of restoring the store and family kitchen and the preparation of the more than 2000 original and reproduction items in the installation and accompanying exhibition. The introductory essays in this book reflect extensive research into the war records of the city of Portsmouth that were filed with the state of New Hampshire in 1947, as well as research in printed and documentary sources available at Strawbery Banke Museum and other repositories. We were privileged to work with Roland Marchand, Mary Drake McFeely, and Harvard Sitkoff, all of whom made extensive use of the local material that we had gathered and placed it within a national and international context.

A great deal of research went into the collecting of 1940s packaging for the project, but because of the huge number of objects involved, it was not possible for us to print catalogue entries for every original example of packaging that the museum owns. We selected 72 items, including printed ephemera and furnishings as well as packaging, to treat in detail, and we have endeavored to illustrate as many related objects as possible throughout the text. Many brand-name items appear throughout the catalogue. Although it has not been possible to include the registered trade mark symbol after every brand name, we have printed all brand names with initial capital letters. All illustrations in the catalogue are from items in the permanent collection of the Strawbery Banke Museum, Portsmouth, New Hampshire, unless otherwise indicated. Bruce Alexander photographed all the museum objects that appear in the book, and took all of the new interior and exterior photographs.

WHEN WE began work on the restoration of Marden House and the installation of the Abbotts' Little Corner Store under a planning grant from the National Endowment for the Humanities, we could already call upon a body of data amassed during an earlier research effort by Alison Fleming and Sherrie Hoyt, research assistants employed by Strawbery Banke in 1984 and 1985. This early effort was instigated by former director James Vaughan and former assistant director John Durel, who first envisioned a three-centuries interpretation for the museum. Unfortunately, the project was put on hold after attempts to obtain corporate funding were unsuccessful. When Jane C. Nylander became director of Strawbery Banke in 1986, she revived the museum's efforts to depict Puddle Dock life in the 20th century, and hired Tekla Haasl in 1988–89, and Judith Moyer in 1989–90, to gather oral histories from area residents. The Drisco House 1954 apartment, the first 20th-century restoration at Strawbery Banke, opened to the public in 1988. In putting together this restoration, museum staff gained significant knowledge of the recent history of the Puddle Dock neighborhood, as well as knowledge of 1940s and 1950s packaging.

Thanks to the insistence of former curator Gerald Ward, and Carolyn Parsons Roy, Karin Cullity, and Rodney Rowland of the curatorial staff, from the very first the museum was committed to furnishing the store with as many original objects as possible. With the support and encouragement of Charles E. Burden, collecting for the Abbott Store project—as it came to be known—began in 1987. Although some items proved difficult to obtain in large enough numbers to fill the shelves—canned goods are particularly rare—the museum has amassed, and will continue to amass, an important collection of 1940s packaging.

Nylander, Ward, Roy, and Cullity began the process of planning for the restoration of the store and kitchen in 1987; in 1989 Strawbery Banke received a small seed grant from the L. J. and Mary C. Skaggs Foundation, and in 1990 the museum was awarded a planning grant from the National Endowment for the Humanities. When I came on board as project coordinator in August of 1990, work on the project—including detailed background research—intensified.

The initial consultants for the planning project—Harvey Green of Northeastern University, Katherine C. Grier of the University of Utah, L. Thomas Frye of the Oakland Museum, Keith Melder of the National Museum of American History, and independent scholars Marjorie Hunt and Jenna Weissman

Joselit—were all struck by the richness of the material that we had at our disposal. With their encouragement, we set out to do a project that was even more ambitious than originally envisioned.

During the course of planning, it became evident that we needed advice on how to conserve the vast collection of 20th-century packages—and often their contents—that we had amassed. We called upon paper conservator Elizabeth Morse of Harvard University (then of the Strong Museum in Rochester, New York), to help us develop a conservation plan. Morse and her colleague at the Strong, Monica Simpson, trained Strawbery Banke personnel in basic conservation techniques and assisted us with particularly difficult problems. Morse's enthusiasm for the project was a great boost to all of us, particularly during those moments when the problems seemed to be insurmountable.

The whole project would not have been possible without the grant from the Skaggs Foundation for the early planning phase of the project; and two grants from the National Endowment for the Humanities, one that provided funding for two years of research and planning, and one that provided funding for the implementation of the project and the publication of this book. I wish to thank Timothy Meagher and all of the panel members who reviewed our grants for their helpful advice.

Stephen Kokolis, Strawbery Banke's director of development, was tireless in his efforts to obtain funding for capital improvements to Marden-Abbott House and for the reconstruction of the garage and the re-creation of the Pecunies's garden. We received a National Endowment for the Humanities challenge grant, as well as grants from the Lou and Lutza Smith Foundation, HCA Portsmouth Regional Hospital, The Davis Family Foundation, and in-kind donations from Cadillac Plastics, Polycast Technical Corporation, and Fernald Lumber.

No project like this can ever come about without the dedication and perseverance of a whole host of individuals. We wish to pay particular tribute to the efforts of the current staff of the Strawbery Banke Museum, and to recognize the key personnel who developed the project and brought it to its final fruition. The project was directed by Jane Nylander and largely carried out by the staff of the collections department: Greg Colati, Karin Cullity, Robyn Mason, Rodney Rowland, Carolyn Parsons Roy, and Gerald Ward. In addition, NEH-implementation funding made it possible for me to hire Ryan Madden and William Moore as research assistants, and Tracey Adkins, Valerie Cunningham, Michelle DeGrappo, and Anne Cullity Hirshberg as project assistants. John Schnitzler was in charge of the physical restoration of the Marden-Abbott House; he was assisted by Terry Flanders, Donald Hickmott, Vera O'Connell, Ronald Raiselis, and Ralph Stevens. The museum's Horticulture department—Anne Masury, Philip Gough, Anne Duncan, and intern Stephen McInnis—researched Victory Gardens and neighborhood gardening patterns, and re-created Emma Pecunies's vegetable and flower garden with the help of Ronald Pecunies. The various facets of the project could not have been completed without the additional help of interns Allan Chin, Dorothy Druvfa, Kate Jones, Sharon V. L. Mullen, Paige Roberts, Rachel Schneider, Sandy

Somers, Scott Strainge, and Susan Wilbur and volunteers Cynthia Nichols, Bruce MacNeil, and Edmund Miller. I would like to thank Peter Hamblett (who served as acting director from June to October 1992), and Dennis O'Toole for their continuing support for the project. They made my job much easier. The education department staff—Mark Sammons, Marcy Samuels, Marlane Bottino, Kathleen Shea, and the museum's interpreters—have made the project come to life for the general public.

In addition to restoring Marden-Abbott House, John Schnitzler and his staff also reconstructed the garage that originally stood behind the Abbotts' house as an exhibition space. Greg Colati, Ryan Madden, and I developed "The Home Front Battlefield, 1940–1945" as the inaugural exhibition. Lisa Blinn did more than just design the exhibition for us; she also worked with all of the subcontractors, helped us to refine our ideas and our label text, and installed the final exhibition. Sonny Gauthier built the finely crafted cases, and helped us in a dozen other ways. Dave Evans silkscreened the often problematic labels. We could not have filled the store shelves without the knowledge and expertise of Jim McIntosh and Donald Daly who made the reproduction boxes, Gary Hoyle of the Maine State Museum who made the remarkable cookies for the bulk cookie containers, and Tracey Adkins who did the original artwork for the reproduction bread wrappers. We would also like to thank Ted Corti and the rest of the staff at Jiffy Copy Center for always being willing to deal with the many special problems involved in making our color photocopies. Russell Rowe at Hovey's Photo Supply made splendid reproductions of period photographs for the book and the exhibition, and Lory and David Pratt of The Framing Alternative framed posters and mounted photographs and advertisements for the exhibition—sometimes at the last minute. Razor and George Burke of Signs by Razor Burke made the reproduction signs for the exterior of the building, and John Foley of Harbour Treats provided candy supplies.

In the course of our research, we called upon hundreds of people who helped us in dozens of ways—both big and small. All in all, 41 people agreed to be interviewed for our oral history archive: Marian and Charles Adams, Nancy Ballard, Rodolphe Blais, Herman Blanchette, Patricia Brackett, Raymond Butler, Catherine Carter, Leslie Clough, Augusta Cunningham, Clarence Cunningham, Valerie Cunningham, Betty Fecteau, George François, Eileen Dondero Foley, William Hersey, Herbert Holt, Muriel Howells, Arthur Hoyt, Joseph Hoyt, Althea Le Beaux, Mike Levy, Robert McManus, Mary McManus, William and Eva Marconi, Joseph Marconi, Dorothy Holt Ober, Kenneth O'Sullivan, Amelia Garland Patch, Sherman Pridham, Anna May and Benjamin Small, Robert Stickles, Ruth Stimson, James Streeter, Alice Sussman, Richard Sykes, Irvin Taube, Blanche Small Washok, and Selvin Watson. We also wish to thank Valerie Cunningham for her generosity in making edited transcripts, from her own oral-history project on the history of Blacks in Portsmouth, available to us for research purposes.

We would also like to thank Gloria Berry, Cynthia Hart, Evelyn Marconi, and Bessie LaCava Sheppard for recommending individuals to be interviewed for the project. Craig Wheeler, director of the Portsmouth City Planning Department, generously provided us with access to the records and reports of his department. Clifford Taylor provided us with a history of WHEB radio, Tony McManus gave us information on the M & M Bakery and on people who could remember its operation, John Taylor shared his memories of the Morley Company and its activities during World War II, and Ronald Pecunies shared memories and provided us with photographs of his mother's garden. Ozzie Henchel provided us with helpful advice regarding antique refrigerators. Andy Mantis of Downeast Donuts shared his astounding collection of local memorabilia with us, and Jim Dolph of the Portsmouth Naval Shipyard provided information and enthusiasm for our effort.

I would like to personally thank all of the students who took my material culture seminar at Tufts University between 1991 and 1993 for their contributions to our research efforts. Philip Jesoraldo, Laura Johnson, Sharon V. L. Mullen, Dorothy Drufva, Amanda Helton, and Alanna Fisher made particularly helpful contributions.

Professional colleagues, dealers, and friends also helped us by distributing information on the project, by leading us to significant resources, and by providing information on specific objects in the collection: We would particularly like to thank John Dumais of the New Hampshire Retail Grocers Association; Debbie Watrous of the New Hampshire Humanities Council; Elizabeth Pratt Fox of the Connecticut Historical Society; Rodris Roth of the National Museum of American History; Richard Nylander of the Society for the Preservation of New England Antiquities; Judy Haven of the Onondaga Historical Association; Henry Duffy of Lyndhurst; Thomas R. Lonnberg of the Evansville Museum of Arts and Sciences; James D. McMahon of the Hershey Museum; Thomas A. Reitz of Doon Heritage Crossroads; Anne Cassidy of the New York State Bureau of Historic Sites; Sally Childs-Helton of the Indiana Historical Society; George Brightville of the Urban Archives at Temple University; Frank Mevers of the New Hampshire State Archives; Bill Ross, Frank Wheeler, and Karen Eberhart of the Dimond Library, University of New Hampshire; Mildred Henshaw of Boynton Public Library; Constance Carter of The Library of Congress; Kate Giordano, Mike Huxtable, and Nancy Noble of the Portsmouth Public Library; Carolyn Eastman and Kevin Shupe of the Portsmouth Athenaeum; Richard Candee of Boston University; Laurel Thatcher Ulrich of the University of New Hampshire; Jonathan Arney of the Center for Imaging Science at the Rochester Institute of Technology; Suzanne and Martin Litschitz of Second Hand Rose; Diane DeBlois and Robert Harris of A Gatherin'; Deborah Ricketts and Lorena Parlee of Cinequest; Richard T. Porter, The Thermometer Man of Cape Cod; Ralph and Terry Kovel; and Alice Kugelman.

Dozens of companies and their employees helped us to gather information on the appearance of wartime packaging and on the history of the various companies and their activities during the war years. Among those who were especially helpful were Elizabeth Adkins of Kraft/General Foods, Jean Toll of General Mills, Roberta Ashe of Brown and Williamson Tobacco, Salvatore Ferrara of Ferrara Pan Candy Company, Tom Frantz of Sheaffer Pen, Desi Gould of Brady Enterprises, Sarah Caldecott of Miles Laboratories, Kathleen Reidy of Morton Salt, Carol Sauchegrow of Pet Inc., Bill Hallier of Sun Maid Growers, James Weidman of Welch's, Walter Marshall of the New England Confectionary Company, E. M. Rider of Procter and Gamble Company, Joyce Rupp of the Kellogg Company, David R. Stivers of Nabisco Brands, Janice Astle of Burnham and Morrill, Marilyn Womer of M&M/Mars, Lori McManus and Philip Mooney of the Coca-Cola Company, Pamela Cassidy of Hershey Community Archives, Jenny Day of the Can Manufacturers Institute, Elizabeth Olenbush of the Steel Can Recycling Institute, Donald Milam of Heekin Can, Thomas DiPiazza of CPC International, Stella Miazga of Canada Dry U.S.A., Paulette Cummings of Hormel Foods, Donna Allen of the John E. Cain Company, and Susan Rogers Killoran of Sands, Taylor, & Wood Company.

Thomas Johnson of the University Press of New England showed initial enthusiasm for the book and continued to encourage us in our efforts to produce a broad treatment of life on the home front. Jonathan Quay of The Stinehour Press saw the book through production and smoothed the way for us at many points during the process. Christopher Kuntze of Stinehour did the handsome design. I would especially like to thank Greg Colati and Michelle DeGrappo for assisting me with the final editing of the book, and for helping me to see the book through the production process. We also wish to thank Angela Thor who undertook the difficult task of preparing the index.

The two men to whom this book is dedicated—Leslie Clough and Charles E. Burden—have been a major inspiration to the project. Before he died in 1991, Leslie Clough was our constant source of information about the Abbotts and their store. The owner of Flowers by Leslie, Clough was always running errands around Portsmouth and would stop by with objects, or to answer a question, at odd times of the day. Charles Burden, as Karin Cullity's essay makes clear, was relentless in his pursuit of period objects for the store. Without his support and enthusiasm we never could have completed the project.

I would also like especially to thank the Abbotts' surviving grandchildren—Joseph Hoyt, Arthur Hoyt, and Herbert Holt—for taking on the job of being our daily consultants on details concerning the store. They have always been willing to drop everything and help us with our minor day-to-day problems. They have become friends.

And last, but not least, all of the authors and I must confess that we often called upon our families to spread the word about the project and to help us to obtain particularly difficult items—we wish to thank them all for their efforts and for their enthusiasm. I would also personally like to thank my family for their love and forebearance during the entire project.

Barbara McLean Ward
PORTSMOUTH, NEW HAMPSHIRE

List of Donors

We wish to thank all of the individuals and corporations who generously donated objects, photographs, and reproductions to the project.

Corrine and Robert Allen
Mrs. F. H. Ameluxen
Lee S. Appel
Claire Audet
James Barclay
Joan Barondes
Nancy E. and Adolph Berounsky
Gloria Ann Berry
Trudy Black
Herman Blanchette
Lisa Blinn
Mr. and Mrs. Henry Blood
Colleen and Greg Bolton
Andy Bosen
Marlane and Robert Bottino
Ronald Bourgeault
Pat and John Brackett
Brady Enterprises
Jessie Bristow
Brown and Williamson Tobacco
Marion Fuller Brown
Pam and Donald Bruce
Virginia Brown
Joan Bullock
Charles E. Burden
Burnham and Morrill Company
Raymond Butler
M. Elizabeth Cady
Capt. and Mrs. John P. Cady, Jr.
John E. Cain Company
Richard O. Card
Margaret S. Carter
Joan and Richard Chalmer
Edith Chase estate

Richard Cheek
Carol F. Clark
Genevieve Clark
Mrs. Norman Clark
Leslie Clough
Mr. and Mrs. D. A. Colati
Connecticut Historical Society
Mr. and Mrs. Fred Connelly
Barbara Cooper
Sally Crockett
Karin E. Cullity
Barbara Dalba
David Darr
Mrs. Ralph Darrin
Edward DeAngelis
Decorative Arts Trust
Del Monte Foods
Clara Devoy
Virginia Dewing Antiques
Mr. and Mrs. David Dickinson
Erica and George Dodge III
Louise C. Donnell
Shawn C. Donohoe
Paul W. Dupre
Colette Dysart
Karen McCarthy Eger
Robert Egleston & Elizabeth Pratt Fox
Dallas E. Elliott
Mrs. Robert Elliott
Dominic Eramo
Charles A. Fagan III
Justine H. Fate
Ferrara Pan Candy Company
Ellen Fineberg & Vincent Lombardi

Gerber Foods
Pauline and John Ford
Margaret Ford
Anne Fowle
Elizabeth C. Foye
Diane and Morris C. Foye III
George François
Mr. and Mrs. Robert G. Fuller
Donna-Belle and James Garvin
General Mills Corporation
Janice Goller
Ida Goodell
Bonnie and Harlan L. Goodwin, Jr.
Nancy and Lane W. Goss
Phyliss Grunert
Great Northern Lights Antiques
Susie and Peter Hamblett
Harbour Treats
Trudy Harrison
Lois R. Hastings
Heekin Can, Inc.
Eugene Hersey
Frank Hersey
Mr. and Mrs. Herbert Holt
Cameron Russell Holt-Corti
Michelle Holt-Corti
Hormel Foods
Katherine B. Howe
Mr. and Mrs. Arthur Hoyt
Mr. and Mrs. Joseph Hoyt
Gary Hume
Mrs. James F. Hunnewell
Sonia K. Johnston
Patricia Joyce
Kellogg Company
Adelia Kennedy
Mr. and Mrs. Kenneth Kincaid
Terry and Ralph Kovel
Kraft/General Foods
Cynthia Lafferty
Sylvia Lahvis
Lawrence Lariviere
Mr. and Mrs. Charles Lawson
Carol and Ralph Lincoln
Stephen Little
Eileen MacDonald

Barbara Marshall
Victor M. Maslov
Mr. and Mrs. Emerson A. McCourt
Peter McDonough
Patricia S. Meyers
Miles Laboratories
George Milliken
Christopher Monkhouse
William Moore
Mr. and Mrs. William Morong
Morton Salt
Janet M. Moulen
Nabisco Brands, Inc.
Nancy Muller
Alex Munton
National Park Service
National Society of the Colonial
    Dames in the State of New
    Hampshire
New England Confectionary
    Company
Christine M. Norris
Elizabeth Nower
Everett R. Nutting
Mr. and Mrs. Donald Nylander
Jane and Richard Nylander
Roberta Nylander
Old Colony Historical Society
Calvin P. Otto
Olga O. and Gerald E. Ottoson
Lois F. Page
Mrs. Jefferson Patterson
Wilton Payne
Laura and Charles A. Phillips
Martha Pinello
Procter and Gamble Company
Lucy Putnam
Ronald P. Raiselis
Milda P. Ringenwald
Rochester Institute of Technology,
    Center for Imaging Science
Sandy Rosnick
Mr. and Mrs. B. A. Rowland, Jr.
Mr. and Mrs. B. Allen Rowland
Mr. and Mrs. Daniel Rowland
Mr. and Mrs. Edward Rowland

Mr. and Mrs. George Rowland
Mr. and Mrs. Rodney Rowland
Margaret and Norman Russell
David Rutherford
Tom Sacramone
Jacquelin and Julius Sadler
Patricia A. Sanderson
Sands, Taylor & Wood Company
Nancy and William Schooley
David Schurman
Seashore Trolley Museum
Nancy Smith
Mr. and Mrs. P.C.F. Smith
Mrs. Philip H. Smith
J. Peter Spang III
Society for the Preservation of New
    England Antiquities
James Stevens
Gail and Ron Stewart, Morley Office
    Supply Company
Glenda Stewart
Margaret Strickland
Sun-Maid Growers
Mr. and Mrs. Alan Swedlund
Mr. and Mrs. William B. Tamplin

Mr. and Mrs. Clayton D. Tenney
Henry Tonole
Gay and Bill Uhde
University of New Hampshire,
    Dimond Library
James Vaughan
Mr. and Mrs. Robert Vibbert
Jeannine and Martin Walsh
Arleen B. Ward
Carolyn and David Ward
Barbara and Gerald Ward
Joan Pearson Watkins
Edith and Edward Watts
Susan Watts
Eric Weinhold
Welch's
Jane Werner
Anne Marie Weston
Ann White
Robert Whitehouse
Barbara Widen
Edith Williams
Nancy and Robert Withington
Mary Ellen Wright
Douglas Woodward

Fig. 1. *Walter Abbott in the "Little Corner Store," ca. 1937. Collection of the late Leslie Clough.*

Crossroads of a Neighborhood in Change, the Abbotts' "Little Corner Store"

by Barbara McLean Ward

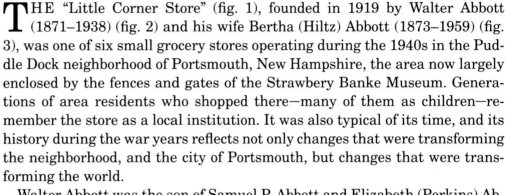

THE "Little Corner Store" (fig. 1), founded in 1919 by Walter Abbott (1871–1938) (fig. 2) and his wife Bertha (Hiltz) Abbott (1873–1959) (fig. 3), was one of six small grocery stores operating during the 1940s in the Puddle Dock neighborhood of Portsmouth, New Hampshire, the area now largely enclosed by the fences and gates of the Strawbery Banke Museum. Generations of area residents who shopped there—many of them as children—remember the store as a local institution. It was also typical of its time, and its history during the war years reflects not only changes that were transforming the neighborhood, and the city of Portsmouth, but changes that were transforming the world.

Fig. 2. *Walter Abbott, ca. 1890, by an unidentified photographer. Gift of Joseph and Arthur Hoyt.*

Walter Abbott was the son of Samuel P. Abbott and Elizabeth (Perkins) Abbott; Samuel's ancestors have been traced back to *Mayflower* passenger John Alden. When Walter Abbott was born, on March 18, 1871, the Puddle Dock neighborhood still had a narrow tidal waterway, also known as Puddle Dock, at its center.[1] His father, a rigger by trade, would have known the area well. Surrounded by warehouses and the homes and shops of craftsmen engaged in the maritime trades, the waterway gave the neighborhood its character as well as its name. The area between Court Street and Puddle Dock contained a mixture of single-family homes and tenements, with a heavy concentration of commercial buildings along the upper end of Water Street facing the Piscataqua River (fig. 4). Both Atkinson Street and Mast Street dead-ended at Puddle Dock.

Bertha Hiltz Abbott was the daughter of Samuel Hiltz and Ellen Powell Hiltz, both of whom were natives of Nova Scotia. Samuel, a fisherman, and Ellen moved their family to York, Maine, about 1870, where Bertha was born. By 1880, Bertha, her older half-sister Georgea, and her younger sisters Isabella and Sarah were living in Portsmouth with their parents and grandparents at 5 Mechanic Street. Three years later they are listed in the Portsmouth City Directories at 9 Charles Street, in the heart of the Puddle Dock neighborhood.[2]

Fig. 3. *Bertha Abbott, ca. 1910, by an unidentified photographer. Gift of Joseph and Arthur Hoyt.*

Walter and Bertha were married in Portsmouth in 1896, and probably settled near the center of town. Although they are not listed in the Portsmouth City Directories until 1908, we know that by 1904 they were living on Nobles Island (see map, fig. 28). In 1908, they are listed in the directory at 7 Mechanic Street, just outside of the Puddle Dock neighborhood, near the riverfront. The Abbotts are first listed as residents in the neighborhood—in an apartment at 96 Jefferson Street (known as the "Block")—in 1910.[3]

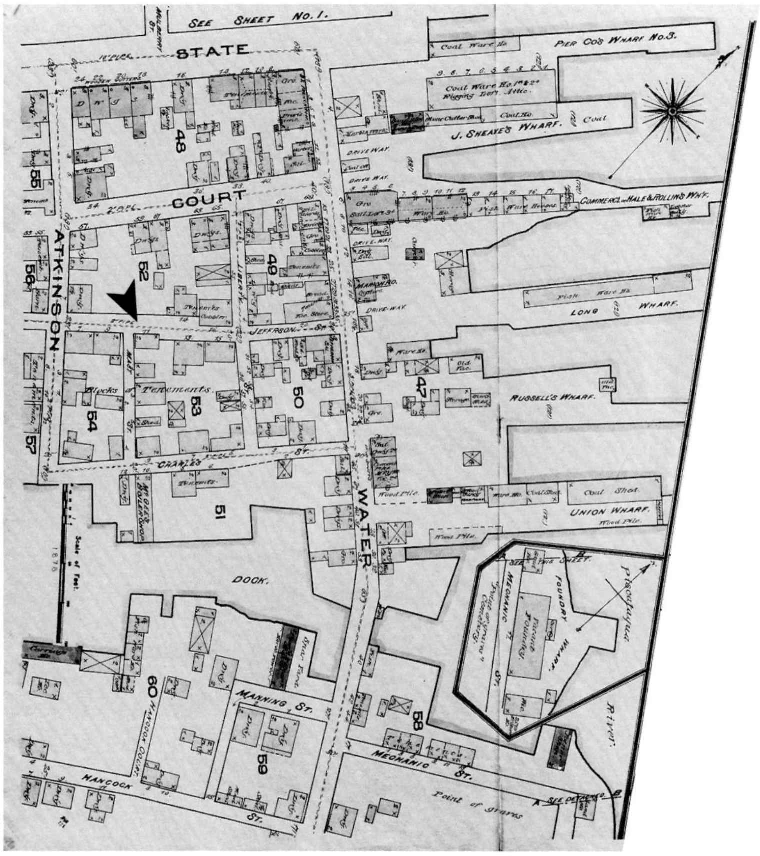

Fig. 4. *Sanborn Insurance Company Map, 1878. The Marden-Abbott House (see arrow) is at the corner of Jefferson and Mast Streets; 96 Jefferson is next door to its right, 95 is directly across from 96. Courtesy of the Portsmouth Public Library.*

The apartment house at 96 Jefferson Street was owned by Bertha's half-sister, Georgea (Georgie) Gould, and her husband Melvin Gould (d. 1916), who operated a successful store at 16 Charles Street (see fig. 62). In 1916 they moved across the street to number 95, and, in 1918, when Georgie, who was recently widowed, and her daughter Etta May Jones decided to sell Marden House and the Block, the Abbotts were the purchasers.[4]

Georgie Gould's decision to sell these two buildings presented the Abbotts with an attractive opportunity. They knew the house at 82-84 Jefferson Street well, and may often have thought that it would make an excellent location for a store. Since at least 1908, Walter Abbott had been employed as a laborer by the Boston and Maine Railroad, where his stepfather, George P. Knight, served as foreman of the freight depot for many years. Bertha, like many other women in the neighborhood, had worked for several years at one of the commercial laundries on Marcy Street. She had also cared for three sons: Walter S., Jr., and Charles Edgar, both of whom died before they were two years old, and Joseph, who was mentally disabled; and three daughters, Grace, Mabel, and Inez. By 1918, all of Walter and Bertha Abbott's daughters were married and on their own. The Abbotts knew that if they bought the two buildings from Gould and her daughter, they could look forward to steady income from rental units in the apartment block, they could fulfill their dream of owning

Fig. 5. *Walter Abbott in the main entrance of the Little Corner Store, ca. 1937. The photograph was probably taken by Abbott's grandson, Walter Holt, who worked for a local photographer. The "Quality Meats" decal on the west window was destroyed when the window broke a few years later. After Walter Abbott died, Bertha Abbott never carried a great deal of meat, and so the decal was never replaced. Collection of Joseph W. Hoyt.*

their own small business (a business in their home would be especially well-suited to Joseph's needs), and, in his new-found spare time, Walter could pursue his interest in local politics. Throughout its history, the Puddle Dock neighborhood has included many buildings which combined domestic and business activities under one roof; the Abbotts' plans for their new house were in keeping with neighborhood tradition (fig. 5).

By this time, commercial waterfront activity had declined significantly on Puddle Dock; public opinion came to favor the idea of filling in the little-used waterway, and the deed was done by 1904 (fig. 6). The resulting open acreage, unusual in this densely settled section of the city, provided an ideal site for scrap metal and other salvage businesses. Salvage businesses quickly occupied converted warehouses and outbuildings along Wallace Avenue (soon to be renamed Newton Avenue) which bisected the former waterway. Immediately following the filling in of Puddle Dock, building density in the neighborhood increased and the population grew with the conversion of some service buildings to dwellings. Notable open spaces began to appear in the neighborhood patchwork as houses and outbuildings were demolished. Many residents engaged in small-scale scrap and junk businesses as one strategy for surviving on marginal incomes.

As the Abbotts' children grew to adulthood, the neighborhood changed in other ways. Increased activity at the Portsmouth Naval Shipyard brought as many as 1500 marines into port at one time, and the brothels along Water Street, as well as the area's many restaurants and boarding houses, attracted large numbers of transients. Crime rose dramatically. During one two-week period in 1912, four murders were committed in the area, and community leaders became increasingly concerned about the district and its hazards.[5]

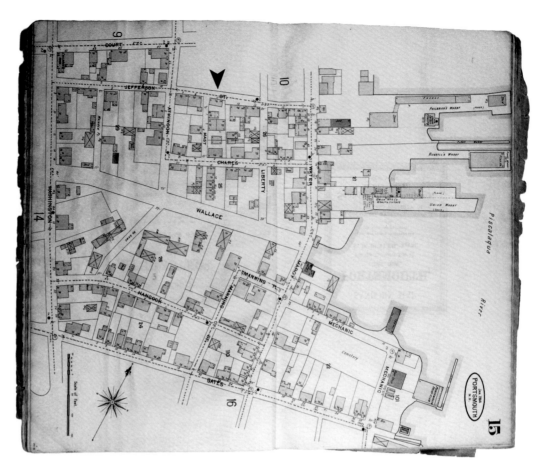

Fig. 6. *Sanborn Insurance Company Map, 1904. Dwellings are identified by "D," stores by "S," and automobile garages by "A." Marden-Abbott House (see arrow) is at the corner of Jefferson and Mast Streets. Courtesy of the Portsmouth Public Library.*

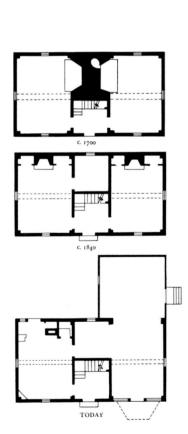

c. 1700

c. 1840

TODAY

Fig. 7. *Evolution of the Marden-Abbott House, first floor plan. Adapted from a drawing by James L. Garvin.*

By the time Walter and Bertha Abbott opened their store, a concerted effort was underway to contain and remove the brothels and saloons. Like most of the other houses in the neighborhood, the house that the Abbotts bought at 82-84 Jefferson Street was an old one. Built about 1722 by mastmaker James Marden, the house had passed through several generations of the Marden family, operators of the Marden Mast Yard at the foot of Mast Lane. In 1827, Marden heirs sold the house to a mariner named Norad Grover. During the 19th century the house had many owners and underwent many physical changes (see floor plans, fig. 7). The house's original central chimney was removed sometime during the first half of the 19th century and replaced with two smaller chimneys along the rear wall. This created a small room behind the staircase on each floor that brought the plan into conformity with several newer homes in Portsmouth. Residents remodeled the house's interior many times during the 19th century; the rear chimneys were removed sometime before the Abbotts purchased the house in 1918.[6]

Before opening the store, the Abbotts made additional changes to the house. They converted the west side of the first floor into a store space by installing shelving and display windows facing Jefferson Street; the lower east room, and the entire second floor, became their living space. They used the downstairs room as their kitchen, but it soon took on the aspect of a "sitting room" during the day when the store was open for business. The domestic portion of the house was set off from the store by the color of the exterior—the store

Fig. 8. *Edith (Abbott) O'Hara, Walter Abbott's sister, on the sidewalk in front of the "Little Corner Store," ca. 1941. Several exterior signs had been added to the building since the time when fig. 5 was taken. Collection of the late Leslie Clough.*

portion of the house was a dark gray, the domestic portion of the house was a lighter shade (figs. 5, 8). Thus, the Abbotts made a clear distinction between domestic space and commercial space, both physically, and psychologically, through the use of barriers, colors, and details such as the formal doorway to the house (see fig. 68).

Inside the domestic doorway, the visitor was confronted with a narrow winding staircase that led to the second floor and an open doorframe that led into the kitchen (see PLATE 2). There was no access to the store from this point; the old door was closed up and blocked off—only a vent to allow the passage of warm air from the house's only register, located in the central hall, was left open. Access from the domestic to the commercial space was through the little room behind the stairs, known as the "Candy Room" because it housed the store's large candy case. From this point family members could easily shift from working in the kitchen to serving customers in the store. Access from the store to the Candy Room was limited—and controlled—by the large case that separated it from the main room of the store (see PLATE 6).

During the 1920s and 1930s the Abbotts, like most owners of Mom-and-Pop grocery stores, shared the work of running the business. There was no separation between female and male work—both partners in the relationship did the same jobs and arrived at business decisions together. We know of only one area over which Walter and Bertha Abbott disagreed: the sale of beer and ale. When prohibition ended, Walter Abbott wanted to add these items to the store's inventory, but Bertha Abbott never liked the idea; she remained steadfastly pro-temperance. Walter Abbott often left the store to tend to his duties as Sealer of Weights and Measures and Bertha Abbott always covered the beer and ale with a sheet during his absence. If asked what was under the sheet, she would reply that it was "nothing"; she refused to sell liquor of any kind.[7]

Whenever Walter Abbott was away from the store, neighborhood children, and the Abbotts' daughter Inez Hoyt, her husband Eugene, and their two sons Joseph and Arthur, helped her in the store. It was a family business, and family members all pitched in to make it work. The hours were long and unforgiving, and Walter and Bertha Abbott always looked forward to their yearly vacation in Owl's Head, Maine. The Hoyts moved into the house during those weeks and took over the operation of the store—it never closed.[8]

The store did well, and the Abbotts soon expanded, adding a small shed onto the house which increased the floor space in the store by approximately 200 square feet (fig. 9, PLATE 1). During the 1930s the Abbotts enjoyed a comfortable lifestyle in spite of the depression. The city welfare department—known then as the office of the Overseer of the Poor—issued vouchers to welfare recipients for groceries and rent. At first the grocery vouchers were general in nature. When city officials saw that welfare recipients tended to spend their vouchers only at the cheaper chain stores, such as the First National or the A&P, they decided to make grocery vouchers specific to certain stores; the stores so favored would change periodically. This policy was meant to support small-store owners at the same time that it supported those in need of welfare

Fig. 9. *Interior view of the shed portion of the "Little Corner Store," ca. 1937. Collection of the late Leslie Clough.*

assistance. For this reason, the Abbott store and others like it prospered in Portsmouth during the depression.[9]

In addition to owning and operating the store Walter Abbott served as Portsmouth's Sealer of Weights and Measures from 1928 to 1934—a position that paid him $400 a year, and provided him with a certain stature in local politics. He ran for the fifth ward City Council seat in 1922 but was defeated; he was elected to the state legislature in 1935. At the time of his death, in April 1938, Walter Abbott was Inspector of Petroleum for the city of Portsmouth. He was mourned by many of the city's most prominent citizens, as well as by the neighbors who he had helped to weather the worst days of the depression.[10]

Walter Abbott saw many changes in the Puddle Dock neighborhood during the nearly 30 years that he lived there. In the mid-1930s, Charles Dale, acting on the instructions of Mary and Josephine Prescott—benefactors of what would eventually become Prescott Park along Portsmouth's waterfront—began to buy up area property. By 1938, the Prescott sisters had demolished many of the buildings along the water side of Water Street, now renamed Marcy Street (figs. 10, 11). Some of these buildings were removed to make way for the park itself, the first phase of which opened to the public in 1940. Two lots facing the park were cleared to make room for two 18th-century houses, moved from elsewhere in the city, that were deemed "appropriate" to face the park.[11] During the same period, other owners had demolished several buildings throughout the neighborhood including the houses that occupied the lots at the corner of Mast Street and Charles Street just down the street from the Abbotts' store. The number of business establishments decreased as well (fig. 12). By 1938, in addition to six small grocery stores, there were four scrap metal yards, a bakery, two shoe-repair shops, and a restaurant operating within the neighborhood's boundaries—Gates Street to the south, State Street to the north, Water Street or Marcy Street to the east, and Washington Street to the west.[12]

As the amount of open land in the neighborhood increased, so too did the number of gardens. Several of the neighborhood's vacant lots were converted into large and elaborate flower gardens; others became vegetable gardens or

Fig. 10. (left) *Marcy Street, Portsmouth, ca. 1938, by an unidentified photographer. This view was taken at the intersection with State Street and looks south toward the Liberty Pole near the intersection of Marcy Street and Newton Avenue. Museum Collection.*

Fig. 11. (right) *Marcy Street, Portsmouth, ca. 1940, by an unidentified photographer. This view was also taken from the intersection with State Street. Museum Collection.*

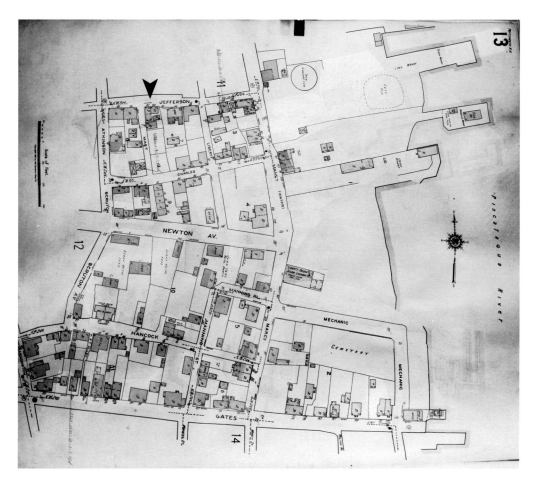

Fig. 12. *Sanborn Insurance Company Map, 1941. Marden-Abbott House is the store, dwelling, and garage located at the corner of Jefferson and Mast Streets. Private Collection.*

the sites for chicken coops. Neighborhood pride, perhaps sparked by the opening of the first phase of the Prescott Park development in 1940, was evident in these garden spots. Some residents remember rose gardens and scrap yards sharing the same lots; others recall that their one most vivid picture of the neighborhood was that it was filled with flowers (fig. 13).[13]

These gardens are intriguing because they represent the neighborhood's response to continuing proposals by outsiders who wanted to change the area. In 1937, Captain Chester G. Mayo, a supply officer at the Portsmouth Naval Shipyard who was intensely interested in the architectural history of the city, resurrected and updated an even earlier plan conceived by Stephen Decatur, member of a prominent local family, and architectural historian John Mead Howells, to combine historic preservation of the area with depression work relief. Colonial Williamsburg was being reconstructed in Virginia, and Mayo became interested in the possibility of developing a similar project in Portsmouth. Mayo was transferred to Brooklyn in 1940, the wartime military buildup began, and the federal government was not concerned with preserving historic buildings. Mayo's project died, but he planted the seed of an idea that would take root in the postwar years, and would add strength to the forces continually working to "rehabilitate" the neighborhood.[14]

After Walter Abbott died, Bertha Abbott's daughters tried to help out in the

Fig. 13. *Re-created Victory Garden of Emma Pecunies, 1993. Leslie Clough's garden was just south of this garden, at the corner of Charles Street and Mast Street.*

store as much as they could, but Bertha Abbott suffered from varicose veins so severe that her mobility was impaired, and eventually they realized that she needed a full-time assistant. Bertha Abbott's granddaughter, and her granddaughter's new husband, moved into the house in 1939 and stayed until 1941. With their departure, again the question arose of who should be asked to help Bertha Abbott with the store. All of her five grandchildren—Dorothy Holt Ober, Walter Holt, Herbert Holt, Joseph Hoyt, and Arthur Hoyt—were either in the service or working in war-related industry; by 1943 all five would be on active duty in the military. Several neighborhood children had helped Bertha Abbott in the store, off and on, for many years. Ultimately, one of the most faithful, a young man then 16-years old named Leslie Clough, was selected for the job. Clough moved into the house in 1941 and stayed until 1949.[15]

During the first few years that Leslie lived with Bertha Abbott he opened the store at 7:00 a.m. and went to school at 9:00 a.m. She then ran the store alone until he returned from school at noon. He cleaned up and stocked shelves, and was back to school within an hour, and then she was on her own again until he returned at 3:00 p.m.[16] Bertha presided over the store from a Windsor chair behind the candy counter, and, according to oral-history informants, rarely moved from that spot unless it was necessary—daytime customers helped themselves to the items shelved in the front room of the store. Although she did not keep seating within the store itself, as her sister Georgie did in her store, Bertha did invite members of her small circle of friends, and some neighborhood children, into her kitchen. She also allowed children to help out with chores around the store, such as dusting the shelves and stocking them with new items.

When Pearl Harbor was attacked on December 7, 1941, Puddle Dock could be characterized as a largely residential area where densely packed older buildings were juxtaposed with scrap metal yards and broad vacant lots. The neighborhood enjoyed a high degree of continuity in its residents, a high level of owner occupancy or near-neighbor ownership, and extended kinship ties reaching over as many as five generations. It was still a viable and vital neighborhood (fig. 14), and its economic base, the scrap metal yards, were important centers of community involvement in the war effort. Zeidman's, the largest of the scrap yards, was particularly active in encouraging the salvage of scrap metal, and paid high prices for it. After December 1941, all salvage metal, rubber, and other strategic materials went to the Allied war effort. Several of the Puddle Dock yards, including the one owned by Sam Hooz, specialized in used auto parts (fig. 15). Piles of tires were particularly valuable when war broke out in 1941 and Japan cut off rubber supplies from Malaysia and the East Indies. More small junk yards appeared in the neighborhood as high wartime prices encouraged individuals to supplement their incomes, as they had during the depression, by collecting salvage materials.

Most residents of the Puddle Dock neighborhood were employed at the Ship-

Fig. 14. *Leslie Clough (right) and a group of neighborhood residents shoveling snow in Jefferson Street, ca. 1940. This view looks west from Liberty Street; the second-story bay window of Marden-Abbott House is visible on the left. Collection of the late Leslie Clough.*

Fig. 15. *Newton Avenue, Portsmouth, ca. 1937, by an unidentified photographer. This view looks east toward the Liberty Pole. Museum Collection.*

yard, in the scrap metal and coal yards (see cat. no. 70), by the military, by the city, or in local businesses. Because of war production and the general scarcity of labor during the war years, nearly everyone who wanted one, could now find a job. Between 1939 and 1943 the neighborhood's population grew slightly. Puddle Dock was within walking distance of the Portsmouth Naval Shipyard, the area's largest wartime employer, and many young married women moved back in with their families while their husbands were in the service in order to free up scarce housing and share child-care responsibilities.[17]

Throughout the history of the store, Puddle Dock was a multiethnic working-class neighborhood. An analysis of the residents in 1943 reveals that 50% of the families in the neighborhood were of Yankee origin, slightly more than 6% were of French extraction (probably French Canadian), a little more than 10% were Jewish, 2% were German or Scandinavian, 13% were Irish, 5% were Italian, 2% were African-American, and one family appears to have been Polish (the ethnicity of the remaining families is unclear).[18]

The Little Corner Store and two others nearby—Georgie Gould's Store and Ethel Smart's Store—seem to have served the predominantly Yankee population (approximately 50%) of the neighborhood, and all three catered to children by carrying penny candy. Oral history informants indicate that the Abbotts' customers were primarily their nearest neighbors. Children were often sent to the store to pick up orders for their parents or to pick out a few items for the nightly meal.[19]

Although the neighborhood was only slightly more than 10% Jewish in the 1940s, Liberson's Market, run by the local rabbi, was patronized by Jewish residents from throughout the city because of the kosher meats offered there.

Black's Market, which stood in close proximity to Liberson's, was also patronized by Jewish customers, but non-Jewish neighborhood residents shopped there as well. Pento's Market probably served an Italian clientele, but not exclusively, for the Italian population of the neighborhood (approximately 5%) was relatively small; the center of the city's Italian community was in the North End of town. Irish residents (approximately 13% of the Puddle Dock population) seem to have patronized Abbotts' and Gould's, and probably Smart's as well. The predominantly Irish neighborhood in town, known as the Creek or "Crick," may have had specialized stores of its own, but by the 1940s in Portsmouth, Italian and Irish foodways were not distinctive from prevailing Yankee foodways. Only the Jewish community remained distinctive in this regard, and as fewer and fewer families worried about keeping strictly kosher, the one thing that set them apart from their neighbors in culinary terms was their avoidance of the local staple—shellfish.[20]

In a neighborhood like Puddle Dock, the profits from a small grocery store were never large. Although no accounts survive from the store, Leslie Clough maintained that the Little Corner Store's business declined during the 1940s.[21] Some items were difficult for small stores to obtain during the war, and the business of operating a store became harder because of wartime measures such as rationing and price controls. Nonetheless, Bertha Abbott knew that her store performed a valuable service to her small community. Her regular customers depended on her for credit and for scarce commodities, and she was determined to serve them for as long as she could.

After the war, however, Bertha Abbott undoubtedly began to notice that her world was changing again. Residents who had saved substantial earnings from wartime work were moving to other parts of town, and to more rural areas. Portsmouth, like many towns that grew rapidly because of war industry, experienced a recession. The number of people on the city's welfare rolls doubled, and many were thrown out of work as the Shipyard reduced its workforce slightly in 1944 and 1945, and then dramatically in 1946. Loan money was not readily available for renovation of older homes, and houses in the Puddle Dock neighborhood continued to suffer from deferred maintenance.

In 1950, at the age of 77, Bertha Abbott was finally persuaded to close the Little Corner Store and to sell her home. She had worked long hours for many years; it was time to retire. She sold Marden House to Bernice and Morris Thurber, and the land on which the Block had stood to her daughter Inez Hoyt. Bertha moved into Inez's home on Hunking Street in the South End where she enjoyed visits from her grandchildren and great-grandchildren. Bertha Abbott died in July of 1959.[22]

1. I am indebted to Joseph and Elizabeth Hoyt for this, and all other genealogical information. Gravestone Record, South Cemetery, Portsmouth, New Hampshire; "Obituary: Walter S. Abbott," *The Portsmouth Herald*, April 21, 1938, p. 12. At the time of Walter's birth, his father, Samuel P. Abbott is listed as residing at 2 Mulberry Street; by 1873 he and his family had moved to 126 Market Street; in 1879 their address was given as 1 Russell Alley; two years later, his widow Elizabeth is listed at the Russell Alley address. *Greenough, Jones, and Co.'s Directory of . . . Portsmouth for 1871* (Boston: Greenough, Jones, and Co., 1871), p. 19; *Greenough, Jones, and Co.'s Directory of . . . Portsmouth for 1873* (Boston: Greenough, Jones, and Co., 1873), p. 15; *Greenough's Directory of . . . Portsmouth for 1879–80*, no. 11 (Boston: Greenough and Co., 1879), p. 3; *Greenough's Directory of . . . Portsmouth for 1881–2*, no. 12 (Boston: W. A. Greenough and Co., 1881), p. 2.

2. 10th Census of the United States, vol. 8, New Hampshire, Rockingham II–Sullivan (microfilm ed.; Washington, D.C.: National Archives of the United States, 1934). *Directory . . . of Portsmouth for 1881–2*, p. 58.; *The Portsmouth Directory for 1883–4* (Boston: W. A. Greenough and Co., 1883), no. 13, p. 71; *1895 Portsmouth Directory*, no. 19 (Boston: W. A. Greenough and Co., 1895), p. 164.

3. *1908 Portsmouth Directory*, no. 25 (Boston: W.A. Greenough and Co., 1908), p. 59; *1910 Portsmouth Directory*, no. 26 (Boston: W.A. Greenough and Co., 1910), p. 57.

4. Rockingham County Deeds, Book 734, p. 481; Book 840, p. 471. Rockingham County Courthouse, Exeter, N.H.

5. Ray Brighton, *The Prescott Story* (New Castle, N.H.: The Portsmouth Marine Society, 1982), p. 59.

6. James L. Garvin, *Strawbery Banke in Portsmouth, New Hampshire: Official Guidebook* (Portsmouth: Strawbery Banke, 1974), pp. 13–15; John W. Durel, "From Strawbery Banke to Puddle Dock" (Ph.D. dissertation, department of history, University of New Hampshire), pp. 166–167.

7. Oral History Interview, July 18, 1990, OH 2 SC 11, Strawbery Banke Museum, Portsmouth, N.H.

8. Oral History Interview, October 2, 1990, OH 2 SC 15.

9. Oral History Interview, February 7, 1991, OH 2 SC 24. This informant worked as a clerk in the office of the Overseer of the Poor during the 1930s.

10. City Records, January 1928–December 1932, pp. 4, 58, 115, 153, 223, Office of the City Clerk, Portsmouth, N.H.; City Records, January 1933–April 1935, pp. 6, 112. In 1932, apparently, the annual salary was reduced from $500 to $400 as part of a cost-cutting measure that reduced salaries of all city officials. Some of the funds generated from these cuts were made available for unemployment relief (City Records, January 1933–April 1935, pp. 9, 50. City Records, January 1921–December 1924, p. 105). Abbott was a Republican and his voting record was generally conservative [Typescript index to *For the Use of the General Court of New Hampshire* (Concord, N.H.: The N.H. General Court, 1901–1949), p. 1, New Hampshire State Archives, Concord]. For further information on Walter Abbott's generally conservative voting record, see the *Journal of the House of Representatives* (Concord, N.H.: Rumford Press, 1935, 1936). "Obituary: Walter S. Abbott"; City Records, January 1936–April 1938, p. 62.

10. "Obesequies: Walter S. Abbott," *The Portsmouth Herald*, April 25, 1938, p. 8.

11. Brighton, *The Prescott Story*, p. 60.

12. *Manning's Portsmouth. . . Directory*, no. 42 (Boston: H.A. Manning Co., 1943).

13. Oral History Interviews, May 11, 1992, OH 2 SC 32, August 27, 1992, OH 2 SC 36, September 28, 1992, OH 2 SC 41.

14. C. G. Mayo Papers, Strawbery Banke Museum.

15. Oral History Interviews, October 2, 1990, OH 2 SC 14, October 2, 1990, OH 2 SC 15, October 12, 1990, OH 2 SC 17. Leslie Clough often said that Bertha Abbott suffered from polio, but family members maintain that she wrapped her legs because she had severe varicose veins. Although her condition limited her mobility, she did not suffer from paralysis.

16. Oral History Interviews, March 25, 1990, OH2 SC2, January 22, 1990, OH 2 SC 2A. Eventually Leslie found the schedule to be too strenuous and he quit school to run the store on a full-time basis.

17. Oral History Interviews, March 5, 1991, OH 2 SC27, April 12, 1992, OH 2 SC 29, September 28, 1992, OH 2 SC 31.

18. Statistics compiled by William Moore,

Greg Colati, and Ryan Madden with the assistance of Cynthia Nichols and Bruce Mac-Neil, from data included in the Portsmouth City Directories for 1939, 1941, 1943, and 1947. *Manning's Portsmouth . . . Directory*, vol. 40 (Boston: H.A. Manning Co., 1939); *Manning's Portsmouth. . . Directory*, no. 41 (Boston: H.A. Manning Co., 1941); *Manning's Portsmouth . . . Directory*, no. 42 (Boston: H.A. Manning Co., 1943); *Manning's Portsmouth and Kittery Directory*, vol. 43 (Boston: H.A. Manning Co., 1947). We would like to thank Valerie Cunningham for providing us with the information about African-American families.

19. Oral History Interviews, May 10, 1990, OH2 SC7, October 2, 1990, OH 2 SC 14, October 2, 1990, OH 2 SC 15, February 15, 1991, OH 2 SC 26, March 5, 1991, OH 2 SC 27, April 12, 1991, OH 2 SC 29, September 28, 1992, OH 2 SC 41.

20. Oral History Interviews, December 12, 1988. OH 1 SC 1; October 18, 1990, OH 2 SC 20, February 12, 1991, OH 2 SC 25.

21. Oral History Interviews, March 25, 1990, OH 2 SC 2, January 22, 1990, OH 2 SC 2A.

22. Oral History Interviews, October 2, 1990, OH 2 SC 14, October 2, 1990, OH 2 SC 15, October 12, 1990, OH 2 SC 17; notes on informal interviews with family members in museum files; "Obituary: Mrs. Bertha Abbott," *The Portsmouth Herald*, July 6, 1959, p. 3; "Obsequies: Mrs. Bertha Abbott," *The Portsmouth Herald*, July 8, 1959, p. 3.

PART I

Fig. 16. *"Her Seven Jobs all Help Win the War!"* Swift's Brands of Beef advertisement published in the January 1944 issue of Good Housekeeping.

The American Home Front

by Harvard Sitkoff

FOR MANY of the people of Asia and Europe, the Second World War brought destruction and grief. The American people, in comparison, suffered very little during the war. The United States was not invaded or bombed. In fact, the war ended the Great Depression: it brought industrial recovery, opened new avenues of opportunity for many women and minorities, and gave the general population its first experience of affluence and prosperity. Despite some serious shortages and inconveniences, most Americans were well-paid, well-fed, and well-housed. Many would remember it as "the good war." Yet it was also a time of domestic upheaval, of drastic and far-reaching alterations in American society. For better and for worse, the war was a watershed, a turning point, in the history of the United States. It profoundly changed the nation; it influenced almost every aspect of American life. It affected the behavior and beliefs of the women (fig. 16), children, and men who stayed home, as well as the soldiers and sailors who fought abroad.

To win the war, the United States first had to mobilize and to convert to war production. To organize this immense task, President Franklin Roosevelt established the War Production Board (WPB) to allocate scarce materials, distribute contracts among competing manufacturers, and limit or stop the production of civilian goods; the War Manpower Commission (WMC) to provide the military, war industry, and agriculture with the necessary personnel; the National War Labor Board (NWLB) to mediate disputes between labor and management, prevent strikes, and curtail excessive wage increases; and the Office of Price Administration (OPA) to check inflation by the imposition of strict price controls. Overall, the federal bureaucracy tripled in size, and the executive branch grew the most. Roosevelt leaned over backward to gain the cooperation of businessmen previously alienated by his policies. "Dr. New Deal" gave way to "Dr. Win the War." The Roosevelt administration appointed many business executives to key "dollar a year" positions in the wartime government, abandoned antitrust actions in all war-related industries, allowed rapid depreciation and huge tax-credits for new plants, and awarded "cost-plus" contracts that guaranteed a fixed profit for war business, all to get vast quantities of war goods manufactured in the shortest possible time. Although these pro-business moves angered some of FDR's liberal supporters, American industry responded by producing a truly astounding 300,000 airplanes, 5600 merchant ships and 79,000 landing craft; 86,000 tanks and 2.4 million military trucks; and millions of rifles, machine guns, and side arms, as well as mountains of ammunition and bombs. Between 1939 and 1944, the peak year of military production, the nation's Gross National Product soared from $88 billion to just under $200 billion. "To American production," Joseph Stalin toasted Roosevelt at the Teheran Conference in November 1943, "without which this war would have been lost."[1]

The United States, the "arsenal of democracy," turned out more than twice as many goods as the Axis countries—Germany, Italy, and Japan—combined. A merry-go-round factory switched to fashioning gun mounts; a pinball-machine maker converted to making armor-piercing shells. Factories that had manufactured silk ribbons began to turn out silk parachutes. To meet the demand for cargo vessels and landing craft, California industrialist Henry J. Kaiser constructed huge shipyards that used revolutionary prefabrication techniques to lower the time needed to build a merchant ship from 105 to 14 days. By 1945, Kaiser, now dubbed "Sir Launchalot," was completing a cargo ship a day. At the Navy Yard in Portsmouth, workers reduced the time required to build a submarine from 469 days in 1941 to 173 days in 1944. That year, in addition to repairing damaged ships, workers at the Portsmouth Navy Yard completed 32 new submarines, compared to four in 1941 and 12 in 1942. In no small part, the United States won the battles of the Atlantic and the Pacific by building ships faster than the Germans and Japanese could sink them. In Detroit, Henry Ford's giant Willow Run factory covered 67 acres, employed 42,000 workers, and at its peak turned out one B-24 bomber every hour. When necessary, whole new industries were created from scratch. The government built some 50 synthetic-rubber plants to compensate for the loss of crude rubber formerly imported from Japanese-occupied areas of Indochina. By 1944, more than 80% of the rubber consumed in the United States was synthetic rubber manufactured from petroleum. Once the world's largest importer of crude rubber, by war's end the United States was the world's largest exporter of synthetic rubber.[2]

The "miracle of production" came at a significant cost. Smog was detected, for the first time, in Los Angeles in 1943. The amount of money the government spent on defense zoomed from 9% of the GNP in 1940 to 46% in 1945; the federal budget mushroomed from $9 billion to $98 billion. Moreover, industrial mobilization accelerated 20th-century trends toward consolidation and oligopoly. Two-thirds of all federal war-production dollars went to the 100 largest corporations. The big had gotten much bigger. The close wartime cooperation between industry and the military, which ensured the defeat of Germany and Japan, created what would later be called the military-industrial complex.[3]

At the same time, with the government providing high support prices for basic commodities, the war years reversed the hard times of the 1920s and 30s for American farmers, agricultural productivity soared, and large commercial farmers mechanized their operations and consolidated many smaller farms into "agribusinesses." While the farm population declined by 17%, farm output rose 20% and farm income quadrupled.[4]

The American worker also profited. Eight million workers who were unemployed in 1939 (17% of the labor force) quickly found jobs, and by 1942 other previously unemployable workers—teenagers, the elderly, minorities, and women—went to work. This rapid expansion of the labor force effectively ended the Great Depression. The number of employees at the United States Navy Yard at Portsmouth rose from less than 1500 in 1933 to 5000 in 1940, 10,000 in 1941, and 20,000 in 1943.[5] Full employment and an increase in the number of two-income families halved the number of American families earning less than $2000 a year, while those making more than $5000 a year increased fourfold.

The war also proved to be a boon to organized labor. In return for a "no-strike pledge" to guarantee uninterrupted war production, the government allowed unions to require workers to maintain union membership throughout the life of a contract. Membership in labor unions grew rapidly, from less than 9 million in 1940 to some 15 million in 1945. Big labor took its seat in the councils of power alongside big government, big business, and big agriculture. Although the National War Labor Board attempted to control wage inflation, and hourly wages increased just 24% during the war, weekly earnings rose 70% as a result of overtime hours and longer work weeks. The real wages of industrial workers increased by 50%. Despite these gains, numerous unions pressed for higher wages and opposed government restraints, and some "wildcat" strikes and other work stoppages occurred, even in war industries. When a strike of coal miners threatened the entire economy in 1943, Congress responded by passing the Smith-Connally Labor Act which imposed a 30-day cooling off period before strikes, prohibited strikes in war industries, and banned union contributions to political parties. This law set the precedent for similar antiunion legislation after the war.[6]

With full employment and lots of overtime pay, and consumer goods scarce, the government endeavored to prevent runaway price inflation. In 1942, the Office of Price Administration froze many consumer prices and rents, and Congress passed an Anti-Inflation Act that regulated agricultural prices and wages. For the most part, government efforts worked: during the last two years of the war consumer prices increased by less than 8% and the total 28% increase in the cost of living between 1940 and 1945 stood in marked contrast to the 62% rate of inflation that had occurred during World War I (fig. 17).[7]

The OPA also instituted a rationing program to conserve scarce materials. Ballyhooing the slogan "Use it up, wear it out, make it do or do without," the OPA rationed canned goods, rubber, gasoline, coffee, butter, shoes, sugar, and meat. Americans endured "meatless Tuesdays" and horsemeat hamburgers, even muskrat meat. They ate sherbert instead of ice cream, and unrationed relish rather than rationed catsup. They put up with imitation chocolate that tasted like soap, imitation soap that did not lather, and ersatz coffee brewed from cracked wheat and soybeans. The walls of the Little Corner Store and others like it were plastered with price ceiling charts and posters indicating the number of ration points for each item. Imported foods disappeared from the shelves, and many products that had once come in metal containers—such as Cashmere Bouquet talc powder and Stickney and Poor's spices—now came in glass jars or paperboard boxes. Storekeepers had to spend a considerable amount of time assisting customers with the frequent changes in OPA regu-

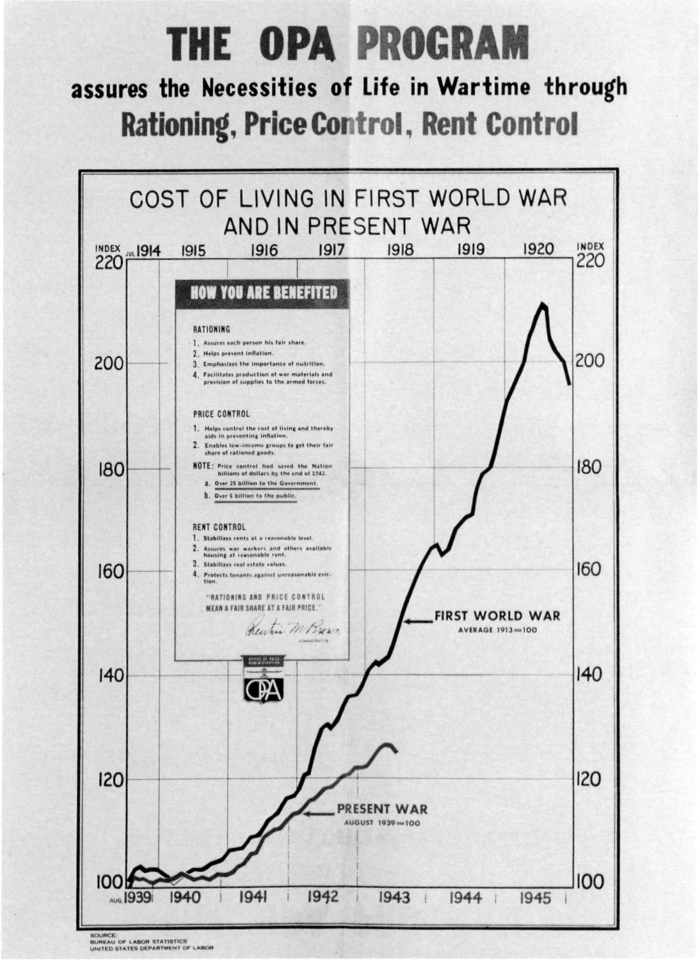

Fig. 17. *"The OPA Program."*
Poster produced using statistics
provided by the Bureau of La-
bor Statistics, U.S. Department
of Labor, 1943. Gift of Richard
Cheek.

lations and in processing their ration stamps. Shortages and changes result-ing from wartime production needs also affected fashion. The need for para-chutes ended the production of nylon stockings, leading to the fad for leg makeup and painted-on hosiery. Skirts and dresses grew shorter to save cloth and the bare-armed look came into vogue, as did zipperless frocks. Fashion retailer Stanley Marcus called the new styles "patriotic chic." For men, the double-breasted, wide-lapeled suit, with vest and cuffed trousers, gave way to the slimmer "Victory Suit"—single-breasted, narrower lapels, no vest, and no cuffs.

In order to speed the production of tanks and airplanes, the government or-dered the automobile industry to stop making cars. On February 10, 1942, the last new civilian car, a Ford, came off the assembly line. Motorists had to make existing vehicles last for the duration of the conflict. Many found it frus-trating, after having had to stint throughout the depression, to be denied what they sought now that they could afford to buy. With fewer goods avail-able for purchase, more income went into personal savings accounts. Some Americans resorted to the clandestine "black market" to get items they de-sired, and many merchants reserved scarce commodities for their best cus-tomers, but most complied with the rationing program as a wartime necessity to speed victory. They learned to handle ration stamps—red for meats and cheese, blue for canned goods—and displayed "A" stamp decals on their car windows to receive three gallons of gasoline per week. (Those with "B" or "C" stickers, doctors, workers officially designated "essential," and congressmen, received a larger weekly fuel allotment.) Both to conserve gasoline and save wear on tires the government also reduced highway speed limits to 35 miles per hour and asked civilians to curtail vacation travel plans (fig. 18). Because of gas rationing, moreover, Americans once again patronized stores within walking distance, giving little neighborhood grocery stores, like the Abbotts', a temporary boost in their battle against the big supermarket chains.[8]

To commute to work, many Americans formed car pools and share-the-ride clubs or switched to public transportation. The Portsmouth Naval Shipyard's newspaper, *The Periscope*, listed rides wanted and rides available. The Shipyard also hired a Portland bus company to transport workers to and from work and operated its own transportation system with 30 old Navy buses.[9] One man who commuted by bus wrote the following lines of poetry in protest:

Fig. 18. *"Is Your Trip Necessary?" Poster published by the Office of War Information for the Office of Defense Transportation, 1943. Gift of Richard Cheek.*

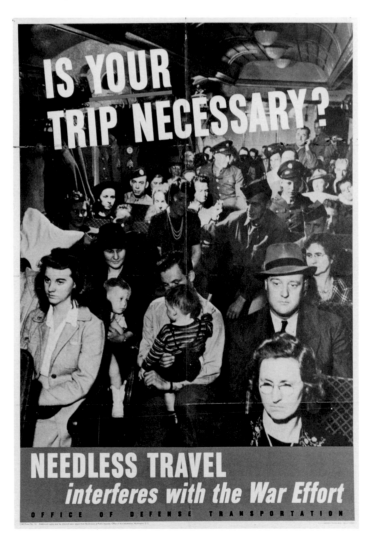

Transportation's a problem
To that we agree
Nevertheless tempting the public
"Travel by bus" signs we see.

   . . . .

Why drape us like monkeys
From the roof of the bus?
Just a case of survival of the fittest
And man you've got to be tough.

   . . . .

Just defense workers trapped
Like rats in a cage.
Re-route half filled buses
Lives and rubber can be saved.

A crack-up surely will be the answer some day
The time to investigate
Is *not then – but today.*

If they can't do the job
Give us gas for the old hack
She got us there before
And by gosh we got back.
      Signed,
      A. I. Harriman
      Oct. 29, 1942.[10]

Some war workers resorted to bicycles; but bicycles also were rationed, and one had to have a certificate of necessity from the local ration board to purchase a new one. So most Americans put up with overcrowded buses and trains.

The liquid assets of individuals, about $50 billion at the time of Pearl Harbor, reached a record $140 billion by the end of 1944. This money would fuel the enormous burst of consumerism, the powerful engine driving the postwar affluent society. Corporate advertisers, eager to keep their names before the public, initially identified their products with the war effort: "Lucky Strike Green Goes to War," "Kleenex to help keep colds from spreading to war workers—America needs every man—full time!" Formfit recommended its brassieres "for the support you need for these hectic days of added responsibility." Many advertisers emphasized bond sales or patriotic messages with their products. "Save your grocer valuable time!" advised Cain's Mayonnaise, "Figure ration points before you shop." The Stetson hat company featured stories of loose talk betraying troop movements under the slogan "Keep it under your Stetson." Gradually, however, advertisers filled their copy with promises of glowing material bounty in peacetime. "Ordnance Today," claimed the Easy Washing Machine Company, "Washers Tomorrow." "When our boys come

Fig. 19. *"Don't Burn Waste Paper." Poster published by the Division of Information, Office for Emergency Management, ca. 1942. Gift of Charles E. Burden.*

home," a shoe manufacturer promised, "among the finer things of life they will find ready to enjoy will be Johnston and Murphy shoes." While American troops still struggled in Guam and Normandy in mid-1944, General Electric cheerfully proposed: *"Now*—we'll be glad to put your name down for the earliest available date on postwar air conditioning and refrigeration equipment."[11]

Government sloganeering—"Slap the Jap with the Scrap!" and "Hit Hitler with the Junk!"—emphasized the need to scrimp, to save, and to salvage used goods such as newspapers (fig. 19), old tires, fats, lipstick tubes, and tin cans. Bing Crosby sang "Junk Will Win the War" and civilians responded with their own slogan, "Give Till It Hurts."

In just three months in 1942, New Hampshire women collected 71,741 pounds of salvage fat, providing enough glycerine to fire 215,223 antiaircraft shells.[12] Countless Americans enlisted as air-raid wardens and civil defense volunteers; others rolled bandages for the Red Cross and participated in scrap paper drives. Children distributed anti-black market pledge cards and enrolled in the Junior Red Cross; they collected old newspapers and discarded tires. The Boy Scouts alone contributed 109 million pounds of old rubber and 370 million pounds of scrap metal to the war effort.

Nearly 20 million Americans planted Victory Gardens. In Portsmouth, the

Chamber of Commerce sponsored rallies, gave out prizes, and printed posters that read "Win the War With Spade and Hoe, Make a Victory Garden Grow." By the summer of 1943 every available plot in town had been planted.[13] Even children became involved: public schools and 4-H clubs promoted the cultivation of home vegetable gardens, and the National Victory Gardens Institute awarded prizes to elementary school students.

The United States spent $321 billion for four years of war (about $250 million a day, ten times the cost of World War I) and to pay for it resorted to deficit financing, borrowing about 60% of the cost of the war. Half of this money was raised through the sale of war bonds. It was hoped that bond sales would discourage inflation by absorbing consumer dollars, and the Secretary of the Treasury confided that the major reasons for promoting bond sales were "to give the people an opportunity to do something," and "to make the country war-minded." Huge bond rallies featured movie stars and other celebrities. While glamorous Hedy Lamarr kissed buyers of $25,000 bonds, her professional rival, Dorothy Lamour, took credit for selling $350 million worth of bonds (fig. 20). Overall, through payroll deduction plans and bond drives, small investors purchased $40 billion in series "E" bonds. Even children bought 25-cent war stamps and faithfully pasted them into albums until they had stamps worth $18.75, enough to buy a $25 bond (fig. 21).[14]

The other 40% of the cost of the war was raised through taxation. The Revenue Act of 1942 increased tax rates and broadened the tax base to make all annual incomes over $600 liable for taxation, thus creating the modern fed-

Fig. 20. *Dorothy Lamour selling war bonds in Portsmouth, N.H., September 16, 1942, by an unidentified photographer. Winebaum Papers.*

Fig. 21. *"Save for Security." Message published in "McCall's Homemaking," section of the April 1942 issue of* McCall's *magazine.*

eral income tax system. In 1943, the Treasury Department instituted the practice of withholding income taxes from workers' wages. By 1945, tax revenues were 20 times larger than in 1940.

The new tax code, with a 94% rate on huge personal incomes and a 90% rate on excess corporate profits, produced the only significant redistribution of income in the United States in the 20th century. The top 5% income bracket, which controlled 23% of the total disposable income in 1939, accounted for only 17% in 1945. While the income of the richest fifth of the population increased by 20% during the war years, that of the lowest fifth of wage earners increased by 68%. Such a reduction in economic inequalities was unprecedented. The size of the American middle-class had doubled; the United States took a giant step toward becoming an economic democracy.[15]

Although only a small portion of the money spent on the war by the United States government was devoted to scientific and technological development, it proved to be decisive in winning what Winston Churchill called the "wizard war." The Office of Scientific Research and Development (OSRD) recruited engineers and scientists and spent approximately $1 billion to perfect vital strategic items such as proximity fuses and radar and sonar devices, as well as to develop jet aircraft, high-altitude bombsights, and the new science of operational analysis. Most notably, about $2 billion went to the ultra-secret Manhattan Project to produce an atomic bomb.[16]

The people of the United States had to be mobilized for the global conflict as well. To restrict the flow of secret information and to shape public opinion, Roosevelt broadened the powers of the Federal Bureau of Investigation to monitor so-called "subversive activities," and created the Office of Censorship and the Office of War Information. These agencies regulated the news media, examined all mail going abroad, and countered enemy propaganda by employing thousands of artists, writers, and advertising specialists to promote patriotism and to present America's role in the war in the best possible light. The OWI worked closely with Hollywood in Frank Capra's "Why We Fight" series and in Louis de Rochemont's "March of Time" newsreels to publicize the nation's official wartime priorities, and to portray Americans in flattering and noble ways. It employed prominent film directors to make documentary films about the war for the armed services. John Ford's "Battle of Midway" for the Navy, Darryl Zanuck's "At the Front" for the Signal Corps, and John Huston's "Battle of San Pietro" for the Army are notable examples. The OWI also produced crude propaganda films like "Letter from Bataan," in which a wounded soldier writes to his mother asking her to save kitchen fats and to his brother-in-law asking him to save razor blades. The film ends with the announcement that the soldier died in the hospital.[17]

The OWI directed Hollywood, radio, and magazine producers to consider the question, "Will this help win the war?" each time they created a new film program or publication. The mass media glorified the American soldier and vilified the Axis troops as sadistic, sinister, dehumanized barbarians. Although the media carefully distinguished between Nazis and other Germans, and between the Italian people and their fascist rulers, no such distinctions were made when it came to the Japanese, all of whom were referred to as Nippos, rats, or subhuman fiends, who always "got what they deserved in the final reel." On the other hand, Hollywood's true-blue Americans, whether John Wayne in "Fighting Seabees" and "The Sands of Iwo Jima," or Humphrey Bogart playing Rick Baines in "Casablanca," always displayed valor and a readiness to sacrifice for the Allied cause. And, whatever the ethnic discord on the home front, the portrayal of Americans on the frontline inevitably highlighted the comradeship between soldiers with different accents and with names of foreign extraction (much like the song "When Those Little Yellow Bellies Meet the Cohens and the Kelleys"). A number of the films that Hollywood turned out in the aftermath of Pearl Harbor, such as "Mrs. Miniver" and "Mission to Moscow," dwelt on the goodness and heroism of our British and Soviet allies. Movie audiences, however, craved escapist entertainment, not propaganda, and Hollywood soon resumed production of its formulaic musical comedies and adventures. The most successful wartime films, like "Meet Me in St. Louis" with Judy Garland and "Yankee Doodle Dandy" with James Cagney, nostalgically portrayed a mythically serene and blissful America.[18]

Popular music also initially featured militantly patriotic themes. "Goodbye, Mama, I'm Off to Yokohama," the first hit tune of 1942, was followed by songs such as "You're a Sap, Mister Jap" and "Praise the Lord and Pass the Ammunition." As the war dragged on, the endless vows of faithfulness ("I'll Keep the Love Light Burning") were superseded by lyrics of lost love and loneliness. "They're Either Too Young or Too Old" and "Don't Get Around Much Any More" expressed the laments of millions of women separated from the men they loved. So, too, did the scores of "dream songs" (such as "I Had the Craziest Dream" and "My Dreams Are Gettin' Better All the Time"), in which love denied in the real world could be achieved only in a dream. By 1945, songs like "Saturday Night Is the Loneliest Night of the Week" and "It's Been a Long, Long Time" implied war-weariness and an impatience for the conflict to end. The single biggest hit of the war years, Irving Berlin's "White Christmas," revealed, in melancholy splendor, the yearning to be home by both soldiers and war workers who were far from their loved ones.

Many stayed home and listened to such music on the radio because of gasoline rationing or the absence of men to go out with. Indeed, radio audiences reached their peak during the war. Listeners especially tuned in for the latest news of the war, and the proportion of broadcasting time allocated to news programs rose from 4% to nearly 30%. The voices of Edward R. Murrow and Eric Sevareid reporting from battlefields became as familiar as those of comedian Jack Benny and singer Kate Smith. Daytime children's programs (and their counterparts in comic books and newspaper comic strips) also went to war. Captain Midnight fought the Japanese on faraway jungle islands; Superman outwitted Nazi saboteurs; and Stella Dallas took a job in a defense plant. Even boxer Joe Palooka enlisted.

Programs analyzing war-related issues, like "Town Meeting of the Air" and "Cavalcade of America," rivaled the popularity of soap operas and situation comedies like "Fibber McGee and Molly." Almost always, radio stations went on and off the air with pleas to their listeners to give blood, become air-raid wardens, donate scrap, and learn first-aid. *The Portsmouth Herald*, like many local newspapers, devoted about half its space to war news, and filled its columns with stories about Portsmouth civilian defense activities, aircraft spotter services, blood bank and bond drives, the recruitment of war workers, collections of fats, clothing, and paper, canning instructions, weekly rationing updates, and recipes for nutritious meals that could be prepared without meat or butter.

The American reading public turned increasingly to nonfiction during the war, although mysteries and historical romances remained popular, and the biggest best-sellers were religious novels like Lloyd C. Douglas's *The Robe,* and *The Apostle* by Sholem Asch. Few war novels were published; readers preferred real accounts of battles like Richard Tregaski's *Guadalcanal Diary,* William L. White's *They Were Expendable*, and the insightful *Here's Your War* and *Brave Men* by Ernie Pyle. Other best-selling works of fiction, such as the autobiographical *See Here, Private Hargrove* by Marion Hargrove, and especially Bill Mauldin's *Up Front*, with its weary, dirty, unshaven Willie and Joe, gave civilians a glimpse of the foot-soldier's irreverence for officers and contempt for men in the rear echelons or back home. The GIs, named after the

"Government Issue" stamped on all their gear, saw their military status as something temporary, a duty reluctantly accepted so that they could return to a familiar, secure America. But home would never be the same again. Sweeping alterations in American society had challenged established values, redefined traditional relationships, and created unaccustomed problems and tensions.[19]

Nothing did more to transform the social landscape than the vast internal migration of an already mobile people. It brought new jobs, new living conditions, new opportunities, new temptations, new problems, new ways of life. In addition to the 15 million young men in the armed forces who left their homes for distant training camps and for service overseas, another 15 million people moved in search of lucrative employment at the booming aircraft plants, munitions factories, and shipyards. Wives and sweethearts followed their loved ones from one job and military base to another; and some six million Americans left farms to live and work in the city. They moved to Portsmouth, Detroit, and Pittsburgh, to Norfolk, Virginia, and Charleston, South Carolina, and, most of all, to the three Pacific coast states, where more than half the wartime shipbuilding and airplane manufacturing took place. California alone added two million to its population in less than five years. One observer of the steady stream of cars heading west thought it was just like *The Grapes of Wrath*, "minus the poverty and hopelessness."[20]

This nation on the move created severe social problems. Housing near war plants was in short supply; hundreds of thousands of Americans took up temporary residence in converted garages, tent cities, trailer camps, overpriced hotels and rooming houses, even in their own automobiles. Despite the opening of several hundred new housing units in the government-built Wentworth Acres and Pannaway Manor housing projects in Portsmouth, and the renting of rooms by homeowners who had never before done so, many of the new workers at the Portsmouth Navy Yard and the Harbor Defenses could never find regular lodging. The overcrowded conditions placed huge strains on family and community life. High rates of divorce, mental illness, family violence, and juvenile delinquency reflected the disruptions caused by the lack of privacy, the sense of impermanence, the uneasiness of the unfamiliar, and the competition for scarce resources. Few boom communities were able to supply their suddenly swollen populations with adequate transportation, or with recreation and social services. Many overcrowded school districts could not find classrooms or teachers for the influx of new students. And the teacher shortage was intensified by the draft and the lure of higher wages in war industries, causing a loss of 350,000 experienced teachers.[21] The Portsmouth Rationing Board complained that their allocations were based on a population of less than 25,000, when the actual population of the area had swollen to more than 40,000.[22]

The demand for workers also led to a dramatic rise in female employment, from 14 million in 1940 to 19 million by 1945. Millions of women responded to songs like "We're the Janes Who Make the Planes" and to advertisements urging them to "do your share," to "help save lives," and to "release able-bodied men for fighting," by donning slacks, putting their hair in bandannas, and going to work in defense plants. Less than a quarter of the labor force in 1940, by the war's end 36% of all civilian workers were women. More startling to many—since the pre-war female work force had been composed overwhelmingly of young, single women—75% of the new women workers were married, 60% were over 35, and more than a third were mothers of young children.[23]

The shock of Pearl Harbor overcame some traditional notions of a woman's place. "Do the job HE left behind," the billboards exhorted. Replacing the men serving in the armed forces, women comprised 70% of the editorial staff of the wartime *Portsmouth Herald*. Women entered industries once viewed as exclusively male, and performed tasks once considered unladylike, such as tending blast furnaces in steel mills, welding hulls in shipyards, running forklifts, and driving taxis and buses. "Rosie the Riveter," in the words of a popular song was "making history working for victory, helping her boyfriend in the Marines by working overtime on the riveting machine."[24]

Throughout the war, however, female workers continued to do jobs classified as "women's work" and to work in the all-female shops of defense plants, under male supervisors and managers. Employers ignored rules requiring them to pay women the same wages as men were paid for the same work, and usually excluded women from management positions. They did so because of the prevailing belief that war work was temporary and women were working not for themselves but simply to support the men at war. "A woman is a substitute," claimed a War Department brochure, "like plastic instead of metal." Wartime work was often pictured as just an extension of women's traditional roles as wives and mothers (fig. 16), and only 18% of the respondents in a public opinion poll in 1945 approved of married women working. Business and union leaders proclaimed that women should give their jobs to returning veterans after the war but many women were reluctant to do so.[25]

Because of these traditional convictions the government generally opposed the establishment of child-care centers for employed women. The clergy opposed them and some people feared they would mean an increased tax burden. The dominant concern, according to the New Hampshire State Planning and Development Commission, was "that if child care centers were established they would encourage mothers to go to work, and make it easy for them to neglect their primary duty and field of greatest usefulness, namely, the care of their home and children."[26]

Consequently, the young suffered. Newspaper stories about "eight hour orphans" and "latch-key children" became common, as did accounts of movie theaters that served as dumping grounds for youngsters, and mothers who locked their children into cars in war-plant parking lots while they completed their work shifts. Numerous articles focused on the unsupervised teenage girls, known as "Cuddle Bunnies" and "Victory Girls," who congregated at bus depots and train stations, dressed in their Sloppy Joe sweaters and bobby sox, waiting to bestow their favors on lonely servicemen. "The chief problem with respect to sexual promiscuity seems to be with the younger girls," the New Hampshire State Planning and Development Commission's survey of

Portsmouth reported, describing them as "those who may be termed amateurs, whose general attitude seems to be that they are working for the cause and are providing entertainment for the servicemen. This is rather a serious problem, and it needs to be checked."[27]

Although the war had an obvious and significant impact on women and the family, the consequences were multifaceted and even contradictory. Although the divorce rate climbed, the marriage and birth rates rose to their highest levels in two decades. The baby boom began: the war years added 6.5 million people to the population, compared to just three million during the 1930s; at the Portsmouth Hospital, the number of births rose from 298 in 1939 to 714 in 1943.[28]

While many women remained content to tend Victory Gardens, or to prepare nutritious meals while respecting the rationing regulations, 300,000 women joined the armed forces, and for the first time in American history they served in positions other than that of nurse. And while millions of women contentedly gave up their jobs in search of the domestic stability that they had sadly missed during the war, just as many sought to maintain the income and self-esteem that they had earned in contributing to the war effort. As nothing had before, the wartime experience proved the capabilities of American women and undermined, however subtly, the long-held belief that woman's *only* proper place was in the home.[29]

The war had an even greater impact on African-Americans. Building on the momentum generated in the New Deal era, Blacks launched the modern civil rights movement during World War II. And by the end of the war, they would be prepared—psychologically, politically, and economically—to battle Jim Crow laws in a manner hardly foreseeable just a decade or so earlier. Unlike the First World War, when W.E.B. DuBois called upon African-Americans to "forget our special grievances" and "close ranks" behind President Wilson, no prominent Black leader or organization declared that the struggle for racial equality at home be halted while the United States fought the Axis powers. Instead, with near-unanimity African-Americans backed the contention of the NAACP that the war provided Blacks with the opportunity "to persuade, embarrass, compel and shame our government and our nation . . . into a more enlightened attitude toward a tenth of its people." This time, the Negro press declared, Blacks would wage a "Double V" campaign, against both the enemy overseas and racism on the home front; similarly, Black politicians demanded that the war be a "Civil War II" to destroy racial discrimination in the United States as well as Nazi racism. African-Americans responded with a militancy rarely before seen in Black communities.[30]

The preparations for war during 1940 and 1941 had effectively ended white unemployment, but Blacks profited little from the revival of prosperity. They continued to be denied equal access to the military and to jobs in the defense industry. Many local draft boards refused to accept Blacks. The Army accepted only a limited number of Black enlistees who were confined to segregated non-combatant units as laborers and stevedores, and maintained a lily-white Air Corps. The Marine Corps and Coast Guard were lily-white as well, and the

Navy accepted an even smaller percentage of Blacks than the Army, most of whom served in menial positions such as mess steward and cook.

In June 1941, Roosevelt issued Executive Order 8802, the first presidential directive on race since Reconstruction. Although it said nothing about discrimination in the armed forces, it prohibited discriminatory employment practices by the federal government and by all labor unions and businesses engaged in war-related work, and it established the President's Committee on Fair Employment Practices (FEPC) to enforce this new policy. Despite the FEPC's lack of effective enforcement powers, the crisis of war eventually brought a dramatic increase in Black employment. The number of Blacks employed by industry increased from some 500,000 in 1940 to more than 1.5 million in 1945. Another 200,000 African-Americans found employment in the federal civil service. The percentage of African-American females employed as servants dropped from 72% to 48% as nearly 300,000 Black women found jobs in manufacturing. By the end of the war, African-American membership in labor unions had doubled to 1.25 million and the number of skilled and semiskilled Black workers had almost tripled. The average wage for African-Americans during the war increased from $457 to $1976 a year, compared to a gain from $1064 to $2600 for white workers.[31]

The war thus brought advancement for African-Americans, but hardly racial equality. Many national trade unions excluded or segregated Blacks. Most government defense jobs open to African-Americans were at the entry level, and attempts to upgrade Black employees frequently led to threats of strikes and walk-outs by white workers. Progress in the midst of continued racism also characterized the experience of the nearly one million African-American men and women who served in the military during the Second World War. Benjamin O. Davis became the first Black brigadier general and an increasing number of Blacks were trained for combat positions—the all-Black 761st Tank Battalion gained distinction fighting in Germany. The Army gradually trained African-Americans as pilots and the 99th Pursuit Squadron won 80 Distinguished Flying Crosses for its strikes against the Luftwaffe. The Navy opened the Marines and Coast Guard to African-Americans, and in 1944 both the Army and Navy began experiments in integration. Whenever and wherever offered the opportunity, African-Americans proved they could do the job. And tens of thousands of Blacks experienced a taste of life with little or no prejudice in places like France and Hawaii.[32]

The great mass of African-Americans, however, served throughout the war in segregated service units commanded by white officers, and encountered frequent racial prejudice. Post exchanges and the USO barred or discriminated against them; even in Portsmouth, the USO held special segregated dances for Blacks.[33] Military chapels proclaimed separate worship for "Catholics, Jews, Protestants, and Negroes," and the Red Cross segregated "white" and "colored" bottles of blood plasma, even though, ironically, a Black scientist, Dr. Charles Drew, had perfected the process of preserving blood plasma. Restaurants in Salinas, Kansas, allowed German prisoners of war to eat at their lunch counters yet refused to serve African-Americans soldiers in uniform. And despite proven battlefield valor, no African-Americans were awarded Medals of Honor in World War II, as none had been in World War I. Military authorities failed to protect Black servicemen off the post, and the use of white military police to keep African-Americans "in their place," sparked conflict and rioting on nearly every southern Army base and on many bases overseas. At least 50 Black soldiers died in racial fights in the United States during the war.[34]

This racial violence mirrored the growing tensions among civilians. Rising expectations and ongoing discrimination brought mounting frustration and evermore militant Black protest. Some Blacks expressed admiration for the Japanese, seeing them as enemies of white colonialism and imperialism. As African-Americans pressed their campaigns for racial equality and justice, many whites stiffened their resistance to any changes in Blacks' inferior economic and social positions. Numerous racial clashes occurred, and, in mid-1943, 47 cities reported pitched battles between whites and Blacks. Race riots broke out in the Harlem section of New York City as well as in Detroit; Los Angeles; Mobile, Alabama; and Beaumont, Texas.[35]

Yet the war brought revolutionary changes that would eventually result in a successful drive for civil rights and first-class citizenship. More than 700,000 southern Black tenant farmers and field workers migrated to the factories of the North and West. This mass movement transformed what was still considered only a southern problem into a national concern. It created a new attitude of independence in African-Americans. Their high concentration in a handful of metropolitan areas provided a new sense of power; more than ever before, African-Americans voting in the cities of the North were viewed as holding the balance of power in close elections. This prompted leaders of both national political parties to pay increasing heed to civil rights issues.

The horrors of Nazi racism made Americans more sensitive to the harm caused by their own white-supremacist attitudes and practices. In 1945 African-Americans looked forward hopefully, and with determination. They were ready to wage the stuggle to end white racism. Like athlete Jackie Robinson, who as a young lieutenant had refused to take a seat at the rear of a segregated southern bus and had fought and won his subsequent court martial, African-Americans in 1945, so unlike those in 1917, militantly and confidently expected that they would soon overcome racial injustice and inequality. An American specialist on racial minorities, Carey McWilliams, wrote at the war's end that "more progress has been made, in this five-year period, toward a realistic understanding of the issues involved in what we still call 'the race problem' than in the entire period from the Civil War to 1940."[36]

Latinos in the armed forces and on the home front shared many of the same experiences as African-Americans: overt discrimination, segregation, lower wages. And they also migrated from rural areas to urban jobs, especially in aircraft factories in California and in petroleum refineries in Texas, improving their economic position substantially. But they still faced racial hostility, as evidenced by the Los Angeles "zoot suit" riot of June 1943. Following a rumor that young Chicanos had beaten a sailor, white servicemen attacked Mexican-American youths dressed in their distinctive long jackets with padded shoulders and billowy, flared pants tightly pegged at the ankles. For four days local and military authorities looked the other way and allowed servicemen to raid the barrios, and the local press blamed the violence entirely on the Mexican-American community. Such expressions of prejudice heightened Latino feelings of ethnic identity and led returning Mexican-American veterans, like their African-American counterparts, to form organizations such as the American G.I. Forum to press for equal rights and an end to racial prejudice and discrimination.[37]

Juxtaposed with the voluntary migrations and significant gains made by African-Americans and Mexican-Americans was the forced relocation of 120,000 Japanese-Americans from the West Coast. Responding to the fears of subversion in California after Pearl Harbor, President Roosevelt approved an Army order in February 1942 to move all Japanese-Americans on the West Coast to remote inland detention camps. More than two-thirds of those forced to sell their businesses and possessions at distress prices, and then herded into desolate, demoralizing camps behind barbed wire, guarded by armed troops, were Nisei, native-born Americans, whose only crime was their Japanese ancestry. Not a single Nisei was ever indicted for espionage, treason, or sedition; nor were any charges of criminal behavior ever brought against Japanese-Americans. Gradually, beginning in 1943, some Nisei were allowed to leave the camps for wartime employment or service in the armed forces. Many of the 13,000 who enlisted fought in the all-Nisei 442nd Combat Team, the most decorated unit in all the military service. Although it was widely acknowledged after the war that the treatment of the Japanese-Americans was a disgrace, it was not until 1982 that a government commission formally declared that the internees had been done "a grave injustice." Finally, in 1988, Congress voted an indemnity of $1.2 billion and a public apology to the estimated 60,000 surviving Japanese-Americans detained during the Second World War.[38]

The surrender of the Japanese following the dropping of atomic bombs on Hiroshima and Nagasaki caught Americans as much by surprise as the Japanese attack on Pearl Harbor. Suddenly, it was over. In cities across the country, civilians and servicemen alike rushed into the streets to celebrate. They snake-danced, formed conga lines, played leapfrog, and embraced one another. Two million frolicked in New York City's Times Square, and many millions more thronged Chicago's Loop, San Francisco's civic center, and thousands of town squares to wave flags, throw confetti, toss their hats in the air, devour as much whiskey as humanly possible, and enjoy the uproar of blaring car horns, the tolling of churchbells, and the howling of factory whistles. It was over, and worries about the loss of jobs due to reconversion or the activities of Soviet troops in Eastern Europe could wait until tomorrow. Today, the "good war" had to be savored. The United States and its allies had destroyed the Axis threat and won the largest war in history. Although the United States experienced some of the war's tragedy, including the deaths of 300,000 servicemen in combat, its losses paled beside those of the nations of Asia and

Europe, now reduced to rubble, where 14 million men under arms and 25 million civilians perished. For Americans, the devastation and horrors of war had taken place elsewhere, far removed from their shores. An almost total unity and the absence of any significant dissent in confronting a clearly defined enemy had made the wartime nation a far more pleasant place to live and work than it had been in the 1930s. Forty-five months of total war transformed the nation into a proud, powerful, prosperous United States that bestrode the world like an international colossus.

The United States had again become a land of opportunity and hope. The mobilization for war had ended the depression, revitalized productivity, redistributed income, and transformed the nation into a genuinely middle-class society, more prosperous than ever, and with restored faith in capitalism, in democratic institutions, and in its ability to solve all problems. Americans had proved they had both the will and the resources to conquer depression at home and aggression abroad; and men and women of every class and race believed that they had contributed to the common triumph. As the Portsmouth Chamber of Commerce, in its final report on its wartime activities, concluded: "its officers and members are proud that the organization could have played even an insignificant part," along with "a hundred other organizations in Portsmouth" and "a hundred thousand civic, service, fraternal, and labor groups throughout the nation," in providing the support that "collectively was instrumental in helping to win World War II."[39]

The war gave millions of Americans a second chance, and millions more a first chance to enter the mainstream of American life. The lowest levels of society harvested the greatest relative gains. And the ideological overtones of the war as a struggle between freedom and totalitarianism, joined with the self-awareness stemming from participation in the war effort, planted the seeds of expectations that would later blossom into full-scale campaigns for equal opportunity for women and minorities.

The war also altered the shape of the economy: tremendously accelerating trends toward bigness in business, agriculture, and labor, and toward making the government an equal partner in management of the economy, while bestowing upon Keynesian deficit spending a legitimacy it had never before possessed. It drastically enlarged the role of the military establishment in various aspects of American life, making it an integral part of the economy and well-being of thousands of communities. It firmly harnessesd scientific research and development to the national interest, it transformed much of the South and West into urban societies, and it decisively enhanced the scope, size, and powers of the federal government. It disrupted family relationships and traditional social values. It altered lifestyles and patterns of behavior. And it ended American isolationism. An internationalist consensus had emerged that perceived the national interest in global terms. The United States would now play a role in world affairs that would have seemed inconceivable just five years before.[40]

The American people in 1945 were eager for the "American Century" they knew lay ahead. A victorious, just war had stimulated great expectations and had restored the self-confidence they had felt prior to the Great Depression. The United States, continuities and limitations notwithstanding, had never before changed so profoundly and fundamentally in so short a time.

NOTES

An earlier version of this essay appeared in Paul S. Boyer, Clifford E. Clark, Jr., Joseph F. Kett, Thomas L. Purvis, Harvard Sitkoff, and Nancy Woloch, *The Enduring Vision: A History of the American People* , Vol. 2, *From 1865* (Lexington, Mass: D.C. Heath, 1990), pp. 935–969. This revision includes substantive changes, including the addition of numerous references to wartime activities in Portsmouth, New Hampshire.

1. United States Bureau of the Budget, *The United States at War: Development and Administration of the War Program by the Federal Government* (Washington, D.C.: U.S. Government Printing Office, 1946); Gladys M. Kammerer, *Impact of War on Federal Personnel Administration, 1939–1945* (Lexington: University of Kentucky Press, 1951); Richard Polenberg, *War and Society: The United States, 1941–1945* (Philadelphia, Penn.: J. B. Lippincott, 1972), pp. 76–89; and Francis Walton, *Miracle of World War II: How American Industry Made Victory Possible* (New York: Macmillan, 1956), pp. 3–5, 521.

2. Allan M. Winkler, *Home Front U.S.A.: America during World War II* (Arlington Heights, Ill.: Harlan Davidson, 1986); "U.S. Navy Yard," MS 96 Portsmouth War Records, Strawbery Banke Museum, box 1:3 [hereafter, reports in this group are cited by the folder title, followed by PWR and, when first cited, the box and folder numbers in which the report may be found in the Cumings Library and Archives, Strawbery Banke Museum]; and William M. Tuttle, Jr., "The Birth of an Industry: The Synthetic Rubber 'Mess' in World War II," *Technology and Culture* 22 (1981): 35–67.

3. John Morton Blum, *V Was for Victory: Politics and American Culture during World War II* (New York: Harcourt Brace Jovanovich, 1976), pp. 124–131; John Brooks, *The Great Leap: The Past Twenty-Five Years in American History* (New York: Harper & Row, 1966), pp. 38–53; Alfred D. Chandler, Jr., and Louis Galambos, "The Development of Large Scale Economic Organizations in Modern America," *Journal of Economic History* 30 (1970): 201–217; and Paul C. Koistinen, *The Military-Industrial Complex: A Historical Perspective* (New York: Praeger, 1980).

4. Walter W. Wilcox, *The Farmer in the Second World War* (Ames: Iowa State College Press, 1947).

5. "U.S. Navy Yard," PWR.

6. Milton Derber, "Labor-Management in World War II," *Current History* 48 (1965): 340–345; and Jane C. Record, "The War Labor Board: An Experiment in Wage Stabilization," *American Economic Review* 34 (1944): 98–101. Polenberg, *War and Society*, pp. 26–27, 176–182; Roland A. Young, *Congressional Politics in the Second World War* (New York: Columbia University Press, 1956), pp. 63–65.

7. John K. Galbraith, "Reflections on Price Control," *Quarterly Journal of Economics* 60 (1946): 476–479; and Harvey C. Mansfield et al., *A Short History of OPA* (Washington, D.C.: Office of Temporary Controls, Office of Price Administration, 1947).

8. Fascinating details of everyday life during the war abound in Richard R. Lingeman, *Don't You Know There's a War On? The American Home Front 1941–1945* (New York: G. P. Putnam, 1970); and Geoffrey Perrett, *Days of Sadness, Years of Triumph: The American People, 1939–1945* (New York: Coward, McCann, & Geoghegan, 1973).

9. "Transportation," MS 96 PWR, box 1:18; Perrett, *Days of Sadness*.

10. "Transportation," PWR.

11. As quoted in Blum, *V Was for Victory*, pp. 101–102.

12. "New Hampshire Women Save 71,741 lbs. of Salvage Fat in 3 Months," *The Portsmouth Herald*, January 7, 1943, p. 8.

13. "Business and Industry," MS 96 PWR box 1:5.

14. Polenberg, *War and Society*, pp. 27–30. Dorothy Lamour raised $310,416 in bond sales when she came to Portsmouth on September 16, 1942. "Thousands See Film Star as She Sells War Bonds," *The Portsmouth Herald*, September 16, 1942, pp. 1, 6.

15. Paul Studenski and Herman E. Krooss, *Financial History of the United States* (New York: McGraw-Hill, 1952), pp. 436–455.

16. Kent C. Redmond, "World War II, a

Watershed in the Role of the National Government in the Advancement of Science and Technology," in *The Humanities in an Age of Science*, ed. Charles Angoff (Rutherford, N.J.: Fairleigh Dickinson University Press, 1968), pp. 167–180. See also James P. Baxter III, *Scientists Against Time* (Cambridge, Mass.: MIT Press, 1968).

17. Allan M. Winkler, *The Politics of Propaganda: The Office of War Information, 1942–1945* (New Haven, Conn.: Yale University Press, 1978).

18. Colin Shindler, *Hollywood Goes to War: Films and American Society, 1939–1952* (London: Routledge & Kegan Paul, 1979). Female roles are closely scrutinized in Andrea Walsh, *Women's Film and Female Experience* (New York: Praeger, 1984).

19. Blum, *V Was for Victory*, pp. 79–89.

20. Henry S. Shyrock, Jr., and Hope T. Eldridge, "Internal Migration in Peace and War," *American Sociological Review* 12 (1947): 27–39.

21. The emotions and strategies of those who coped are vividly conveyed in two compilations of oral histories: Mark Jonathan Harris et al., *The Homefront: America during World War II* (New York: Putnam, 1984), and Studs Terkel, *"The Good War": An Oral History of World War II* (New York: Pantheon, 1984). They are also poignantly described in Harriette Arnow, *The Dollmaker* (New York: Macmillan, 1954), a moving novel of one woman's experience in wartime Detroit.

22. Herman L. Smith, "Excerpts from 'History of War Price and Rationing Board, 14-8-1'" (1946), Portsmouth War Records Committee Report Files, Portsmouth Public Library, Portsmouth, New Hampshire.

23. William H. Chafe, *The American Woman: Her Changing Social, Economic, and Political Roles, 1920–1970* (New York: Oxford University Press, 1972), pp. 135–148.

24. "Medical," MS 96 PWR box 1:6; and Maureen Honey, *Creating Rosie the Riveter: Class, Gender, and Propaganda during World War II* (Amherst: University of Massachusetts Press, 1984).

25. Ruth Milkman, *Gender at Work: The Dynamics of Job Discrimination by Sex during World War II* (Urbana: University of Illinois Press, 1987).

26. N.H. State Planning and Development Commission, ed., "Health and Welfare Survey," MS 96 PWR, box 2:14. A child-care center was eventually established in Portsmouth in 1944 at Wentworth Acres.

27. "Health and Welfare Survey," PWR.

28. "Medical," PWR.

29. "Health and Welfare Survey," PWR; Karen Anderson, *Wartime Women: Sex Roles, Family Relations and the Status of Women during World War II* (Westport, Conn.: Greenwood Press, 1981); and Chafe, *The American Woman*, pp. 180–182.

30. Harvard Stikoff, "Racial Militancy and Interracial Violence in the Second World War," *Journal of American History* 58 (1971): 671–675.

31. Norval D. Glenn, "Changes in the American Occupational Structure and Occupational Gains of Negros during the 1940s," *Social Forces* 41 (1962): 188–191; and John Hope II, "The Employment of Negros in the United States by Major Occupations and Industry," *Journal of Negro Education* 22 (1953): 309–314.

32. A. Russell Buchanan, *Black Americans in World War II* (Santa Barbara, Calif.: ABC-Clio Press, 1977); and Neil A. Wynn, *The Afro-American and the Second World War* (New York: Holmes and Meier, 1975).

33. Oral History Interview, August 20, 1991, Strawbery Banke Museum, Portsmouth, N.H. Courtesy Valerie Cunningham.

34. Sitkoff, "Racial Militancy and Interracial Violence," pp. 668–669.

35. Sitkoff, "Racial Militancy and Interracial Violence," pp. 661–681. For a full description of the Detriot race riot see Harvard Sitkoff, "The Detroit Race Riot of 1943," *Michigan History* 53 (1969): 183–206.

36. Neil A. Wynn, "The Impact of the Second World War on the American Negro," *Journal of Contemporary History* 6 (1971): 50–52.

37. Carey McWilliams, *North From Mexico: The Spanish–Speaking People of the United States* (Philadelphia: J. B. Lippincott, 1949), pp. 259–272.

38. Roger Daniels, *Concentration Camps U. S. A.: Japanese Americans and World War II* (New York: Holt, Rinehart & Winston, 1972); and Peter Irons, *Justice at War* (New York: Oxford University Press, 1983). See also Bill Hosokawa, *Nisei: The Quiet Americans* (New York: Morrow, 1969); and Michi Weglyn, *Years of Infamy: The Untold Story of America's Concentration Camps* (New York: Morrow, 1976).

39. "Business and Industry," PWR.

40. Arthur M. Schlesinger, Jr., *The Imperial Presidency* (Boston: Houghton Mifflin, 1973), pp. 124–130. See also David Brinkley, *Washington Goes to War* (New York: Knopf, 1988).

Victory Begins at Home: Portsmouth and Puddle Dock during World War II

by Gregory C. Colati and Ryan H. Madden

> *Hundreds of thousands of Americans, working in or around defense areas, have had their lives turned topsy-turvy by the war. In some cases they face problems they never dreamed of; in others, the compensations are great and they are happier than ever.*

New York Times, *October 5, 1942*

APRIL 10, 1940. President Franklin Roosevelt makes his third and final visit to Portsmouth. He arrives by train and drives in an open car (fig. 22) through the city; his characteristic profile and wave are familiar sights to the thousands who line the streets of his route over the Memorial Bridge to the Portsmouth Naval Shipyard. After a brief inspection of the facility he boards the Presidential yacht *Potomac* and heads down the Piscataqua River, bound for Boston. He makes no public statement, nor is one issued to the press in his name. He is in town for a total of 55 minutes.

The Presidential visit was a brief but symbolic event in the history of the city. Once again, the federal government called upon the people of Portsmouth to produce the naval vessels necessary to meet wartime demands. Once again, after a period of decline and stagnation, the city experienced the explosive growth of a war economy. Once again, the people of Portsmouth faced the possibility that this boom would be as ephemeral as the last.

It was natural that the government would again expect substantial wartime production from the Portsmouth Naval Shipyard (fig. 23). The long-standing maritime tradition of the city, its geographic location, its experience in building submarines during the First World War, and its pool of skilled manufacturing labor were all in its favor.[1] Well before Pearl Harbor, federal, regional, and state agencies developed plans and were creating bureaucracies to mobilize Portsmouth's resources for war.[2]

Portsmouth became, like many other communities in America, reliant upon war industry for its livelihood. Not everyone saw this as a benefit. The Portsmouth members of the State Council of Defense remembered the aftermath of the First World War: abruptly closed shipyards, the exodus of jobs, population, and prosperity. A 1943 "Survey of Health and Welfare in the Portsmouth Defense Area" warned of the potential costs of the current military build-up. The writers predicted that there would be a large group of unemployed and that vacant housing projects, with costly sewer and water services built to meet the war emergency, would be left as burdens upon the com-

Fig. 22. *President Franklin Roosevelt riding in an open car along Daniel Street, Portsmouth, N.H., 1940. Photograph by Frank Hersey. Gift of Frank Hersey.*

munity. The survey charged the federal government with a "direct and unavoidable responsibility to see that when contraction occurs, the least possible dislocation of life and services is experienced."[3] Unlike the situation at the end of the First World War, after the Second World War the federal government did remain a potent force in Portsmouth, and in many other American towns and cities. But the government did not, and could not, restore the prewar status quo.

Prior to 1940 the Portsmouth Naval Shipyard completed an average of two submarines per year. By 1944 capacity increased to 32 submarines a year. While employment expanded and round-the-clock shifts were instituted to meet this increased demand, other factors also contributed to this outstanding productivity. The shipyard pioneered new "quasi-assembly-line" techniques that decreased the number of calendar days it took to build a submarine from 469 to only 173. Additionally, total workdays required to build a single submarine shrank from 193,000 to 83,000. However, in order to meet wartime demand, the Shipyard had to attract large numbers of new workers. Using radio advertising and even sound trucks cruising neighborhoods, workers were recruited from as far away as Portland, Maine, and Lawrence, Massachusetts. The Shipyard was so desperate to attract workers that it contracted a private transportation company to run nearly 100 buses a day to the Shipyard from towns within a radius of 60 miles.[4]

The outbreak of the war caused expansion in other industrial areas in town as well. By June 1942 almost half of the industrial plants in Rockingham

Fig. 23. *Aerial photograph of Portsmouth, N.H., 1925, by an unidentified photographer. This view shows the Memorial Bridge, at the middle left, with the Puddle Dock neighborhood just to its right. The Portsmouth Naval Shipyard in Kittery is visible in the upper right. Historic Photograph Collection.*

county were engaged in some type of defense work.[5] The Morley Company, a manufacturer of buttons, was one of many production plants able to survive, thrive, and expand during the war years by converting to war-related manufacturing. Morley made gas mask face-pieces (fig. 24), eye shields and gas-resistant sacks for chemical warfare, fiber and molded plastic buttons for uniforms, tufting for war workers' clothing, and fiberboard for lunch boxes. Housewives, USO Hostesses, Y.W.C.A. "girls," and office "girls," after their regular workday was completed, turned up in large numbers to work at Morley when a government contract was due, and the company received four Army-Navy E awards for efficiency in meeting contract deadlines.[6]

Some local industries, unable to make the transition to wartime production, were forced to suspend operations for the duration. National Gypsum Company could not secure the raw materials necessary to continue its work and on February 27, 1943, the plant closed. Although 100 employees were thrown out of work, the high demand for skilled labor meant that they easily found positions in other industries. National Gypsum did not resume operations in Portsmouth until 1946.[7]

From 1940 to 1943 workers and their families poured into Portsmouth and the surrounding area by the thousands to fill jobs in war-related industries. The civilian population of the Seacoast Defense Area (which included the city of Portsmouth, and the towns of Newington, Greenland, Rye, and New Castle in New Hampshire and Kittery and Eliot in Maine) increased 34.3% at the same time that the overall population of New Hampshire declined by 8%.[8]

Fig. 24. *Employees of the Morley Company assembling gas masks at the company's Manchester, N.H., plant. Photograph by G.W. Badger, ca. 1943. Due to wartime demand, the Morley Company expanded production beyond its Portsmouth factory. The Morley Company was awarded four Army-Navy "E" awards for productivity. Gift of the Morley Office Supply Company.*

Some people moved permanently, others came just for the duration, still others lived in outlying areas and commuted long distances using an uncertain public transportation system.

Most people who came to work in the Shipyard and other war industries looked for places to live that were either on a bus route or within walking distance. The Puddle Dock neighborhood, home of the "Little Corner Store," was within sight of the Shipyard; after only a few minutes walk over the Memorial Bridge a worker could be at the entry gate. The availability of low-cost, short-term housing within its boundries made Puddle Dock an ideal place for transient workers to live. But the proximity of the neighborhood to the Shipyard had an even more significant effect on the permanent population.

The war brought opportunities for jobs, the accumulation of capital, and social mobility, and reinforced the continuity of the Puddle Dock area. However, it was also the harbinger of the loss of the traditional close-knit urban neighborhood. The experience was typical of many urban neighborhoods in America. As in so many other communities, Puddle Dockers supported the war and accepted its attendant changes as a consequence of global conflict.

The war years themselves brought fewer changes than might be expected to a neighborhood that was familiar with shortages, hardship, and "making-do." An informal support system was already in place because of the significant percentage of women heads of household and women who worked outside the home. The coming of the war demanded activities (such as finding child care, stretching food dollars, procuring adequate housing, and relying on neighbors) that may have been new to some Portsmouth residents, but which were all too familiar to Puddle Dockers. Oral histories reveal a strong sense of community and identification with the neighborhood in times of crisis. Residents solved their problems by relying on a time-tested network of informal relationships rather than on a state-sponsored bureaucracy.

The multitude of programs and agencies spawned by the war did not have as direct an effect on the residents of Puddle Dock as on people in other parts of the city. The neighborhood retained much of its insularity, and, except for brief interest in the availability of rental units in the area on the part of the housing authority, the neighborhood was essentially left alone by local government. And Puddle Dockers stayed away from many city-wide volunteer efforts. Of the 26 volunteer committees created by the Portsmouth Council of Defense (PCD), Puddle Dockers served on only 11. There was significant participation on only two of these groups: Air Raid Wardens (fig. 25) and the Utility Repair Squad. The committees that Puddle Dock residents served on generally were those, such as the Auxiliary Firemen or Auxiliary Policemen, that directly benefited the neighborhood, rather than the larger community. Although it consumed huge numbers of volunteers by virtue of its 24-hour-a-day schedule, only one resident helped staff the PCD's Report Center.[9] Considering that neighborhood residents had never looked to the government as a partner, it is not surprising that they relied more on traditional family and close-friend relationships than on government to carry them through the war years.

There are no specific figures available on median income for the neighbor-

Fig. 25. *Air Raid Warden Garland Patch's Station, 386 (rear) Court Street, ca. 1943, by an unidentified photographer. The station was located on the lower level of a brick building that was constructed in 1908 as a museum honoring 19th-century author Thomas Bailey Aldrich. The museum building still survives in its original use on the grounds of the Strawbery Banke Museum. Portsmouth War Records Collection.*

Fig. 26. *"Zeke" Pridham (left) and Joe Pridham (right) pose with their friend "Ike" Peirce in the backyard of their mother's home, 1944. The photograph was taken to send to their brother, Sherm, who was in the Army. Reproduced from an original in the collection of Hazel Pridham.*

hood, but oral-history informants confirm that incomes were low to moderate. Twenty-one percent of all households in the neighborhood were headed by women; of these 12% were widows. Eight percent of all adult women worked outside the home; their occupations ranged from bookkeeper to maid; three were grocers—Ethel Smart, Georgie Gould, and Bertha Abbott. Four women are listed as either shoe workers or employees of Continental Shoe, one worked at the First National Store, and one served as the dietician at Camp Langdon, an army camp in nearby New Castle. Eighteen percent of the adult males in the neighborhood were serving in one of the branches of the military in 1943 (fig. 26). Others worked in local businesses and for the city.

The Shipyard always exerted a strong influence on the neighborhood. In 1943, 49 men (25% of the employed males) in the neighborhood worked at the Portsmouth Naval Shipyard. Many more men and women worked at the Shipyard at one time or another, either prior to, or after, 1943 (see table 1). For some it was their first job, and they stayed until they were drafted into the service, to be replaced by others following the same path. Others finally found steady employment there after years of doing odd jobs or being unemployed. The Shipyard had a negative impact as well. As soon as the war ended the Navy drastically cut the work force. By 1947 only 14 residents (4% of working men) worked at the Shipyard and, of those, only ten had worked there in 1943. During the war, the physical condition of the neighborhood attracted attention from outside, especially government agencies desperate to find housing for Shipyard workers. A 1943 survey commissioned by the Portsmouth Council of Defense found that "some of the houses in the poorer district are of early construction and possess exteriors of good architectural design and can be re-

Fig. 27. *Aerial View of the Puddle Dock Neighborhood, Prescott Park, and the Portsmouth Waterfront, ca. 1958. Photograph by Douglas Armsden. Armsden Collection.*

stored" (fig. 27). The survey went on to determine that "their less desirable neighbors should be removed."[10]

Neighborhood residents resisted efforts of outsiders to dictate to them. Contrary to the stereotype of low-to-moderate income neighborhoods, the properties in Puddle Dock were not owned by absentee landlords. Many multi-family dwellings were owner-occupied; most landlords were neighborhood residents. The Abbotts, for instance, owned the apartment building (known as the "Block") directly next to their own home and store. Some large houses became apartment buildings that housed people who were at or near the pov-

Table 1: Population Survey of Puddle Dock Area

	1943	1947
Population surveyed	970	845
Men	510	420
Women	460	425
Households	199	181
Female heads of household	42	39
Vacancies	N/A	12
Widows	23	19
Working men	227	167
Working women	41	28
Navy Yard employees	49	14

erty line. Smaller houses, like the Abbotts', remained single-family dwellings and were occupied by individuals with strong ties to the neighborhood—through relatives and friends—who enjoyed a modest level of prosperity.

Nevertheless, rents in the Puddle Dock neighborhood continued to decline even in the face of an extreme housing shortage. A factor working against the neighborhood was its waterfront location. All waterfront housing, regardless of its condition, was considered a security risk. The Shipyard was easily visible from even the ground floors. If tenants were to be permitted, a government directive cautioned that "they should be above suspicion and unoccupied houses should be under surveillance."[11]

There is also a noticeable lack of bank financing evident in the recorded deeds for Puddle Dock addresses. The banks believed that, as soon as the war ended, the neighborhood would revert to its "sub-standard" character which would "preclude amortization and regular income from the investment."[12] As a result, most properties were transferred for one dollar, with grantors evidently holding mortgages for grantees. Although the deeds reveal that one or two families may have intended to buy up considerable amounts of land for potential commercial or industrial development, most land transfers appear to have been between family members and friends. Because house values and rents were declining, and banks were reluctant to grant home improvement or mortgage loans to area residents, some owners demolished their houses rather than continue to try to repair them. Bertha Abbott, for instance, was unable to afford to make repairs on the Block; finally the building decayed to the point where it was condemned by the city, and it was torn down in the early 1950s. Hers was probably a typical situation. The Health and Welfare Survey described Puddle Dock as a "low-class tenement district which includes a junk yard among the neighborhood features." It cited one two-family house as an "outstanding fire hazard." When the city ordered this house razed, the owner of one half complied, the other owner refused to "remove the debris" and left the structure "partially collapsed."[13]

For many residents the opportunity to obtain jobs at the Shipyard or in other war-related industries was what made the war years the best economic times they had seen in decades. Nationally, unemployment dropped to a record low of 1.2% by 1944.[14] Employment statistics are more difficult to determine for Puddle Dock residents. City directories do not always list occupations, even when a person was employed. Nevertheless, a survey of listed occupations in the 1939, 1943, and 1947 directories shows that a significantly larger percentage of people had listed occupations in 1943 than in 1939.

The war brought changes to all facets of city life. It changed the physical face of the city and the social character of its people. The citizens of Portsmouth rallied to the cause of the war even as they fought to control its effects on their town. Shipyard expansion strained public utilities, schools, housing, transportation systems, medical care, and other public services well beyond their peacetime capacity. Ultimately, more than 17% of the entire Seacoast population would come to work at the Shipyard.[15]

The single most important problem facing the community's leaders was the shortage of adequate housing for the thousands of people pouring into the city. That Portsmouth's situation was more desperate than other New Hampshire cities was self-evident. The Portsmouth City Planning Board reported that a survey of housing made in 1941 showed that more than half of the 4021 "dwelling units" in Portsmouth were more than 80 years old, while less than one quarter of the units in Manchester were even 40 years old. The situation in Portsmouth was so bad that the report only considered 28 housing units as "unfit for use" even though 70 units had no running water, 160 had no gas or electric lights, 162 had no toilets, and 879 had no bathtubs or showers.[16]

In order to deal with the influx of war workers, entire neighborhoods were created almost overnight (fig. 28). A federal survey conducted in 1940 determined that there was a need for 2200 new housing units within a 25-mile radius of the Shipyard. The Defense Homes Corporation responded by planning two developments, 200-unit Pannaway Manor and 800-unit Wentworth

Fig. 28. *Map of Portsmouth, N.H., published by the Seacoast Regional Development Association, 1943. The Puddle Dock neighborhood is located along the waterfront, just south of the Memorial Bridge. Courtesy of the Portsmouth Public Library.*

Acres, the two most visible examples of the long-term impact of World War II on Portsmouth.

Pannaway Manor, a subdivision of moderately priced single-family homes, was completed in 1941. City Council minutes indicate that although the expense of extending the city's sewer lines to the new neighborhood was considerable, few councilors resisted the development.[17]

Wentworth Acres, however, was a controversial project from the beginning.[18] Plans for its development pitted federal bureaucracies against local civic leaders; control of the project lay in the hands of the federal government, the city could only offer advice, most of it contrary, and hope the federal government would heed the warnings. Unlike Pannaway Manor, Wentworth Acres was made up of multifamily rental units, with common recreational areas, including a swimming pool, for community use. The government conceived the complex as temporary housing for workers at the Shipyard. The Portsmouth Council of Defense and the Portsmouth Planning Board feared, with good reason, that however temporary the project was planned to be, once built, it would remain. The PCD complained that units were being constructed with substandard materials. Local legend, probably apocryphal, has it that the building materials for the New Hampshire project were shipped to Portsmouth, Virginia, and that the Virginia materials, not designed for winter weather, arrived in Portsmouth and were put up before anyone uncovered the mistake. The PCD predicted that "if all the multifamily houses were retained in their present conditions Wentworth Acres may easily degenerate into a blighted area." The report inferred that multifamily rental units were undesirable.[19] The Planning Board was also concerned that the city was being asked to pay the cost of running sewer and water lines to the outskirts of town for a project that was only temporary.

Transportation, schools, child care, and public utilities all had to be created to serve these new parts of the city. New schools were built, and bus lines altered to accommodate the new patterns of travel. When the PCD finally established a day care center in 1944, it was located in Wentworth Acres.[20]

Residents of these new areas had mixed reactions to their situation. One newcomer from Nebraska was pleased to live in a three room "cottage" in Wentworth Acres and make "more damn money" than he had ever made in his life. His wife also felt more comfortable in Wentworth Acres than she had when they lived downtown. She felt a bond with other newcomers who, like her, sometimes found it difficult to fit into the local social scene. Although she learned to like seafood, she thought Portsmouth natives were unfriendly and talked "just like people from England." However, other residents complained about the noise and lack of privacy in the complex.

Some Portsmouth natives were nonplussed by the influx of new people into the area. "It used to be fun to go down town on a Saturday," said a local taxi driver in 1942, "Everyone always smiled at you and said hello. Now you don't know a soul."[21] In order to alleviate some of the strain and promote support for the war effort, federal, state, and local agencies sought to mobilize public opinion and public resources through volunteer programs. The Office for

Civilian Defense (OCD) was the federal agency created to coordinate the national volunteer effort through regional, state, and local offices. The New Hampshire State Council for Defense (SCD) was created through legislative action on April 4, 1941, and the Portsmouth Council of Defense was created in November of that same year.[22] The PCD office was staffed 24 hours a day from December 9, 1941, until February 20, 1944. The PCD was organized into two main divisions: The defense corps and the service corps. The defense corps cooperated with other government agencies, such as police and fire departments, to organize defense-related activities in the area (fig. 29). The service corps was designed to assist citizens of the community "to do more collectively in winning the war than each citizen could do as an individual." The service corps itself was divided into twelve areas: Agricultural Interests; Salvage; Recreation; Information; Health and Welfare; Housing; War Savings; Nutrition; Consumer Interests; Child Care; War Transportation; Home Participation.[23] Practically every area of civilian life was covered by a committee whose job it was to gather volunteers and encourage participation. This was the point at which national programs met the American public. It was up to the local committees to sell programs to the general population. The emphasis was on cooperation and sharing. The objective was to win the support and enthusiasm of the local population and procure the materials necessary to continue the war overseas. These agencies and their programs met with uneven success and sometimes unintended results.

Fig. 29. *"When the Bombs Drop." Poster published by the New Hampshire State Council for Defense, 1942. Widespread fear on the New England coast of a Nazi attack prompted the development of elaborate civilian defense strategies. Gift of Richard Cheek.*

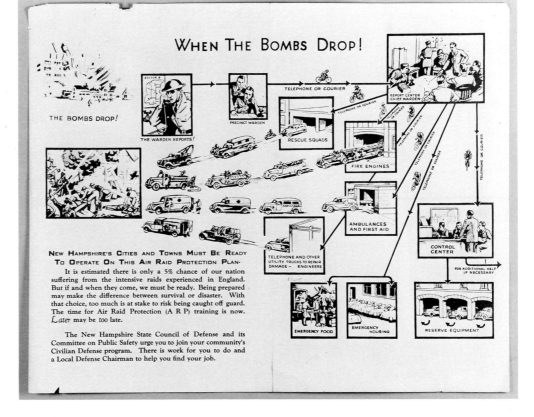

Portsmouth residents turned out in large numbers to staff the wartime committees. Approximately 10% of the population volunteered in some official capacity, many on more than one committee.[24] Thousands of others did their part simply by participating in scrap drives, rubber drives, and numerous other salvage efforts; buying War Bonds; and working in war industries (fig. 30). Committee leadership in the volunteer effort fell to familiar faces and families. The chairs of the committees of the PCD reflected the political and social leadership of pre-war society in Portsmouth. In order to be able to volunteer for the war effort, one had to have extra time beyond the time needed to procure the necessities of life or to look for a job. Residents of the less affluent or less politically connected parts of the city viewed these organizations with some skepticism, if indeed they thought of them at all. Competing with the volunteer movement for the attention of the less affluent resident were the more immediate and familiar issues of food, housing, jobs, and transportation. Nevertheless, Portsmouth residents participated in an impressive

Fig. 30. *"OK Tojo—you asked for it."* Government directed message printed in The Portsmouth Herald, *May 19, 1943, p. 5. The image of retribution against Japan was a common theme used to encourage community participation in volunteer programs. Courtesy of the Portsmouth Athenaeum.*

array of federally and locally sponsored efforts to support the war, the soldiers who fought it, and the families they left behind. Private agencies, religious groups, and other concerned citizens and businesses all contributed something to the cause.

Radio stations and newspapers cooperated with government guidelines on the dissemination of information. Local radio stations refrained from broadcasting weather reports for the duration, to prevent potential enemy commandos, bombers, or commerce raiders from receiving current weather information. The ban even extended to discussing conditions at baseball games. If a game was canceled due to rain, the information appeared only in the next day's newspaper, it was not reported over the airwaves.[25] Even before Pearl Harbor, the local radio station WHEB assisted the war effort. On April 17, 1941, Portsmouth, New Hampshire, Mayor Stewart Rowe addressed the citizens of Portsmouth, England, via shortwave linkup. After a short musical selection from the Portsmouth Male Chorus, Mayor Rowe delivered a speech that stressed the "true and sincere friendship" between the two cities. The broadcast was part of a program of "New England Towns to Old English Namesakes" sponsored by the Committee to Defend America By Aiding the Allies. Ralph May, Portsmouth resident, historian, and another of the speakers that day, recalled later that it is unlikely that the speeches were ever heard in Portsmouth, England, which was under heavy bombardment by the Germans on the night of the broadcast.[26]

Beginning the day after Pearl Harbor, WHEB radio broadcast a daily half-hour program devoted to round-table discussions of preparedness and emergency response. Topics included what to do in case of an air raid, how to deal with unexploded bombs, and so forth. The station also gave free publicity to virtually all wartime agencies and programs.

The Portsmouth Herald was similarly involved in promoting the war effort. Although circulation suffered because of a lack of delivery vehicles, the scarcity of spare parts for its presses, and the loss of 20% of its staff to the armed forces, the *Herald* was a continuous booster of the war effort on the home front. One of the newspaper's many efforts was to sponsor a special cooking clinic featuring Miss Ruth Bean (fig. 31), a "topflight home economist" who showed Portsmouth women how to cook nutritious meals with available foods.[27] The newspaper also ran daily and weekly columns aimed at helping local people deal with rationing and shortages.

Like all commercial establishments, the media were eager to devote time and resources to promote the war effort. Supporting the war would not only bring victory, but it would also bring reader or listener goodwill and loyalty that would translate, they hoped, into increased circulation and larger audiences after the war. The war effort also helped the *Herald* to obtain new advertisers as businesses rallied to the cause by adding their names to the list of sponsors supporting the government wartime "messages" which appeared almost daily in its pages.

Portsmouth's social and fraternal organizations altered their usual activities to become involved with the war effort. Sometimes these activities were

Fig. 31. *"Nutritional Cooking is a Fine Art." Advertisement for* The Portsmouth Herald's *four-day seminar on wartime cooking, conducted by Ruth Bean, "America's top flight food expert,"* The Portsmouth Herald, *April 2, 1943, p. 3. By its own account, the* Herald's *program was a complete success; on April 9, the newspaper reported "Throngs Crowd Last Cooking Class." During her talk, Bean warned women not to waste vegetables, offered remedies for the "leftover dilemma," and featured a "special orange nut cake to keep a family happy." Courtesy of the Portsmouth Athenaeum.*

coordinated by the Portsmouth Council of Defense, other times they were completely self-directed. With a profusion of opportunities available, it was an unusual person who was not involved in some way with supporting and sponsoring the soldiers at the front. Although these activities had little impact on the total war effort they did boost morale in the town, giving everyone a sense of involvement and helping with the vital services of a burgeoning community.

After the bombing of Pearl Harbor, the De Molay group (a fraternal organization of young men) dedicated themselves to becoming the Auxiliary Fire Department for Portsmouth. "The support of the members of this organization was most enthusiastic and at the next regular meeting of the organization it was reported that five companies had been formed from volunteers from the chapter."[28]

Throughout the war, the Y.W.C.A. was open for 24 hours a day. It gave over its first floor to the USO and filled the permanent rooms with 15 resident women, "all war workers." It became a meeting place for women working at the Shipyard along with "wives, mothers, and sweethearts" of armed men and "Waves and Wacs." Edith Brewster, the House Director, recalled "one case of the restless girl stirred by the tensions of the war period" who, when she arrived asking for a room, told "fabulous tales of her life in Mexico and Texas. It finally developed that she was a run away from the state of Maine. Her parents, thankful to find her, came to Portsmouth for her."[29] Brewster also reported a case of a serviceman's wife who telephoned one evening to say that her husband had arrived in New York for two days. She told the Y.W.C.A. director that she must see him and that her bus was scheduled to leave within the hour. "What should she do with the baby?" she asked. "The Y.W. found a way, and she caught her bus."[30]

The Family Welfare Association assisted in war work in Portsmouth by sponsoring a much needed child-care center at Wentworth Acres and by finding foster homes for children of servicemen where placement was necessary because of the mother's illness or employment.[31]

The Y.M.C.A. realized that Portsmouth would grow rapidly in numbers because of the Shipyard. Their goal was to "provide recreation and council" to the new families of Portsmouth, especially the youth. In that vein they established a youth center that accommodated more than 100 children per day. The Y Dormitory was occupied entirely by men employed in the Shipyard—"these men were given preference over others, so that they might be able to live near their work."[32]

The members of the Women's Christian Temperance Union did their best to cope with the changes in Portsmouth. They took part in parades, gave away free lemonade, gave lectures to servicemen and Shipyard employees, and sent a protest to the Governor "about the waste of precious tin caps for alcohol carriers." They also requested that if liquor was to be sold, it be rationed. In fact, "every monthly gathering had some reference or plan connected with the war."[33]

Youth groups also contributed significantly to the war effort. The Girl Scouts made International Friendship Bags that contained toilet articles, sewing equipment, and other household material. They packed Christmas boxes for the men of the Merchant Marine. A correspondence was kept up with the "Girl Guides of the St. Edmund's Company of Northhampton, England" during the war. The Northhampton girls received a "party" package from Portsmouth on D-Day filled with "gingerbread, cocoa, candy bars, gum, peanuts, raisins, dates, figs, and candied orange peel." They immediately had a party with these presents from the "Scouts of Troop 2, Portsmouth to celebrate the Invasion of Europe."[34]

The Boy Scouts "quickly learned that their organization, their training and their ideals had fitted them for many services in a total war which found the home front as much a part of the war effort as the battle front." They tested blackout measures; distributed posters, literature, and questionnaires; picked crops that would have rotted; and collected aluminum, waste fat, and paper as well. The Scouts accounted for 85% of all the aluminum collected in Ports-

committee that organized clothing drives or did sewing for the Red Cross. A spirit of cooperation and generosity infused the city.[41]

And then, suddenly, but certainly not without warning, it was over. Rationing, scrap drives, carpooling, and other types of volunteerism, were discarded almost as quickly as they were taken on. The end of the war in Europe in May of 1945 was the beginning of the end of wartime cooperation on the home front. The collapse of the Japanese resistance in August (fig. 33) and the return of veterans released the long suppressed desire for material prosperity. Many people were eager to spend enforced savings from wartime wages. Although the federal government tried to convince Americans that the end of the fighting did not mean the end of the struggle, Americans demanded, and got, a rapid dismantling of wartime agencies and programs. President Truman was appalled at a nation gone almost "insane in selfishness," but there was little he could do to stop it. "Everybody wants something at the expense of everybody else and nobody thinks much of the other fellow" Truman wrote in late 1945.[42] The citizens of Portsmouth and the Puddle Dock neighborhood were no different than their counterparts throughout the country. They wanted what they considered to be their rightful share of postwar prosperity. After all, they had earned it, hadn't they?

In Portsmouth, not everyone received their share. Some parts of the city benefited more than others. Even though increased employment allowed Puddle Dockers, as a group, to accumulate capital, it was generally not enough to renovate their houses without help from banks, who were still unwilling to lend the money. Federal Housing Authority (and, after 1944, Veterans Administration) programs encouraged and supported the purchase of new con-

Fig. 33. *V-J Day in Portsmouth. The news of Japan's surrender sparked celebrations throughout Portsmouth and the country. Photograph by Frank Hersey, August 15, 1945. Gift of Frank Hersey.*

struction single-family houses. By insuring loans against loss, these federal agencies allowed lenders to loan to less-affluent home buyers. The federal government consciously supported the creation of suburbs at the expense of urban neighborhoods; subdivisions were supported over multifamily homes in urban areas, and loans for the repair of existing structures were discouraged to the point where it was easier to purchase a new home than it was to modernize an old one. According to historian Kenneth Jackson, "FHA programs hastened the decay of inner city neighborhoods by stripping them of much of their middle class constituency."[43] A demographic comparison of the neighborhood in 1943 and 1947 reveals a decline in the total population. A significant number of residents who left were not, as would be suspected, transients who came to work in the Shipyard and left at the end of the war, but rather members of established families. By 1947, 96 residents who had lived in the neighborhood in 1939 had moved out. Some moved to other neighborhoods, others left the city altogether. Many did not leave the area completely but rather ventured out to the rapidly expanding suburbs. The combination of new-found wealth, and the lack of resources to help to improve the neighborhood drove them from the area. Some moved only a few blocks, but those few blocks meant a new world, a new neighborhood, a new status.

Before the war, a typical Puddle Dock resident would move several times within the neighborhood, sometimes only as far as across the street. One resident recalled that when she got married, it seemed only natural for her to stay in the neighborhood, close to her family. Unable to afford their apartment on Mechanic Street after her husband entered the service, she moved in with her mother and sisters on Marcy Street. By pooling their ration coupons she and her mother and sisters were able to provide for their entire extended family. She took care of her sisters' children while they worked in war industries. When her husband returned, the family left the neighborhood once and for all, and, ultimately, moved to Mariette Drive in a new subdivision because "there was nothing good in town, this town was starting to go downhill."[44]

Some residents did use the neighborhood as a stepping stone, living in Puddle Dock only long enough to accumulate enough money to move out and up. Roland Cadarette and his wife lived on Atkinson Street in 1943 while he worked at the Shipyard. Not listed as living in town in the 1939 directory, by 1947 the couple had moved to Pannaway Manor, the federal subdivision on the southern outskirts of town. Sixty-three other neighborhood residents shared a similar experience.

A long-time Puddle Dock resident recalled that there was a "real exodus" of people to other parts of the city after the war. "People saved money . . . bought land . . . and had their own homes built, for $6000, nice homes today. If they moved [out of the neighborhood], they never came back."[45]

Young people also left the neighborhood. Not old enough to be listed in the directory in 1939, many worked in defense-related industries or were in the service in 1943. By 1947 they had disappeared from the neighborhood, many from the city. The Hersey family, long-time residents of Puddle Dock, are representative of the trend. In the Navy in 1943, by 1947 William Hersey mar-

22. Guyol, *Democracy Fights*, p. 57.

23. Gerald D. Foss, "Brief History of Portsmouth Council of Defense," MS 96 PWR, box 3:1.

24. "Public Safety Division: Portsmouth," PWR. See Guyol, *Democracy Fights*, pp. 224–230 for further treatment of Portsmouth volunteer groups and their support of the war effort.

25. "Radio Transcripts, Entertainment, & the Media," MS 96 PWR, box 1:16.

26. A second attempt to broadcast greetings was made in October, 1942. This one was heard in Portsmouth, England. The Lord Mayor cabled Mayor Rowe: "Thanks for the personal greetings . . . Reception excellent. All good wishes to you and your citizens." "Radio Transcripts, Entertainment, & the Media," PWR.

27. "Radio Transcripts, Entertainment, & the Media," PWR; *The Portsmouth Herald*, April 5, 1943.

28. "Social and Fraternal Organizations," MS 96 PWR, box 1:10.

29. "Social and Fraternal Organizations," PWR.

30. "Social and Fraternal Organizations," PWR.

31. "Children," PWR.

32. "Social and Fraternal Organizations," PWR.

33. "Social and Fraternal Organizations," PWR.

34. "Social and Fraternal Organizations," PWR.

35. "Social and Fraternal Organizations," PWR.

36. "Children," PWR.

37. "Animals," MS 96 PWR, box 1:13.

38. "Portsmouth Civilian Committees and Agencies," MS 96 PWR, box 1:11.

39. "Medical," MS 96 PWR, box 1:6. In 1939 there were 298 births at Portsmouth Hospital; in 1943 the Hospital recorded 714 births. The numbers of patients admitted, minor and major operations, and accidents that the Hospital handled also increased in similar proportions during the war years.

40. "Government Agencies," MS 96 PWR, box 1:8.

41. "Religion," MS 96 PWR, box 1:17.

42. David McCullough, *Truman* (New York: Simon and Schuster, 1992), pp. 68–71.

43. Kenneth Jackson, *Crabgrass Frontier: The Suburbanization of the United States* (New York: Oxford University Press, 1985), p. 217.

44. Oral History Interview, October 7, 1992, OH 2 SC 20, Strawbery Banke Museum, Portsmouth, N.H.

45. Oral History Interview, October 18, 1990, OH 2 SC 20.

46. Portsmouth Directory, vols. 40, 42, 43 (1939, 1943, 1947).

47. Diggins, *Proud Decades*, p. 181.

48. *Your City Government 1945–1946–1947* (Portsmouth, N.H.: Office of the Mayor, 1947), p. 17.

49. *The Portsmouth Herald*, June 9, 1941.

50. Inaugural Address by Mayor Mary C. Dondero—January 1, 1945. *Your City Government*, p. 4.

A Fair Share at a Fair Price: Rationing, Resource Management, and Price Controls during World War II

by Barbara McLean Ward

> *Then one Sunday afternoon came Mr. Tojo's bombs. One by one, the plastics, the foils, the cellophane, the metal, the bottle caps, the fancy papers, transformed into bombers, tanks and shells, went to war.*
>
> Modern Packaging, *November 1943*

FOR EVERYONE who remained on the home-front battlefield, rationing, shortages, and price controls were a fact of life. Few Americans remember these conditions as hardships; most remember them as their contribution to the global conflict. Thousands of government-sponsored advertisements created and fostered this attitude, working especially hard to convince the public that food was a weapon of strategic importance. If folks on the home front used food wisely, it would "fight for freedom," as one advertisement explained:

> It just won't "happen" that there will be enough food. America has got to work at it. Food is fighting today for freedom on many fronts. Here at home, too. If you enlist in this fight, you'll help speed the day of Victory. We know you will do anything you can to help—if you just have the facts.[1]

Government messages bombarded consumers with information on how they could help to ensure victory by taking action at home. The "Seven Point Plan" for holding down prices, the "Home Front Pledge" campaign, the "Health for Victory Club," and other efforts, all pointed out the urgency of avoiding waste; using food, clothing, and other essential items wisely; acting fairly and in the community interest; and scrimping and saving to hold down inflation and make scarce items available for everyone. The slogans "Food Fights for Freedom," and "Produce, Conserve, Share and Play Square," "Use it up, Wear it out, Make it do," appeared everywhere—in newspapers, magazines, posters, and pamphlets (fig. 35, PLATE 14). New campaigns were launched even as late as January 1945 to enlist volunteer cooperation with wartime measures and to maintain civilian morale throughout the war. Although many efforts remained strictly volunteer—the Victory Garden and home canning programs are examples—by early 1943, it was clear that some conservation measures would have to be made mandatory. These programs touched the lives of consumers on a daily basis. The three types of federal economic and production controls that had the greatest impact on the purchase and sale of food and gro-

Fig. 35. *"Use it up, Wear it out, Make it do!" Poster published by the Office of War Information, 1943. Gift of Richard Cheek. (See also plate 14)*

cery items of the kind sold in establishments such as Bertha Abbott's "Little Corner Store" were commodities rationing, quotas and limitations affecting the packaging of consumer goods, and price controls.

Not only were these programs key elements in the bureaucratic machine that engineered the United States' war effort, they also played an important role in President Roosevelt's efforts to bring about the nation's long-term economic recovery. Government economists knew that if significant inflation was allowed it would negate the benefits resulting from full employment in war industries. They also realized that the diversion of supplies to war production would dampen civilian morale unless citizens clearly understood that adequate supplies of food and of most consumer goods would continue to be available for everyone. Nonetheless, if the United States ultimately entered the war, many industries would have to be retooled and mobilized for war production, and this conversion would essentially stop the manufacture of consumer durables such as washing machines, refrigerators, and automobiles for the duration of the war.[2]

The bureaucratic engine needed to put rationing, materials allocations, and price controls into place was already in the planning stages in 1940. Even before U.S. entrance into the war, the War Department was involved in allocating critical materials to defense contractors producing armaments and military hardware under lend-lease. On May 29, 1940, Roosevelt revived the National Defense Advisory Commission (NDAC) and its four divisions: Price Stabilization, Consumer Protection, Agriculture, and State and Local Cooperation. The NDAC and a host of other defense-oriented boards and commissions would soon give way to wartime administrative structures with greater powers and more clout. Nonetheless, from the outset the Roosevelt administration was determined to avoid the mistakes of World War I; the NDAC and its successors began planning stricter controls—price ceilings and monitoring of every aspect of wartime production—to prevent inflation and encourage rapid expansion of war industries.[3] United States' entrance into the war would make it necessary to put ceiling prices into effect and to monitor and control every aspect of wartime production.

War emergency programs placed restrictions on all aspects of the American economy by controlling the flow of strategic materials to industry. By cutting down on the supplies available to businesses making consumer goods, the War Production Board encouraged manufacturers to convert to war production, or to sell most of what they produced to the military.[4] As a result, the numbers of consumer goods produced for the domestic market fell, and it was ultimately necessary for government agencies to step in and regulate the distribution and sale of these goods to civilians.

These war emergency programs were created by executive order during the last half of 1941 and given legislative sanction during the first weeks of 1942. On April 11, 1941, the President signed Executive Order 8734 establishing the Office of Price Administration and Civilian Supply; in August the name of the agency was changed to simply Office of Price Administration (OPA). The OPA was created to set, publicize, and enforce ceiling prices, and to gather statistics and develop a plan for rationing consumer goods that would allow the most equitable distribution of available resources. Once the United States entered the war, things moved even more quickly. In January 1942, President Roosevelt replaced the Office of Production Management and the Supply Priorities and Allocations Board with the War Production Board (WPB). The WPB had the power to determine the supply of materials to all types of industries, to set quotas for war production, and to ensure that war industry received sufficient allocations of strategic materials such as rubber, aluminum, steel, glycerine, tin, and petroleum. By WPB directive no. 1 the OPA was authorized to ration consumer goods on January 24, 1942, and on January 30, 1942, President Roosevelt signed the Emergency Price Control Act which gave the OPA the authority to regulate commodities prices and residential rents.[5] In addition to the WPB, the OPA, and the Army and Navy departments, two other key governmental agencies were involved in determining the supply of goods to the American public: the War Food Administration (WFA) of the Department of Agriculture; and the Petroleum Administration.

While most WPB orders affected only suppliers, manufactuers, and wholesalers, the OPA, as the administrator of rationing and price controls, directly interacted with consumers through its 93 district offices. During the initial weeks of the war, the OPA utilized the already-existing network of State Defense Councils to help organize citizen rationing boards across the country.[6] The overall strategy was to gain public support by enlisting influential local people as volunteer enforcers of price control and rationing programs. Herman L. Smith recalled, in his history of the Portsmouth War Price and Rationing Board, that this "enlistment" happened soon after war was declared:

> During the last days of December, in 1941, several men from Portsmouth, New Hampshire, received telephone calls from the County Civilian Defense Chairman, Alvin F. Redden. These men were told that they were respected members of the community and were asked to serve as members of a tire rationing board. They were told that this would take very little of their time, that the job might not last too long, but that they would be doing a very valuable service to their country.[7]

The volunteer boards were critical to the success of differential rationing programs—such as for gasoline and fuel—which required an intimate knowledge of local conditions and of the needs and habits of specific individuals. The boards also provided grass-roots support for potentially unpopular measures. Government officials recognized that some people would resist price controls and rationing measures, and that a massive "information" campaign would be needed to make citizens see the connection between shortages at home and the all-out mobilization of the country for war. In 1947, historian Harvey C. Mansfield stated his opinion that average Americans resisted price controls because they believed they constituted unfair government regulation of free enterprise, and because they associated rationing with critical shortages that admitted weakness to the enemy.[8] The propaganda campaign to promote price controls and rationing, therefore, had to be constructed in such a way that American civilians were not frightened by the measures, but nevertheless understood the need for them.

Ultimately there would be four different programs for rationing consumer goods.

1. Certificate Rationing. This was the first type of rationing to go into effect. Certificates were issued, on the basis of need, for the purchase of single items that were in scarce supply such as tires, automobiles, stoves, and rubber boots.
2. Differential Coupon Rationing. Commodities in this program were rationed on the principle that some people required more of certain resources—such as fuel oil and gasoline—than others. These programs were the most difficult to administer because every case had to be reviewed individually and appeals and applications for additional allotments were frequent.
3. Uniform Coupon Rationing. This was used for such items as shoes, sugar, and coffee, on the assumption that everyone "should share alike" in the purchase of available supplies of certain items. Stamps (first issued in War Ration Book I) were periodically vali-

dated for these goods according to WPB determinations of availability, and consumers were notified through the news media.

4. Point Rationing. Under this program, every man, woman, and child received his or her own individual coupon book. The first of these point ration books—War Ration Book II—was issued to consumers in February of 1943 for point rationing of meats, butter, margarine, canned fish, cheese, canned milk, fats, and oils (red stamps) and most canned and bottled foods (blue stamps) beginning in March. The point rationing program was based on the British model, and allowed consumers to choose foods according to individual tastes and eating habits.[9]

Certificate rationing began with tires in January of 1942; automobiles were added to the list less than a month later (fig. 36). In Portsmouth all residents were required to report in person, during the first week of May 1942, to the Ration Board to register for War Ration Book I which included stamps for the uniform coupon rationing of sugar, (and later for coffee). The following week, differential coupon rationing began with the rationing of gas and the distribution of gas coupons and stickers. The OPA immediately recognized that the distribution of ration coupons and the assignment of need in differential

Fig. 36. *"I'll Carry Mine Too."*
Poster published by the Office of War Information for the Office of Defense Transportation, 1943. This poster was meant to encourage people to accept tire and gasoline rationing. Gift of Calvin P. Otto. (See also plate 15)

coupon rationing would be a massive undertaking. Officials ultimately decided to use the largest comprehensive network available to them—the nation's public school systems—to help them carry out the task of distributing rationing materials. Consumers registered for ration coupons at schools throughout the country, and schoolteachers and board clerks handled applications and distributed ration coupons and certificates. On May 2, 1942, Louise Grant, a second grade teacher at Portsmouth's Haven School, distributed gas rationing materials and commented in her diary that she "minded it more than sugar."[10]

Oil and gasoline were first rationed in New England and the Northeast where oil shortages were caused by restrictions on shipping. Temporary measures were followed by permanent gas rationing on July 22, 1942, and heating oil rationing in October. Gas was rationed by means of A, B, and C stickers, each type allowing the holder different amounts of gasoline per week. According to Philip Guyol, official historian of New Hampshire during World War II, many abuses of this system occurred, especially during the first year that rationing was in effect.[11] Heating oil rations were determined by the size of the area to be heated and the resident's previous usage. Deciding allotments was an onerous task, and requests for further rations were frequent. In his history of the Portsmouth board, Smith records the following incident.

> We had one dear old man who lived alone in an old and drafty house.
> . . . He knew the thermometer reading in every corner of his home.
> . . . It was too much for us to take too seriously when he introduced,
> by lengthy notation, such detail as: "Bed temperature (10 p.m.), 70°.
> Room temperature (same time), 55°. Bed temperature (3 a.m.), 82°.
> Room temperature (same hour), 50°."[12]

Although the availability of fuel oil affected nearly everyone, it was point rationing that most affected the retail grocer's workload and the average consumer's eating and buying habits. On December 27, 1942, National Food Administrator Claude R. Wickard broadcast plans for the upcoming food rationing program on national radio. Officials feared that consumers would rush to local stores to buy up as many cans and jars as they could before the program went into effect, and Wickard warned consumers that hoarding excess supplies of processed food was a serious misdemeanor.[13] In Portsmouth, consumers were limited to six items of canned food "per visit" in the weeks just before rationing began. Although this measure was primarily meant to discourage hoarding, it also gave people the opportunity to buy the maximum number of items that they would be allowed. When consumers registered for Ration Book II, they were asked to declare the number of cans and jars of rationed foods—in excess of a certain maximum per person—that they had on hand at home. Declarations were made on what was essentially an "honor system." In early January 1943, reporters for *The Portsmouth Herald* interviewed local grocers, and found that some store managers had noticed unfamiliar customers coming into their stores to purchase their six-can limit. As a result, stocks of canned foods were "dwindling," especially at the chain stores. Within two weeks, an editorial reported that canned foods were difficult to come by.[14]

The proprietor of the local People's Market remembers that during this period there was one elderly lady who came into his store and purchased one five-pound can of shortening every day. When he compared notes with another grocer, he learned that the same woman was buying shortening in that store as well. To this day he remains baffled over what this woman could possibly have planned to do with all that shortening, but she undoubtedly remembered World War I shortages, and wanted to be prepared (fig. 37).[15]

The announcement that food rationing would soon be a reality made people wonder what it would mean to them, and how the system would work. Newspapers and magazines ran stories illustrating the stamps in War Ration Book II along with question-and-answer columns that helped people to understand what rationing would be like. OPA officials were kept busy speaking to local civic organizations and talking with what must have seemed like an endless stream of reporters. *The Portsmouth Herald* editors referred to the shortage of food as "the most formidable problem" of 1943 and helped local residents to understand the necessity for rationing.[16] When Book II finally appeared, it took people quite some time to become used to point rationing, even though the book was produced in a fairly straightforward manner. Grocers bore the burden of explaining this system to customers and of sorting coupons for their

Fig. 37. *"Rationing Means a Fair Share for All of Us." Poster published by the Office of Price Administration, 1943. In government publications, hoarding consumers were usually portrayed as elderly women. Gift of Richard Cheek.*

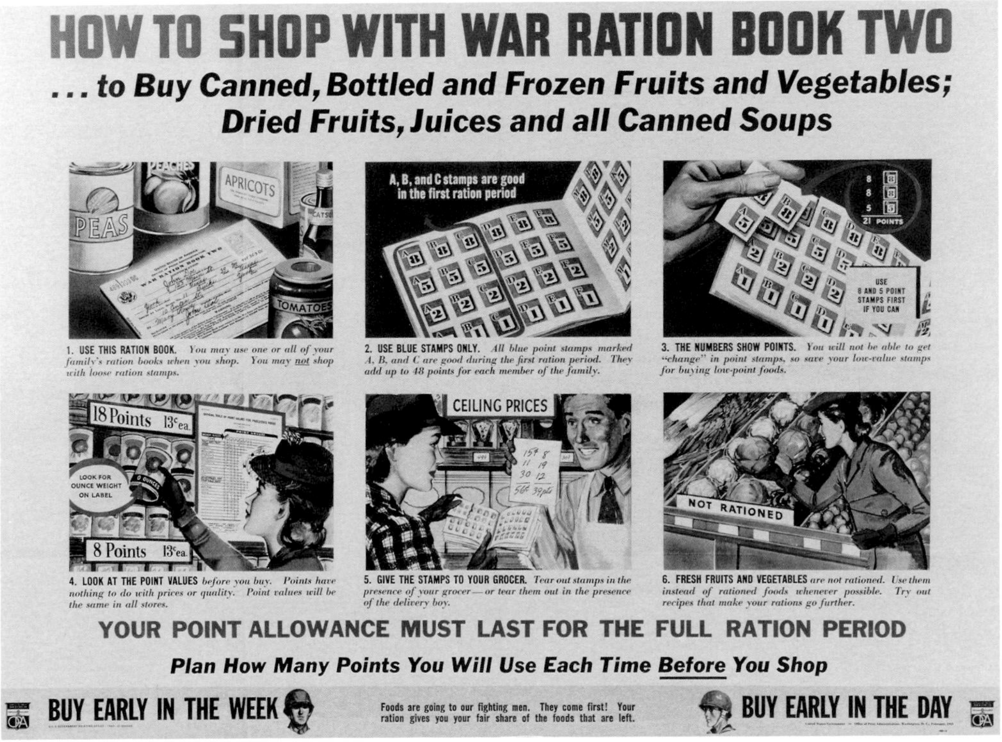

Fig. 38. *"How to Shop With War Ration Book Two."* Poster published by the Office of Price Administration, 1943. Gift of Charles E. Burden.

wholesalers, but government posters assisted their effort (fig. 38). Although oral-history informants contend that some Puddle Dock grocers did not collect ration coupons from their customers, it is unlikely that this was the case unless goods were purchased on the black market, because grocers had to pay wholesalers the requisite number of ration coupons in order to receive their supplies. Wholesalers paid packers in stamps which were eventually deposited in ration banks and ultimately turned in to government agencies (fig. 39). At the outset, the OPA hoped to be able to issue ration currency in the form of coupons, in set denominations, with tokens that could be used as change. Unforeseen difficulties arose over the minting of tokens, however, and only stamps could be printed in time for the beginning of the first point-rationing programs.[17] Coupons in War Ration Book II, therefore, were printed in point denominations of eight, five, two, and one to allow for the greatest number of possible combinations. Consumers were cautioned to use their eight-point stamps whenever possible and to keep their one- and two-point coupons for times when they made small purchases, because grocers would have no way to issue "change"—stamps would not be valid once they had been torn from the ration books.[18]

OPA officials in Washington could not fully anticipate how many rationing programs the coupon books might be used for, and therefore the books were designed for maximum flexibility. Book I, issued in early May 1942 for sugar rationing, was eventually used for coffee and shoe rationing as well. In New Hampshire, the state OPA board mailed Ration Book III to consumers on July 15, 1943, and the stamps became valid on September 12.[19] Book III included

Fig. 39. *"Where Coupons Go."
Illustration from* The Story of
Wartime Rationing. *Published
by the Office of Price Administration, Washington, D.C.,
1945, p. 31. Courtesy of the
Portsmouth Public Library.*

four pages of stamps bearing images of ships, planes, tanks, and guns that
were meant to be used for a clothing-rationing program that was never put
into effect. Although most of these stamps never had any purpose, a few of
them were eventually validated for shoe rationing. The brown stamps that
comprised the remaining four pages of Book III were used for meat rationing.
War Ration Book IV, which consumers again had to apply for in person at the
nearest public school, were issued in the fall of 1943 for processed-food rationing. Book IV included stamps labeled "spare" that could be validated for
commodities under special circumstances and some of these were used as part
of the program that enabled home canners to receive extra sugar rations.[20]
One and one-quarter billion ration tokens, each worth one red point or one
blue point, were put into circulation in February 1944 (fig. 40). At the same
time, all coupons in the meat and food rationing programs were given a face
value of ten points, and retailers used the tokens to make change. Blue tokens
were discontinued in October 1944 when all blue-point foods were given point
values in even multiples of ten.[21]

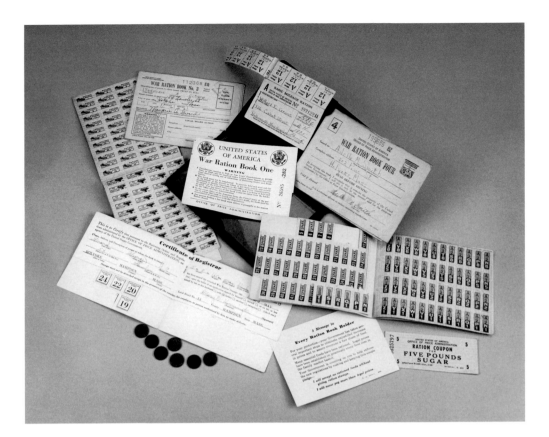

Fig. 40. *Assortment of War Ration Books, Coupons, Tokens, and Folders, 1943–45. Gifts of Patricia Dillon Brackett; Lois R. Hastings; Doris Linden Heerdt; Mr. and Mrs. Donald M. Knapp; Calvin P. Otto; Donald Randall; and Mr. and Mrs. B. Allen Rowland.*

In addition to a numerical value, each stamp also had a letter designation. Coupons with different letters had different validation and expiration dates.[22] For instance, green stamps G, H, and J in War Ration Book IV were valid between January 20, and February 20, 1944.[23] This system made it possible for the OPA to create validation periods of varying lengths coinciding with the availability of certain items. In many ways, in spite of the fact that they had British experience to learn from, OPA officials were only experimenting when they assigned the first point values to rationed foods. As they developed a better understanding of consumer buying patterns and the effect of high point values on the distribution of available stockpiles, OPA officials came to understand that they could significantly affect the distribution of most types of food by periodically raising or lowering their point values. For instance, when the Victory Garden and home-canning programs caused a reduction in the demand for commercially canned foods, some items were removed from the list of rationed goods, and others received lower point values.[24] The validity dates of stamps within the books, and even the values assigned to individual stamps, became so confusing that *The Portsmouth Herald*, and newspapers across the country, ran weekly "Ration Reminder" columns to help consumers keep track of changes.

Food rationing was, perhaps, the program most difficult to "sell" to the American people. Most people just did not understand the connection between food rationing and the war effort. The government enlisted the assistance of local newspapers and the largest of the food processors and distributors in a massive campaign to convince the average American that food was "a weapon of war." Friendly cartoon-like images were devised to explain the need for food allocation and food rationing programs (fig. 41), and posters and other Office of War Information publications and "messages" stressed the consumer's role in supporting the war effort in a positive, thought-provoking, but nonthreatening manner (fig. 48, PLATE 16).[25]

These campaigns were basically successful. By early 1943, consumers had already experienced the impact of reduced stocks of certain goods, and knew what it was like to have to run from one store to another—and one line to another—to buy *any* meat or butter at all. While Portsmouth residents stood in the pouring rain waiting for a share of the large shipment of butter that arrived at the local First National Store in early February, by mid-March, under rationing, people could choose whether to spend eight points on butter, or to settle for margarine at five points.[26]

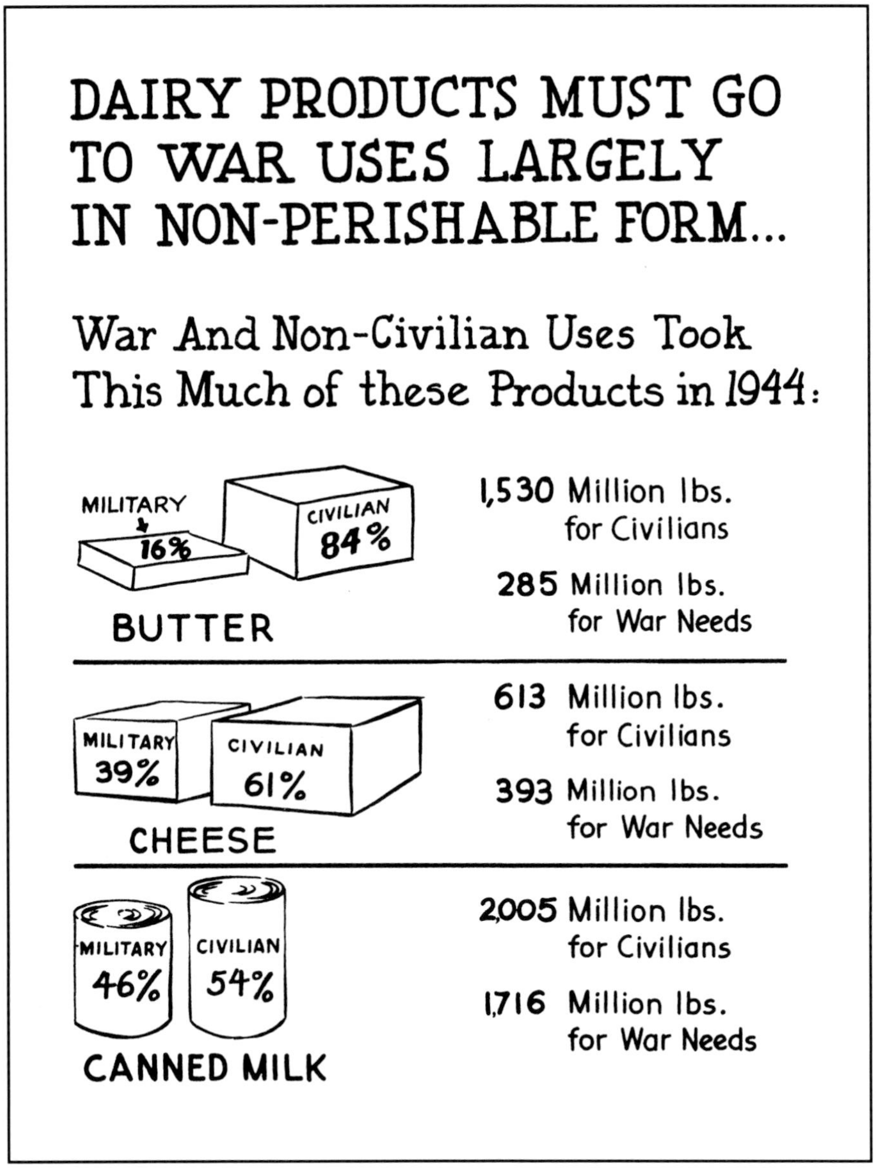

Fig. 41. *"Dairy Products Must Go to War Uses. . . ." Illustration from* The Story of Wartime Rationing. *Published by the Office of Price Administration, Washington, D.C., 1945, p. 76. Courtesy of the Portsmouth Public Library.*

DAIRY PRODUCTS MUST GO TO WAR USES LARGELY IN NON-PERISHABLE FORM...

War And Non-Civilian Uses Took This Much of these Products in 1944:

BUTTER
MILITARY 16%
CIVILIAN 84%
1,530 Million lbs. for Civilians
285 Million lbs. for War Needs

CHEESE
MILITARY 39%
CIVILIAN 61%
613 Million lbs. for Civilians
393 Million lbs. for War Needs

CANNED MILK
MILITARY 46%
CIVILIAN 54%
2,005 Million lbs. for Civilians
1,716 Million lbs. for War Needs

Fig. 42. *"Rationing Safeguards Your Share." Poster published by the Office of Price Administration, 1942. Gift of Richard Cheek.*

Once it became clear that rationing would actually *increase* the likelihood of finding one's favorite foods at the local grocery store (fig. 42), consumer advocacy groups became strong supporters of food rationing. At the beginning of processed-foods rationing, approximately 600 processed food items were included; in January 1944 ready-to-serve soups were removed from rationing, and in September 1944 jams, jellies, fruit butters, asparagus, lima beans, corn, peas, pumpkin or squash, mixed vegetables, baked beans, tomato sauce, and tomato puree were eliminated from the list of rationed foods.[27] The decision, by a new group of administrators at OPA, to remove many items from rationing in anticipation of a quick end to the war in Europe, was regarded by the OPA's Consumer Advisory Committee as a "tragic mistake." In a letter to OPA Administrator Chester Bowles, the Committee asserted that

> OPA has not realized how popular rationing has been among consumers. In our experience housewives have not only accepted rationing as necessary, but have been glad for the assurance it has given them of being able to buy the foods they need.[28]

The Committee predicted that the termination of rationing on some commodities would "enable well-to-do families to buy up stocks of canned foods while low-income families and those living in crowded quarters cannot possibly do so," would "encourage hoarding," and would "discourage the victory garden program." But, worst of all, the move would erode confidence in the rationing program, and "undermine civilian war morale."[29]

The Committee's fears were realized when, in mid 1944, the Allied invasion forces in Europe found their progress to be slower than expected, supplies dwindled, and shortages again became the order of the day. By the end of the year, even Louise Grant, normally a public-minded citizen, felt betrayed by OPA policies that reduced the available supply of foodstuffs.[30] By January 1945, nearly all commodities removed from rationing were again placed on the ration lists, and most would remain under rationing until V-J Day.[31] Feeling the need to justify the renewal of rationing, and to explain why it was again necessary, the OPA issued a pamphlet entitled "The Story of Wartime Rationing," in February of 1945. In headlines, charts, and line drawings, the pamphlet explained that because meat supplies were drastically lower for 1945 than they had been for 1944, and because as many as one-third of all retailers had no rationed beef or pork on hand at all, broader meat rationing had been put into effect in December of 1944. Processed foods were becoming scarce as well. According to the pamphlet, although "production of Processed Foods reached an all-time peak in 1944 . . . civilian supplies, allocated from the yearly pack, [were] less" than at any time since the beginning of the war.[32]

At the same time that consumers faced the problem of how to accommodate their eating habits to food rationing, they also began to notice that the foods they bought were appearing in a new variety of containers. Changes in the packaging and shipping of consumer goods affected the types of goods that consumers could buy, but in a different way than rationing did. In addition, the problems that arose from limitations on the availability of packaging materials taxed the ingenuity of manufacturers, and forced further reductions in domestic supplies of processed foods. Nonetheless, these restrictions resulted in a wide variety of creative solutions that have had a major impact on product packaging ever since, and demonstrate that concerted industry-wide conservation efforts can dramatically reduce waste.

The restrictions on the use of various materials in product packaging were administered through the War Production Board. In October 1945, WPB chairman J. A. Krug summed up the job of his agency in the following manner:

> The job of the War Production Board and its predecessor agencies, stated in the simplest terms, was to keep our economy strong and mobilize the nation's industry to assure the fighting forces of the material they needed to win the war as quickly as possible. That job resolved itself into two parts: first, to build up production, and second, where production could not be built up rapidly enough, to divide the shortages so that those requirements least essential to the war effort stood at the end of the queue.[33]

The WPB was probably the most powerful of federal agencies on the home front, but under the Controlled Materials Plan, although the WPB set quotas, it was up to the Army and Navy, the Maritime Commission, the Lend-Lease Administration, and the Office of Civilian Supplies, to actually select war production contractors.[34] When the Morley Button Factory of Portsmouth, for instance, slowed down production of mattress buttons, they applied for government contracts to manufacture decontamination bags, gas mask packaging assemblies, and gas mask faceplates for the Chemical Warfare Division of the

War Department. Soon the Morley Company was so busy that they were able to employ nearly every available housewife in town, and their plant became so cramped that they were compelled to open a second plant in Manchester (see fig. 24).[35]

The WPB "curtailed civilian output" in order to make "facilities available for military production," by issuing a seemingly endless series of L (for limitations) and M (for materials) orders which limited the production of specific nonessential products in an attempt to bring the demand for materials "somewhere near the available supply." These regulations also "prohibited the use of designated scarce materials for nonessential purposes," some of which included the packaging of consumer goods for the domestic market.[36] Container manufacturers and food processors responded to these WPB orders by adapting their products and creating a wide variety of "conversion" solutions (fig. 43).

It is difficult to read through the endless lists of L and M orders printed monthly in the pages of *Modern Packaging* without drawing parallels between the efforts of the WPB and current efforts to reduce solid waste by cutting back on the amount of paper, styrofoam, plastic, and other materials used in consumer packaging. The significant difference between the two efforts was that WPB orders and the resultant conversion packages were affected not only by the need to reduce the amount of raw material used in shipping and packaging, but also by the need to significantly reduce the amount of ma-

Fig. 43. *Spry can, ca. 1940, and Spry jar with paperboard lid, ca. 1942–1945. In addition to the substitution of glass jars for metal cans, paperboard lids also replaced metal ones on a wide variety of consumer goods. Gift of Charles E. Burden.*

chinery and labor involved in container production. Every aspect of the economy was involved in every production order.

The WFA informed the WPB of packaging needs for all food, and the WPB set limitations on the amounts and types of materials that could be used to package consumer goods.[37] These orders affected everything from types of materials allowed, to weights and thicknesses of paperboard containers, and sizes and shapes of bottles and cans. In March 1943, government planners estimated that the new limitations on the production of tinplated cans as packaging for foods would result in a savings of more than 300,000 tons of steel a year (fig. 44).[38] New glass and paper containers replaced cans. Glass container quotas for products such as coffee and shortening increased during 1943, but the strain that the production of these jars put on industry, because of problems of "manpower" and shipping prompted the Glass Containers and Closures Section of the Containers Division of the WPB to attempt to increase production by limiting the variety of glass bottles that could be produced. Such regulations are endless, but L-103, which listed standard containers of simplified designs, was fairly typical. In September 1943 the order was amended to allow 18 sizes of lightweight "Boston round bottles."[39]

The WPB prided itself in being flexible and responsive to manufacturers' needs. As a result, orders were often countermanded almost immediately after

Fig. 44. *"What Single Container . . . ." Advertisement for the Can Manufacturers Institute, Inc., published in the January 1944 issue of* Good Housekeeping.

they had been issued. Limitation Order L-239, for instance, imposed restrictions on the thickness of paper boxes for frozen foods. It was soon amended to remove some restrictions, "because of confusion in the trade." So many varieties of packages were in use, that "it was practically impossible to comply with the order." Finally, in desperation, the WPB eliminated restrictions entirely, and decided to "permit processors to continue as they had been doing in the past, until new, standard specifications [could] be worked out. . . . " Another order, L-317, also meant to conserve paper, was amended in March of 1944. The editors of *Modern Packaging* commented that the amendment was "the crowning blow to any doubters who may have felt re-use [of paperboard containers] was simply a job thought up by WPB to keep a lot of people busy." They went on to add that "several changes were made in the order before the sweeping changes which are about to be announced," and noted that they were calling "attention to these changes in order to show that WPB has no intent to be arbitrary and is more than willing to listen to reasonable protest."[40] Numerous orders and counterorders of this type undoubtedly spread confusion.

Although the variety of packaging in which food and other grocery items were now available often was bewildering, consumers soon became accustomed to the idea that some products would appear on the shelves in more than one form. For their part, manufacturers tried hard to create packages that helped consumers to recognize their "old favorites." Boraxo, for instance, reproduced an image of its familiar metal can on the front of its wartime paperboard package in order to maintain loyal customers, and other manufacturers followed suit. Nonetheless, the restrictions on materials for packaging some products became so limiting that companies experimented with a variety of package types—Procter and Gamble's experience with Crisco (see cats. 40–42), and Swift's experience with Prem luncheon meat—which was packaged in jelly-type glass jars, oblong tins, and tall cans—demonstrated that the most flexible and imaginative production planners stood the greatest chance of finding a way to get their product into the hands of consumers.[41]

It seems ironic that while the WPB took pains to reduce the variety of containers in production—the idea being to save labor and allow for the conversion of some packaging machinery to wartime production—it also *created* the need for a bewildering variety of packages. And, in fact, most WPB orders only standardized a few container types—most notably cans—and even these standardized containers were allowed to incorporate some custom-design elements—such as the embossed letters "Spry" and "Crisco" which appear on the otherwise-identical glass jars used for these two different brands of vegetable shortening.

Restrictions on the use of metal in packaging—from the reduction in the numbers of items that could be packed on cans, to orders limiting the use of metal in caps for glass jars and the thin metal strip closures used to secure the tops of coffee bags—meant that needs for glass and paper packaging skyrocketed. The radical increase in the demand for paper became a real concern. An August editorial in *Modern Packaging* explained the situation:

Long ago we all knew that for a considerable time packaging would not be as usual. First pinch was metal. As it was denied to an increasing number of products for packaging purposes, many of those products moved into glass. The glass industry has nearly doubled its normal capacity . . . . Even so, the industry is 15 to 20 per cent oversold. . . . Up to the present time [August 1943], paper has played the versatile and willing part of making up for those other shortages. . . .[42]

So, while in May 1943 the same journal advocated the production of counter cards with rationing and other product information, by August editors and advertisers were urging industry executives to think of paper as a strategic material, and to support reuse and salvage campaigns. One editorial even pointed the finger at expensive and unnecessarily elaborate advertising publications, and asked that paper shortages be shared equally by all paper users. By November the reuse and salvage campaign for paper and paperboard was in full swing.

Nonetheless, it would seem that the paper used to issue some WPB orders did more to eat up precious supplies of paper pulp than paperboard production, and undoubtedly paper use in government agencies was astronomical. One reader of a particularly lengthy report issued by the New Hampshire office of a wartime agency penciled a comment on his or her copy of the document that suggests that this irony was not lost on agency employees. "Mr.———," it reads, "Isn't there a paper shortage?"[43]

The many orders and counterorders issued by the WPB must have constituted an enormous headache for producers and retailers, but most individuals viewed the changes in the kinds of packaging available as only a minor annoyance. T. E. Manwarring of the WPB included a personal story in an article he wrote for *Modern Packaging* that sums up the essence of the situation:

The other day I called at the neighborhood drug store to buy a pint of ice cream. The young lady said she was sorry but she could not sell it in bulk as she had no container for it. But she added brightly "I could put it in paper cups for you." So I bought my ice cream in a cone-shape container designed for soda water. The point is I was able to get the ice cream, even though it wasn't on a "business as usual" basis.[44]

The imposition of price controls on consumer goods constituted a similar administrative headache for producers and retailers. To avoid the damaging effects of inflation, by 1940, the Roosevelt administration began preparing data that eventually would be needed to regulate prices. Although at first prices were allowed to rise according to the law of supply and demand, early indications were that inflation would reach World War I levels if it was allowed to continue unchecked (see fig. 17). In 1941 and 1942 the cost of food and other key consumer commodities rose more than 12%. Price-control measures held increases in food prices to 4% over the remainder of the war.[45]

Price controls were first put into effect under the Emergency Price Control Act in January 1942. This statute instituted only selective price controls, and required individual monitoring of manufacturing, wholesale, and retail conditions. So many exceptions were allowed, however, that the law became virtually ineffective. It was replaced by the General Maximum Price Regulation (GMPR) on May 18, 1942, which froze prices at the highest levels charged in March 1942 (fig. 45). The OPA strictly adhered to the measure, but the freeze technique was fraught with complications. Many people felt that the new measures merely represented more New Deal efforts to control the economy. Washington officials pleaded with consumers to understand that price controls were necessary because, with full employment and high wages, people had more money to spend on a slowly dwindling supply of consumer goods (fig. 46). Prices were creeping upward, and if the law of supply and demand was allowed to operate unchecked, they would continue to do so. "The Home Front Pledge" campaign (see cat. 1) and other propaganda efforts sought to dispel consumer resentment over price controls and restrictions on the production of consumer goods by outlining the cause-and-effect relationship between these factors.[46] As Caroline F. Ware explained in 1942:

> The fundamental cause of rapidly rising prices . . . is, too much money and too few goods. We consumers have more money to spend than

Fig. 45. *"How to Display Ceiling Prices." Form published by the Office of Price Administration, 1942. Gift of Charles E. Burden.*

Fig. 46. *"Look Out, Lady."*
Poster published by the U.S.
Government Printing Office,
1943. Gift of Richard Cheek.

there are goods for us to buy. As we try to spend our money for the limited supply of goods, we bid against each other. . . . and so we force prices up. . . . Our economic system is like an intricate machine. If skyrocketing prices are allowed to throw it out of order, it will fail to turn out weapons for war and produce a living for civilians. The fight against inflation is a major battle for the home front. Every consumer and every business man has a place in that battle line.[47]

In the words of one government pamphlet:

With Demand much higher and Supplies much lower than pre-war days . . . it was apparent that many wouldn't get their fair share. This could only lead to . . . *Buying runs, Hoarding, Aggravated shortages,* AND . . . People with the most money—People with the most shopping time—Would get the best and the most.[48]

Price regulations were usually expressed in terms of percentage mark-ups over previously charged prices but so many contingencies were built into them, that even where intentions were good, and profiteering was frowned upon, retailers violated the new price regulations because they did not understand them. In Portsmouth, because volunteers and regular staff of the Price Control Board were busy processing rationing applications and certificates, they were unable to handle the influx of questions and complaints regarding ceiling prices. On October 2, 1942, Congress simplified price control with the passage of the Economic Stabilization Act which established ceiling prices for nearly all consumer foodstuffs. Prices continued to climb, however, and on April 8, 1943, Roosevelt issued his famous "Hold the Line" order which effectively prevented the Price Administrator from approving any further price increases. This order allowed for a simpler "dollars and cents" series of price controls, and permitted fewer exclusions than were possible under the GMPR.[49]

In order to establish equitable price ceilings, OPA district offices conducted community price surveys, one of which took place in Portsmouth. Herman L. Smith recorded that "the stores gave these representatives very good cooperation, and the results were gratifying. One of the most successful accomplishments of the panel was in obtaining refunds from various dealers or individuals in behalf of customers."[50] To the prices gathered in these price surveys, OPA officials added a "set of percentage markups," ultimately arriving at a series of figures that "were uniform throughout the country for each of four classes of retailers." Small independent stores, and stores that offered delivery or credit (such as the Little Corner Store) were classified as Groups 1 and 2, and allowed to charge slightly higher prices than stores classified in groups 3 and 4, which were large self-service stores and chain stores.[51]

These new price ceilings went into effect on August 1, 1943. In Portsmouth, the local OPA board posted the new prices on July 1, 1943, and on July 28, after much advance publicity, *The Portsmouth Herald* published the first of the new ceiling price lists. These early charts included ceiling prices for all groups of stores, printed in parallel columns, on large sheets of paper. Grocers were required to post the charts in their stores, and the government even initiated a program whereby consumers received ceiling-price brochures that could easily be tucked into pockets and purses for easy reference while shopping. The OPA felt that:

> The classification of stores among four "groups," according to volume of sales and type of service rendered, with small differentials in the mark-ups permitted was the technical key to the success and fairness of the program. Completely uniform prices, even within a single community were out of the question, as necessarily either too high for the self-service chains or too low to be fair to the small independents or to stores providing delivery or credit.[52]

Although grocery-store owners essentially agreed, they resented the fact that government charts advertised "to the public that groceries could be bought more cheaply in chain stores than at the corner grocery" and price lists were eventually printed so that prices for Group 1 and 2 stores appeared on separate sheets from prices for Groups 3 and 4. Newspapers periodically printed full ceiling price information for consumers.[53]

In Portsmouth, a new head was named to the Price Panel, and the Price Control Board held a two-day meeting at the Portsmouth High School where specialists from the District Office discussed problems and questions with local merchants. Although promotion, rather than enforcement, took up much of the local OPA board's time, violations did occur, and consumers were quick to bring them to the board's attention. As soon as the public found that the Portsmouth Board was "handling these complaints in a satisfactory manner, the cases increased proportionately."[54]

During the war, the federal government instituted rent controls which were to be exercised at the discretion of state OPA officials. Understanding that pressures would occur in areas where housing was limited, and that the need for war production workers was great, rent controls went into effect in Portsmouth on December 1, 1942, retroactive to March 1, 1942.[55] The shortage of labor in the Portsmouth Defense Area—Portsmouth, Greenland, Rye, and Newington, New Hampshire; and Kittery, and Eliot, Maine—was critical, but housing to accommodate an influx of new workers was extremely limited. Housing constructed for war workers by the Defense Homes Corporation in two housing developments—Pannaway Manor, and Wentworth Acres (see fig. 28)—did much to alleviate Portsmouth's housing shortage, but they had their drawbacks as well. The city now found itself saddled with providing services to new neighborhoods which it feared would become ghost-towns when the war ended.

In fact, employment at the area's major war production facility, the Portsmouth Naval Shipyard, reached its peak in late 1943, and cutbacks began in early 1944. The war production "battle" had been largely won by November of 1943, and although food supplies remained tight, some commodities were slowly becoming available for distribution to consumers. Advertisements in popular magazines featured the words "now back on sale" as items from baked beans to scouring pads were allowed to again grace the grocer's shelves. By the summer of 1944, advertising in national magazines asked consumers to think increasingly about how they would spend their money after the war when consumer durables would be available again. Housewives were even prodded to dream about their new postwar homes, and to begin gathering home decorating ideas (fig. 47).[56]

"Reconversion" of the American economy to domestic production began in May of 1945 (V-E day was May 8). According to OPA historians, in the fall of 1944, administration officials began to realize that "total military production was so great, and the share of it going to Europe obviously so large," that even "allowing for very heavy increases in the flow of supplies westward, it was plain a Pacific war alone could not use up all the country could produce." As a result, WPB and OPA officials decided to make metals and other strategic materials temporarily available for the manufacture of some consumer goods. Officials in the commodities branches of the OPA were asked to recommend

Fig. 47. *Window Display,
Winebaum's News Shop,
Portsmouth, N.H., October 1944,
by an unidentified photographer.
Winebaum Papers.*

products and services that could be safely removed from the list of prohibited or controlled items.[57]

In the summer of 1944, when manufacturers of pianos and electric irons were allowed to again make a certain number of these items for domestic civilian consumption, OPA officials got a small taste of what the difficulties of reconversion would be. One of the biggest problems that the OPA faced was how to price consumer goods during the reconversion period. Most agency officials favored the continuation of price controls throughout the entire reconversion process, that is, for months or even years after the war ended, but most politicians disagreed. On V-J Day the OPA issued 184 price decontrol orders covering aluminum, nearly all military goods, numerous types of industrial equipment, many foods, and consumer goods and other items unimportant to the cost of living or to business costs. A price-control extension bill passed through Congress on June 28, 1946, but was vetoed by President Truman. Congress did not override the veto, but instead passed a new price-control bill on July 25. During this 25-day hiatus in price controls, confusion reigned, but many leaders became convinced that the suspension of price controls would not result in runaway inflation, and all price controls were lifted by November 1946.[58]

World War II had taxed the productive capacity of the United States to its utmost, and government planners worked wonders in rerouting the economy to war production. Enormous strides were made in materials conservation that continue to have an impact on the way we transport and package goods, and we can learn a great deal from the lessons of 50 years ago as we face the challenge of finding places to put the garbage generated by the world's ever-expanding population.

What is perhaps most impressive about the regulations placed on the American economy during World War II, however, is that they were instituted with relative ease utilizing an astounding number of volunteer workers. The federal government for the last time, instead of creating new bureaucracies, took efficient advantage of local governmental and educational structures to help introduce and enforce federal regulations. Never again would the grass-roots organizations of the United States be so effectively mobilized in one cause. Never again would big government reach down to individuals with such a personal touch. Population growth and the expansion of the "partnership" that Eisenhower referred to, in his second inaugural address, as the military-industrial complex, would serve to make individual citizens feel insignificant and anonymous in the face of governmental power. Wartime propaganda made every individual feel that he or she could make a difference in bringing about victory, and gave individuals a sense of personal responsibility that has been all but lost in the postwar world. In a way, we can see this depersonalization epitomized in the demise of the corner grocery store and the expansion of the conglomerate-owned super-supermarkets and warehouse megastores that continue to proliferate along the Cold War "defense highways" which now nearly obliterate much of what was once rural America.

NOTES

1. Supplement to *Health for Victory Club Bulletin* no. 19, August 24, 1943, Strawbery Banke Museum.

2. Geoffrey Perrett, *Days of Sadness, Years of Triumph: The American People 1939–1945* (New York: Coward, McCann & Geoghegan, 1973), pp. 255–261.

3. Harvey C. Mansfield et al., *A Short History of OPA* (Washington, D.C.: Office of Temporary Controls, Office of Price Administration, 1947), pp. 13–36.

4. J. A. Krug, *Wartime Production Achievements and the Reconversion Outlook* (Washington, D.C.: War Production Board, 1945), pp. 6–7.

5. Mansfield, *Short History of OPA*, pp. 14–21; Bureau of Demobilization, Civilian Production Administration, *Industrial Mobilization for War* (Washington, D.C: U.S. Government Printing Office, 1947), pp. xiii-xiv.

6. Mansfield, *Short History of OPA*, pp. 15–19.

7. Herman L. Smith, "Excerpts from 'History of War Price and Rationing Board 14–8–1'" (1946), p. 1, Portsmouth War Records Committee Report Files, Portsmouth Public Library, Portsmouth, N.H.

8. Mansfield, *Short History of OPA*, p. 143.

9. *The Story of Wartime Rationing* (Washington, D.C.: Office of Price Administration, 1945), pp. 24–29.

10. Philip N. Guyol, *Democracy Fights: A History of New Hampshire in World War II* (Hanover, N.H.: Dartmouth Publications, 1951), p. 104; Diary of Louise Grant, May 2, 1942, S. Louise Grant Papers, Strawbery Banke Museum, Portsmouth, N.H.

11. Guyol, *Democracy Fights*, pp. 103–105.

12. Smith, "History of War Rationing Board 14–8–1," p. 10.

13. "Local Grocers Say Canned Food Users are 'Chiseling' Here," *The Portsmouth Herald*, January 4, 1943, pp. 1, 3.

14. "Local Grocers Say Canned Food 'Chiseling,'" pp. 1, 3; "Paging New England," *The Portsmouth Herald*, January 19, 1943, p. 4.

15. Oral History Interview, February 13, 1992, OH 2 SC 33, Strawbery Banke Museum, Portsmouth, N.H.

16. "Point Rationing Puzzle," *The Portsmouth Herald*, January 26, 1943, p. 11; "Point Rationing System Complicated? Not if You Use Coupons as Money," *The Portsmouth Herald*, February 4, 1943, p. 7; "OPA Lists Questions Answers on Rationing of Processed Foods," *The Portsmouth Herald*, February 8, 1943, p. 9; "Point Rationing to Be Explained to Lions Here," *The Portsmouth Herald*, January 9, 1943, p. 9; "Kittery, Eliot to Hear Talk on Point Rationing," *The Portsmouth Herald*, February 15, 1943, p. 2; "Paging New England," *The Portsmouth Herald*, January 19, 1943, p. 4.

17. Mansfield, *Short History of OPA*, pp. 179–180.

18. Mansfield, *Short History of OPA*; "How to Use War Ration Book Two," poster issued by the Office of Price Administration, 1943; Judith Russell and Renee Fantin, *Studies in Food Rationing* (Washington, D.C.: Office of Temporary Controls, Office of Price Administration, 1947), pp. 86–87.

19. For details on expiration dates see "Ration Book 3 Goes into Effect Here Sept. 12," *The Portsmouth Herald*, August 26, 1943, p. 5.

20. Mansfield, *A Short History of OPA*, pp. 171–176.

21. Mansfield, *Short History of OPA*, 180–182; Russell and Fantin, *Studies in Food Rationing*, pp. 171–172.

22. During 1944 the OPA temporarily suspended expiration dates, and told consumers that all coupons would be valid until the end of the war unless notice was given in advance of the imposition of new expiration dates. When it was determined that the no-expiration policy was making it impossible for OPA officials to predict possible shortages, the policy was rescinded, and new expiration dates were imposed without notice to the consumer. Mansfield, *Short History of OPA*, pp. 182–185.

23. "Your Ration Reminder," *The Portsmouth Herald*, January 20, 1944, p. 4.

24. Russell and Fantin, *Studies in Food Rationing*, pp. 99–103, 109–111, 114, 168.

25. Mansfield, *Short History of OPA*, p. 144.; John Morton Blum, *V Was for Victory: Politics and American Culture during World War II* (New York: Harcourt Brace Jovanovich, 1976), p. 21.

26. "Portsmouth Hunts Butter in Rain Downpour," *The Portsmouth Herald*, February 5, 1943, p. 9.

27. Russell and Fantin, *Studies in Food Rationing*, pp. 86, 152, 166–167.

28. Russell and Fantin, *Studies in Food Rationing*, p. 156.

29. Russell and Fantin, *Studies in Food Rationing*, pp. 156–157.

30. Grant diary, January 18, 1945.

31. Russell and Fantin, *Studies in Food Rationing*, pp. 166–167.

32. *The Story of Wartime Rationing*, pp. 67–73.

33. J. A. Krug, *Wartime Production Achievements*, p. 7.

34. Blum, *V Was for Victory*, pp. 117–124.

35. Personal communication with John Taylor, former employee and owner of the Morley Company, May 20, 1993.

36. Bureau of Demobilization, CPA, *Industrial Mobilization for War*, pp. 308, 309.

37. "What is the Relation of WFA to WPB Containers Branch?" *Modern Packaging* 17, no. 2 (October 1943): 96–97, 126."

38. "New Glass Jars Save 300,000 Tons of Steel Yearly in Food Cans," *The Portsmouth Herald,* March 18, 1943, p. 3.

39. "Last Minute News from Washington" *Modern Packaging* 17, no. 1 (September 1943): special insert; T. E. Manwarring, "WPB Member Explains Glass Order Amendments," *Modern Packaging* 17, no. 2 (October 1943): 95, 130.

40. R.L. Van Boskirk, "Washington Review," *Modern Packaging* 16, no. 10 (June 1943): 102; 17, no. 7 (March 1944): 190.

41. "You Will See Favorite Brands in More than One Container," *Modern Packaging* 17, no. 2 (October 1943): 81–83, 130.

42. "We Must Share the Shortages—Or Else," *Modern Packaging* 16, no. 12 (August 1943): 41.

43. Publication 3057, New Hampshire War Records, State Council for Defense OCD file, Box 276044, New Hampshire State Archives, Concord, N.H.

44. Manwarring, "WPB Member Explains Glass Order Amendments," p. 130.

45. Mansfield, *Short History of OPA*, p. 59.

46. Mansfield, *Short History of OPA*, p. 21, 43–51; Guyol, *Democracy Fights*, p. 107.

47. Caroline F. Ware, *The Consumer Goes to War: A Guide to Victory on the Home Front* (New York: Funk & Wagnalls, 1942), pp. 33, 36.

48. *The Story of Wartime Rationing*, pp. 8–9.

49. Mansfield, *Short History of OPA*, pp. 52–59.

50. Smith, "History of War Rationing Board 14–8–1," p. 10.

51. Mansfield, *Short History of OPA*, pp. 59–63.

52. Mansfield, *Short History of OPA*, p. 61.

53. Mansfield, *Short History of OPA*, pp. 43–45, 61.

54. Smith, "History of War Rationing Board 14–8–1," p. 9.

55. "Official Rent Control Goes into Effect in Rockingham, Strafford Counties," *The Portsmouth Herald*, December 1, 1942, p. 1.

56. See also advertisements in the January and February 1944 issues of *Good Housekeeping*.

57. Mansfield, *Short History of OPA*, p. 81–83.

58. Mansfield, *Short History of OPA*, pp. 81–83, 99, 100–101.

Fig. 48. *"Food is a Weapon."*
Poster published by the U.S.
Government Office of War In-
formation, ca. 1943. Gift of
Richard Cheek. (See also plate
16)

The War in the Kitchen

by Mary Drake McFeely

IN Portsmouth, New Hampshire, Louise Grant, a schoolteacher who lived with her mother and father, recorded in her diary changes in civilian life that took place as the nation went to war. On December 9, 1941, two days after Pearl Harbor, an air-raid warning sounded; at school, Grant and her students spent an hour in the basement, while at home a neighbor "rang our bell & told Ma to stay in & fill the tub with water." A few days later, Grant entered a first-aid course. Her father went to an air-raid wardens' meeting. She and her mother made blackout curtains for the windows and blue cellophane dimmers for their flashlights; they filled buckets with sand and put shovels next to them in case of fires caused by bombing. The Grants bought their first war bonds. The Japanese dishes from the sideboard in the dining room "went into exile." Louise Grant went shopping for new rubber boots; she and her mother ordered new shoes, anticipating that they would become scarce. They decided to replace their old radio, and when the new one came, "Pa got London & Buenos Aires on short wave, & that made him happy." At the grocery store, "The store manager told Ma tea was going to be scarce." But Christmas celebrations went on much as usual. They roasted turkey and made maple nut squares and stewed apricots. They baked sugar cookies and made chocolate ice cream. On New Year's Eve, they cooked a pork shoulder.[1]

The sense of emergency and preparation for anticipated further attacks that prevailed in the immediate aftermath of Pearl Harbor dimmed in time, even in vulnerable coastal towns like Portsmouth, where sometimes watchers on shore heard the diesel engines of German submarines. For civilian Americans the war became a war of the imagination.[2] Fostering a sense of participation among civilians required forging a symbolic link between the people at home—dreading casualty reports, dealing with shortages, rationing, blackouts, and frustrations—and the American and Allied forces fighting the war in Europe and Asia, as well as beleaguered British and Russian civilians. The metaphor of the home front affirmed that every civilian act contributed to or detracted from the war effort.

The woman who cooked for the family, now enrolled as an officer to fight the war in the kitchen, found herself making an abrupt change of focus (fig. 48, PLATE 16). The consumer role conceived and elaborated in the early part of the century assigned women the responsibility for watchful, educated, and enthusiastic consumption of the products of an industrial society. In the 1930s, the decade of the Great Depression, cooking from scratch and making do had a renaissance as many women became skilled at making the best of meager resources. Rather than compete with men for scarce jobs, they were encouraged to stay at home and to expend their energy in unpaid, frugal work. For women, the most important job was to see to it that the family was amply fed and spiritually nourished as well.

If her husband was unemployed, a wife was expected to support him, if only psychologically. "Should a man out of a job afford pie?" asked Ida Bailey Allen, a well-known advisor on housekeeping, poignantly. The answer she gave was a firm "yes"—and it was up to the wife to make the pie. Cookbooks of the 1930s recommended reviving the first course as a way of making people feel that they had plenty to eat. *The Most for Your Money Cookbook* suggested a threadbare Economy Soup. "Boil a minced onion in 1½ quarts stock or water, with a cup of bread crumbs. Press all through a sieve. Bring to a boiling point and season. Remove from fire and stir in 2 egg yolks beaten with a couple of tablespoons milk. Sprinkle grated cheese over each plate after serving."[3]

When the nation went to war, the rhetoric changed. Concern for family was replaced with a call to enlist in a great national effort. Military imagery made home cooking part of meeting the challenge of war. "Mother, captain of the kitchen, guards the health and strength of the family these difficult days," wrote Louisa Pryor Skilton in *American Cookery* magazine in March 1943. "Kitchen Commandos" found themselves deluged with recipes for such dishes as "Victory Medley" and "Military Meat Balls." The slogan, "Food is a weapon of war," appeared everywhere (fig. 48). "Every American housewife . . . is all out for victory on her own home front," said Harriet H. Hesler, in her *300 Sugar Saving Recipes*.[4]

Housekeeping became more complicated and time-consuming as both ingredients and equipment grew scarce. At the same time, women were urged to take jobs in war production, replace men who had gone to war, and do volunteer work (see fig. 16). Stretching meat became more important than stretching budgets as war industry put many people back to work. The cook's usual responsibilities included keeping up the health, strength, and morale of the family. In wartime, she now learned, she was also in charge of conserving the national food supply and participating in salvaging critical strategic materials.

Government programs to conserve fuel, tin, and rubber, and to supply food, not only to American armed forces, but to Allies through the lend-lease program, went into effect in the early months of war. All of them affected the kitchen. Food rationing began with sugar in the spring of 1942, but as soon as America had entered the war government officials had urged conservation of resources and had tried to discourage the hoarding of coffee, canned food, and other items.

Government agencies—existing ones such as the Cooperative Extension Service and new wartime ones such as the Office of Price Administration (OPA)—put forth volumes of advice, recommendations, and rules. The men in Washington issued pronouncements—sometimes avuncular, sometimes stern—emphasizing the need to supply food to American and Allied fighting forces, but other, less picturesque goals were at least as important. Seeking to avoid wartime inflation, the government emphasized saving money and investing in war bonds. To conserve metal for war supplies, commercial canning had to be reduced to a minimum. The rubber shortage required cutting back on transportation of freight—including foodstuffs—as well as on personal automobile travel. Housewives were instructed to save used cooking fats and to turn them in for reuse in the manufacture of munitions (see cat. 2). One full-page advertisement in popular magazines showed the actress Helen Hayes, in her kitchen in Nyack, New York, demonstrating for two beaming visiting sailors how she strained used kitchen fat to return to her meat dealer. "I don't know as much about making explosives as most soldiers and sailors do about the stage," Hayes was quoted as saying, "but lately I've learned these things: that kitchen fats make glycerine, and glycerine makes the powder charge that drives millions of shells from the guns of the United Nations."[5]

To meet national goals, the government had to make women alter their homemaking habits. "Meatless days" and other voluntary measures were introduced, followed gradually by a program of food rationing. Cooperative Extension Service staff members gave local demonstrations of canning and preserving techniques, organized community Victory Gardens, and distributed food bulletins. They taught classes in clothing remodeling (making children's clothes from men's and women's) and presented slide lectures on the role of food in winning the war.

Gas rationing and unpredictable food shortages made shopping more complicated. Louise Grant (fig. 49) met her mother downtown after school to do the shopping on foot commenting that it was the "Only way we can get our heavy bundles home with this nuisance of a gas situation."[6] Some shortages of familiar "basics"—sugar, butter, meat—lasted for the duration or longer. Others were less predictable. Grant bought a half-pound of coffee—the smallest amount she had ever purchased—on September 30, 1942, and stood in line for another half pound two-and-a-half weeks later. A few days after that, she heard the sound of the coffee grinder as she was shopping in the A&P, and acquired another half pound there.[7] Coffee rationing was announced shortly thereafter. While there was always plenty to eat in the United States, varying supplies combined with transportation pressures and shortages of packaging materials required the cook to constantly rethink menus. The home cook's challenge was to find substitutes and stretchers and to prepare them in ways that the family would accept—contriving "stick-to-the ribs" main dishes with little or no meat and comforting desserts without sugar (fig. 50).

By the winter of 1942 Louise Grant complained, "Everything is so muddled. No meat only a few fowls & some minced ham & hot dogs. No fish in the First National" (this in a seaport).[8] An Agriculture Department official explained in the pages of *Woman's Day*: more Americans were working than during the depression, and with more money to spend, they wanted to buy meat; American soldiers must have their meat; and the United States was shipping meat to Britain and Russia.[9] Housewives were bombarded with information on how to keep meat from spoiling (fig. 51) and on how to cook meat in ways that reduced shrinkage. Even before meat rationing began, the government called for a voluntary "meatless day" each week and suggestions for meatless and low-meat dishes and meat substitutes appeared everywhere.

Fig. 49. *Louise Grant, seated at front center, with her Portsmouth Training School for Teachers graduating class, 1932. S. Louise Grant Papers.*

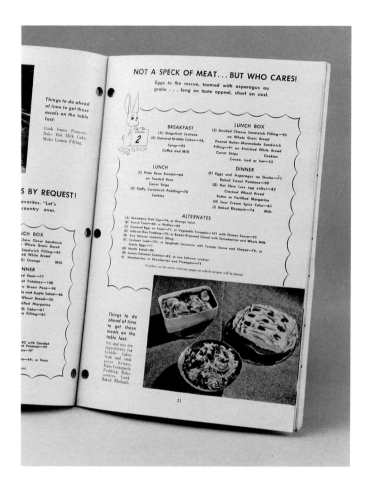

Fig. 50. (left) *Selected recipes from* Health-for-Victory Meal Planning Guide. *Published by the Westinghouse Electric & Manufacturing Company, Home Economics Institute, Mansfield, Ohio, 1944. Museum Collection.*

Fig. 51. (right) *"How to Keep Meat." Advertisement for the Frigidaire Division of General Motors Corporation published in the January 1944 issue of* Good Housekeeping.

Meat eaters explored less familiar cuts—spareribs, pork tails, oxtails and innards—to compensate for the scarcity of steaks and roasts, and advertisers joined government agencies in providing housewives with nutrition and food storage information. In February 1943, Louise Grant triumphantly reported "Got a piece of corned beef!" and remarked wistfully, "How I would like a little smoked shoulder or ham."[10] While the recipes using less popular, tougher, bonier cuts were similar to those that appeared in depression-era cookbooks, the motivation was no longer thrift, but patriotism.

But Americans were not in the habit of cooking vegetarian meals. The 1927 edition of *The Boston Cooking-School Cookbook* listed only one recipe for a main dish using dried beans—Boston Baked Beans. Other non-meat dishes—vegetable timbales, dainty egg dishes, and cheese rarebit—were clearly intended for ladies' luncheons and evening suppers, not for the main meal of the day. To make a little meat go farther, wartime recipes added oatmeal or corn meal to meatloaf mixtures, creating more bulk, if not more taste. In November 1942, *Woman's Day* printed a group of recipes all of which provided dinner for four using only a half pound of meat: baked lima beans with sauerkraut and pork, sausage scrapple with peanut butter gravy (peanut butter was a popular protein additive), spaghetti with frankfurters, hamburger stew with barley and vegetables, and liver balls with noodles served with a sauce made of condensed vegetable soup.

Macaroni and cheese was almost the only meatless dish based on pasta that appeared with any frequency; vegetarian dishes of any kind were few and presented apologetically. No more auspicious moment could have existed for the triumph of vegetarianism, but widespread enthusiasm for that change would have to wait for a generation. Herbs and spices were still foreign to most Americans, and few recipes took advantage of them to enliven the taste of otherwise bland concoctions. A 1942 Helen Hokinson cartoon in *The New Yorker* showed her well-known garden club ladies seated for luncheon; the hostess says, "If everything has a funny taste, don't worry. It's just herbs."[11]

Woman's Day invited its readers to submit favorite meatless recipes. The contest winners included Fried Cheese Squares, strips of cheese dipped in egg-flour batter and fried in drippings, and Green Pepper and Cheese Patties. These recipes gave an impression of valiant effort but little experience with non-meat cooking. Even though Wisconsin dairies diversified their production to supply Americans with equivalents of European cheeses—such as Roquefort—that the war had made unavailable, nearly all of the cheese recipes published in popular magazines during the war called for processed American cheese.

The sharp cutback in commercial canning removed standard ready-made main dishes like baked beans and Chef Boy-ar-dee spaghetti with sauce from the grocery shelf and forced people to try to reproduce them from scratch. A wartime cookbook, in a section headed "IF IT MUST BE—BEANS!" gave recipes for Chili Con Carne made with soybeans and "Baked Beans, U.S.N." made with pork tails or feet instead of the traditional salt pork.[12]

And butter. In the well-known A. A. Milne poem, the king says plaintively,

> Nobody, my dear, could call me a fussy man.
> But I do like a little bit of butter to my bread.
> The answer, which pleased him not at all, came back:
> Many people nowadays like marmalade instead.[13]

But in 1942, there was not enough sugar to make marmalade, and butter was at first scarce, and then rationed. American ingenuity focused on stretching butter—mixing it in various proportions with margarine, evaporated milk, and gelatin. Margarine had been manufactured in the United States since 1881, but most people still preferred butter, in part because of appearance. Margarine, naturally chalky white and unappetizing-looking, was subject to a 10% federal tax if colored to look like butter. (Eleanor Roosevelt campaigned for repeal of this law but it was not until 1950 that restrictions on coloring margarine were lifted.) An orange capsule enclosed in the box had to be mashed in to color the spread—a job often assigned to children (see cat. 25).

Dessert, as Ida Bailey Allen knew in the 1930s, has a substantial reputation as a morale-builder. Sugar and butter rationing inspired creations combining oatmeal and prunes or bread crumbs and figs, as well as sensible uses of alternative sweeteners, as in a lemon-prune pie sweetened with honey or a raisin pie sweetened with molasses. To celebrate her parents' 46th wedding anniversary, Louise Grant managed to produce a cake using only half a cup of sugar. As a substitute for whipped cream, Margaret Rudkin suggested an ingenious blend of dried milk, ice water, and lemon juice.[14]

Many women turned back to almost-forgotten methods of home food production, learning anew skills their grandmothers might have known and making their households more self-sufficient than they had been for decades. Margaret and Henry Rudkin were New Yorkers who had chosen to live a country life in Connecticut while he commuted to Wall Street on the railroad club car. Margaret Rudkin's genius for putting old skills to work has become legendary; having learned to bake in order to provide wholesome bread for her children, by 1937 she began selling her homemade Pepperidge Farm bread, sending it to Charles & Co. in New York with her husband on the morning train, and was on her way to fame. When the war came, the beautiful farm that had been a hobby took on a new significance. Rudkin wrote to the Department of Agriculture for pamphlets about raising and butchering pigs and steers. The Rudkins raised the animals, installed refrigerating machinery and a freezer room, cured their own meat (a butcher came to perform the slaughter), and made lard and sausage. "It really was very little trouble, and the quality of the meat was excellent," she recalled.[15] Rudkin also made her own butter during the war, again following the instructions in a United States government pamphlet.

The Rudkins had space and money to deal with wartime shortages by becoming self-sufficient producers for the duration. In more modest circumstances, people did what they could to grow and preserve their own vegetables and fruits. Where space was limited, community gardens occupied empty lots and corners. In Portsmouth, Louise Grant and her parents converted nearly all of the space in their tiny backyard on Cabot Street into a Victory Garden. They sent away for seeds and planted tomatoes, peppers, beets, carrots, lettuce, and other vegetables. Louise spent much of her time with the vegetable garden and its products, from starting seeds indoors in late winter, to setting out plants in spring, gardening in summer, and harvesting and preserving the crops in late summer and fall.

Before the war, aggressive marketing had taught people to appreciate the convenience of commercially processed foods. Americans had learned to appreciate canned and frozen vegetables and fruits, already trimmed and cut and sometimes cooked, and to take for granted the availability of green beans in February and peas in November, even in New Hampshire. Now, out of duty, not pleasure, they were required to reacquaint themselves with cooking and eating fresh locally grown produce in season. "We'll search for quick easy methods of preparing fresh vegetables because we will have to eat more fresh foods," wrote Cora Anthony in March 1943.[16] Anthony suggested kale with potatoes, baked vegetable hash, and scallions, peas, and cabbage served with an egg. People who very likely had never heard of such things were urged to eat soybeans, use soy flour, and grow their own bean sprouts. Soybeans were presented as "Hitler's secret weapon" now available to Americans, too, to beat the food shortages, but the propaganda was more dramatic than the unimaginative, unspiced recipes. The spirit of sacrifice for country, it appeared, was not fulfilled by cooking savory casseroles.

Nothing must go to waste. Waste was still a major sin, but now the reason not to transgress was concern for those distant others—fighting men and allies—rather than for the family budget. "You haven't saved it until you've used it," chided *Woman's Day* in May 1945, introducing a chart showing how to use leftovers. Government officials turned to homemakers to use up surplus crops, sometimes grown with excessive encouragement from the government. "It is up to you and me to eat the things that the farmers grow for us," a Department of Agriculture representative wrote, "even if it means eating the same food several days in a row." In 1943, a billion-pound peanut crop far exceeded the demand for peanut butter sandwiches, and food editors responded with sometimes bizarre inclusions of peanut butter in bean casseroles and in sauces. When farmers grew too many sweet potatoes, women were expected to use them, and *Woman's Day* supplied an assortment of sweet potato recipes. Save the home-grown white potatoes for later, the voice of government warned, for we must keep the farmers happy. "There's a long winter ahead and it may be a hard one. There is a war to win, and it may be a long one."[17]

"Bluntly speaking," announced the president of the Gourmet Society in New York in the fall of 1941, "it is exceedingly important to our total happiness that we enjoy our dinner."[18] Besides experimenting with new ingredients, women who had never put up food now found themselves pressed to learn home canning. Women who had never cooked (nearly half of all upper-middle-class households before the war had household help) had to learn to do so in these somewhat hampering circumstances. Women had to juggle with changing regulations and shortages.

By the summer of 1942, *Woman's Day* warned of a shortage of containers for commercial canning and published an article on methods of preserving food at home. The supply of glass jars, and rubber rings and lids seemed adequate (though later it would become a problem) (fig. 52). The article explained techniques of hot-water-bath and pressure-cooker canning. It also described methods of cold storage in basements, storage banks or pits, and outdoor root cellars—methods that a generation earlier would have been familiar to most rural people (fig. 53). Drying parsley, celery, and onions was relatively simple—more esoteric was a suggestion for tomato paste, cooked until thick, then dried a half-inch thick in a shallow pan and cut in pieces for storage. Among techniques of the past to be revived were salting fish and making sauerkraut.

Martha Garland, a Cooperative Extension Service agent in New Hampshire, held 27 demonstrations on community canning. A follow-up questionnaire in September 1942 revealed that 212 participants (about half the total) had put up 39,874 quarts of food. A woman in Danville, New Hampshire, wrote, "Canned everything in sight." In the summer of 1942, Louise Grant and her mother laid in a supply of jars for canning. In September and October they put up 61 quarts of tomatoes from their garden. They also made mincemeat and piccalilli. The Grants augmented the produce of their own garden

Fig. 52. (left) *Ball brand Canning Jars and Ball, Crown, Good Luck, and Bull Dog brand jar rings, caps, and rubbers, ca. 1940–1947. Museum Collection and gifts of Charles E. Burden and Mrs. Philip Horton Smith.*

Fig. 53. (right) *New Hampshire woman with her jars of home canned foods, ca. 1944, by an unidentified photographer. Reproduced from a photograph in the New Hampshire State Archives.*

by buying wax beans and peas to can from local farmers. They also exchanged fruits and vegetables with friends.[19]

The next year, Grant recorded that she and her mother had put up 299 jars of "stuff" from their garden—tomatoes, beans, peas, carrots, pears, applesauce, as well as ketchup, relishes, chili sauce, and jam. By the fall of 1943, jars were hard to come by. Grant describes bottling their homemade ketchup in "an odd asst of bottles—1 pt Coldwells' rum with a ship pressed in—1 pt M1-31, a Hubbards germicide bottle, a pepper sauce bottle, an olive jar, & a candy jar."[20] Nonetheless, the campaign to "Grow More and Can More" continued into 1944 (fig. 54, PLATE 10).

Pressure cookers, the safest equipment for home canning, were in short supply and were subject to rationing. During the war, there were only approximately 325 pressure cookers in the entire state of New Hampshire. People who were lucky enough to own one were urged to share it. Community canning centers were organized where women could share equipment and beginners could learn techniques.[21] Such centers became the scene of convivial gatherings not unlike the old quilting bees.

In addition to producing more of their own food at home, women also found that they had to devote more time than usual to shopping. Instead of going to one grocery or supermarket, they shopped from store to store to get what they wanted, standing in line for a share of one grocer's shipment of sugar or coffee, hunting (sometimes unsuccessfully) for a turkey for Thanksgiving or Christmas, using their favored-customer status at the local grocery to obtain sugar and butter, and shopping the supermarkets when they heard of the arrival of fresh shipments of meat or other scarce commodities.

Advice was plentiful. Magazines, newspapers, and radio programs kept audiences informed about availability of foods and changes in restrictions. *Woman's Day* added a special section, with a last-minute deadline, so that it could provide women with the most current information, amplified with articles by government officials from OPA and the Department of Agriculture, that

Fig. 54. *"Grow More . . . Can More . . . in '44." Poster published by the U.S. Government War Food Program, 1944. Gift of Calvin P. Otto. (See also plate 10).*

explained why shortages of particular foods occurred, how the ration point system worked, and why wage and price freezes were put into effect. Jessie Young, the "radio homemaker" of Iowa radio station KMA, broadcasting from her own kitchen, suggested recipes like Marbled Macaroni with tomato sauce and Spam, and Mock Hamburgers made of oatmeal and eggs flavored with onions and sage and cooked in tomato juice. Billie Burke, better known as the Good Witch in "The Wizard of Oz," played a point-perplexed housewife talking to guest authorities from government and industry about the latest food information on a weekly radio program called "Fashions in Rations."[22]

While the food supply was always adequate, America restructured its cooking and eating habits. The National Nutrition Conference for Defense, called by President Roosevelt in the spring of 1941—before Pearl Harbor—had established standards for a healthy diet in the form of seven "food groups" (fig. 55). The conference report recommended one pint of milk daily for adults, and one quart for children over the age of two; one serving of meat, one egg or one serving of a protein substitute such as beans; two servings of vegetables, one of them green or yellow; two servings of fruit, including one good source of vitamin C such as an orange or a grapefruit; whole grain or enriched bread, flour, or cereal; butter or margarine; and dessert at least once a day.

The nutrition message was delivered as widely as possible. Nutrition experts even wrote songs emphasizing the importance of milk, vegetables, and protein. In one of these wartime songs, "Food—a Weapon of Our Nation," sung to the tune of "The Battle Hymn of the Republic," a verse was dedicated to nutrition requirements for the lunch box:

Fig. 55. *"For Health. . . ." Poster published by the U.S. Government Department of Agriculture, 1943. Gift of Richard Cheek.*

In the lunch box you must put a hot and creamy soup, not tea,
Make the sandwiches of whole wheat bread with meat loaf, cheese,
 poultry,
You must sometimes add an egg and always fruit or celery
In all our factories,
 Pack a lunch a man can work on
 Pack a lunch a man can work on
 Pack a lunch a man can work on
In all our factories.[23]

Women had to provide lunches for the members of their families (sometimes including themselves) who worked factory shifts or worked too far away to waste precious gasoline coming home for midday dinner. Factories allowed as little as 15 minutes for lunch, often not enough time to get to the cafeteria even if there was one.

 The magazines, like the songs, urged ample lunches. They encouraged efficient production, establishing an area of the kitchen where lunch boxes were packed, and planning ahead. In "Victory Lunches: Hearty Food for Sturdy Men," Louisa Pryor Skilton proposed a community effort. "Why not take turns packing these Victory lunches? It is no more trouble to plan for two, four or six men, and by taking turn and turn about, it would certainly lighten the work."[24] While men relied on their wives to provide individual lunches, women workers sometimes brought food to share, broadening their fellow-workers' tastes by providing ethnic dishes to brighten the night-shift meal.[25]

By late 1944, patriotism in the kitchen had become a dreary task. There were not enough turkeys to go around for the holidays, and many people settled for pork, veal shoulder, or braised fowl. The Grants were lucky at Thanksgiving, but on December 21, with "no birds in view," they settled on a hen and a smoked shoulder. Dried apricots were so scarce that finding some merited a comment in Louise Grant's diary. Canned grapefruit and orange juice were rationed again, and the Grants, hearing commentator Gabriel Heatter announce on his news broadcast that shortening would return to the ration list, hurried to the store before closing time to stock up. Louise Grant scornfully renamed the OPA the Office of Perfidious Administration.[26]

By summer, the Grants considered themselves lucky to get a piece of meat even when it took two trips to the store. One Saturday morning, Louise Grant and her mother went shopping but had "No luck for food." Louise went back in the afternoon and "stood & stood & was lucky. Got a nice piece of ham." Two weeks later she left off shelling peas to get to the store early, only to find that the butcher did not expect meat until the afternoon. She returned and "Stood from quarter of 2 until 3 but got some," then returned to shelling and canning 23 pints of peas, making soup, and cooking the hard won piece of lamb.[27]

Wartime cooking had little permanent effect on the American diet. Patriotic rhetoric firmly defined it as a response to the exigencies of war; "doing without" was a way of supporting the boys at the front and licking Hitler and Hirohito. The "boys" came back hungry, and not for Spam. The lunch boxes were discarded. The shortages ended, though not immediately or all at once. Well before the war ended, the advertising industry was whetting appetites for new refrigerators. The war recipes were happily abandoned; it would be 25 years before serious vegetarian recipes commanded any sizeable audience, and by then the postwar enthusiasm for ethnic cooking would have changed American attitudes about herbs and spices and cooking with wine.

The war in the kitchen was over. Abundant good food for all was one of the things we had fought to preserve. One of President Roosevelt's Four Freedoms was Freedom from Want. In the Norman Rockwell poster that illustrated it, a comfortable, motherly woman in an apron sets before the family a magnificent, enormous, well-browned, luscious turkey surrounded by platters and bowls of buttered vegetables, mashed potatoes, rolls, and well-sugared cranberry sauce, sure to be followed by apple pie.

1. Diary of Louise Grant, December 12–31, 1941, January 8, 27, February 12, 1942, S. Louise Grant Papers, Strawbery Banke Museum, Portsmouth, N.H.

2. John M. Blum, *V Was For Victory: Politics and American Culture During World War II* (New York: Harcourt Brace Jovanovich, 1976), p. 16.

3. Cora, Rose, and Bob Brown. *Most for Your Money Cookbook* (New York: Modern Age Books, 1938), pp. 14–15.

4. Louisa Pryor Skilton, "Victory Lunches: Hearty Food for Sturdy Men," *American Cookery* 46 (March 1942): 348. Harriet H. Hesler, *300 Sugar Saving Recipes* (New York: M. Barrows & Co., 1942), p. vii.

5. Advertisement, *The New Yorker*, September 5, 1942.

6. Grant diary, May 29, 1942.

7. Grant diary, September 30, October 17, 19, 1942.

8. Grant diary, December 19, 1942.

9. Harry Henderson, "Why the Meat Shortage?" *Woman's Day*, November 1942, pp. 35, 62–63.

10. Grant diary, February 1, 13, 1943.

11. *The New Yorker*, August 22, 1942, p. 21.

12. Prudence Penny, *Coupon Cooking* (Hollywood, Calif.: Murray & Gee, 1943), p. 57.

13. Grant diary, June 28, 1945.

14. Margaret Rudkin, *The Margaret Rudkin Pepperidge Farm Cookbook* (New York: Atheneum, 1963), p. 164.

15. Rudkin, *Pepperidge Farm Cookbook*, pp. 64–65.

16. *Woman's Day*, March 1943, pp. 1–3.

17. Roy F. Hendrickson, "If Men Would Only Listen," *Woman's Day*, September 1943, p. 1.

18. *American Cookery* 46 (August/September 1941): 122.

19. Ruth G. Stimson, "Chronology of Events Significant to the Cooperative Extension Service and Its Clients . . ." Part 4, 1942 and 1943, entry for September 1942; Grant diary, June–October 1943.

20. Grant diary, October 23, October 3, 1943.

21. Ruth Stimson, Panel Discussion, March 27, 1993. OH 2 SC 43 Strawbery Banke Museum, Portsmouth, N.H.

22. Evelyn Birkby, *Neighboring on the Air* (Iowa City: University of Iowa Press, 1991), pp. 42, 46, 109; Advertisement, *American Cookery* 48 (December 1943).

23. Students and Faculty of Sarah Lawrence College, *Nutrition Melodies* (Bronxville, N.Y.: Sarah Lawrence College, 1943).

24. Louisa Pryor Skilton, "Victory Lunches: Hearty Food for Sturdy Men," *American Cookery* 46 (March 1942): 348–49.

25. "Nell Giles Packs a Victory Lunch Box for Girls on the Aircraft Assembly Line," *American Cookery* 47 (October 1942): 86–87.

26. Grant diary, December 21, 1944; February 3, January 18, 1945.

27. Grant diary, June 23, July 6, 1945.

Suspended in Time: Mom-and-Pop Groceries, Chain Stores, and National Advertising during the World War II Interlude

by Roland Marchand

WORLD WAR II brought both temporary advantages and onerous burdens to America's multitude of tiny, neighborhood groceries. Although their ranks had been severely depleted by more than three decades of devastating competition from national and regional retailing chains and the emerging supermarkets, during the war the surviving Mom-and-Pop stores found momentary refuge by serving certain intensified local demands. The stringent wartime rationing of gasoline, the increased participation of married women in the workforce (sometimes on graveyard or swing shifts), and the increasing income levels of poorer urban families all expanded the tenuous economic niche that still allowed for the survival of many small-scale urban grocers.

But the Mom-and-Pop corner stores could not serenely enjoy this brief respite from a mismatched commercial rivalry. The war also brought daunting reminders of the disproportions of scale that relegated them to the vulnerable margins of the food industry. Leslie Clough, who spent much of his youth working in Bertha Abbott's tiny corner store in the Puddle Dock neighborhood of Portsmouth, New Hampshire (fig. 56), later remembered vividly the emotions stirred and the values challenged by these drastically unequal relationships. At the height of the war, he recalled, a salesman from one of the giant meatpackers came to the store and announced that he was not "going to be able to call on the neighborhood groceries any more." In response to dire meat shortages, the giant packers were going to have to restrict their sales to "the big markets, the A&P, the First National." Bertha Abbott had no illusions about the powerlessness of the corner grocery in its relations with the great meatpackers and their nationally advertised brands. "She was mad as a hornet," Clough recalled, "but she understood. She didn't say anything."[1]

Soon after the war, the encounter was rejoined. Now Bertha Abbott called righteously upon that cluster of values that have sentimentally enshrined such institutions as the corner store—and that intuitively have equated economic disproportion with moral disparity. The same salesman came to the door of the Abbott grocery to report that his company was "picking up some of our old customers." But Bertha Abbott had staggered through the last years of the war with meager meat supplies obtained from a small supplier and from another larger retailer in the area. Now she was determined to stay with those suppliers who had "carried" her along then, and who needed her now. When the packers' representative persisted by asking, "What can I sell you," Bertha Abbott retorted, "Nothing! . . . you threw down the little neighborhood grocery stores when they needed you most . . . You left once and you can leave again

Fig. 56. *The Abbotts' "Little Corner Store," 82 Jefferson Street, Portsmouth, N.H., ca. 1937. Reproduced from a photograph in the collection of the late Leslie Clough.*

and don't ever come back!" Clough listened to the confrontation, at first with apprehension and then with admiration. "That's what you call loyalty," he remembered thinking.[2]

The feeling of moral triumph that Clough recognized in himself and attributed to his employer was closely linked to the other qualities that set the Mom-and-Pop store apart from the giant grocery chains and constituted its primary shelter from the economic efficiencies of its larger competitors. Prices at the tiny neighborhood store were almost invariably higher than those at the chain stores and supermarkets.[3] The advantages accruing from volume buying, rapid stock turnover, and the efficiencies of vertical integration could not be matched by the small independent grocery store. It could only hope to command a smaller trade through its convenience of location, longer hours, liberal credit policies, friendly ambience, and miscellaneous personal services.

Appeals to customer loyalty often proved insufficient to counter the larger modern facilities and lower prices of the chains and large independents. During the 1920s, chains like A&P and First National surged forward to capture more than a third of all grocery sales. They then held their own in the face of a furious counterattack—in the form of anti-chain laws, both proposed and enacted, in state legislatures and the national Congress during the 1930s.[4] The circumstances of World War II would tip the competitive balance, temporarily and marginally, back in favor of the neighborhood grocery. But even with their marginal gains through temporarily enhanced functional roles during the war, the Mom-and-Pop stores could hardly escape the ominous realization of the vast disproportions in their crucial relationships with giant producer cooperatives, with wholesale and retail chains, with national advertisers, and—particularly during wartime—with the federal government.

In the federal programs of food rationing and price controls, corner grocers suddenly came into direct, and sometimes onerous, contact with the federal

Fig. 57. *"My Pledge to You."*
Poster published by the United
States Government Printing
Office, Washington, D.C., 1943,
as a part of the Home Front
Pledge campaign. Gift of
Richard Cheek.

wartime bureaucracy (fig. 57). Powerful new agencies, such as the Office of Price Administration (OPA) and the War Food Administration (WFA), armed with the immense moral authority as agencies of war mobilization, intruded into grocers' daily operations. Vexed in their realization that Americans had "not yet learned the necessity of sacrifice and self-denial," federal officials and their eager allies in the press of the wholesale and retail grocery trade harangued retail grocers on their duty to act as the local agents of mobilization.

Federal agencies and administrators deluged local grocers with requests to promote the sale of food commodities that were in plentiful supply (for instance, Irish potatoes were "hereby designated" by the Federal Food Administrator as "a Victory Food Selection for the period of October 21 through November 6, 1943") and to educate their customers with posters such as "The Victory Food Special" (fig. 58) or the Office of Price Administration's "How to Shop With War Ration Book Two" (see fig. 38).[5] The grocery journals, eager to demonstrate the patriotism of the food industry and sanctimonious in flaunting their moral authority as Uncle Sam's wartime helpers, regularly prodded retailers with queries such as: "Are *you* doing *your* part? Are you *mobilized* and in *action*?" Not only did grocers acquire the duty to serve as collectors of

monials by "grocers everywhere" from "a flood of letters" recounting the help that Del Monte was providing in helping them to "meet their wartime problems." Featuring copies of its national advertising in the trade journals, Del Monte appealed to local retailers by calling attention to efforts to convince consumers to buy groceries for a full week at a time, to recognize that shortages of foods were not the grocer's fault, and to shop early in the week and early in the day. This campaign was intended to help grocers, Del Monte observed, by keeping women from crowding stores at later times when those with demanding work schedules had to shop.[15] "Here's What We Are Doing—to make every woman realize what grocers are up against—and what she must do to get better service in wartime," Del Monte proclaimed. "We know the spot you're in this year!" Del Monte assured grocers in the Spring of 1943. "More foods rationed—less to go around—customers wondering who to blame." The company promised that its national ads, by instructing customers to do their part in "licking our food problem," would "take complaints off your shoulders" (fig. 59).[16] Still, for all of this vaunted sacrifice and assistance, the national

Fig. 59. *Del Monte Foods Advertisement,* American Grocer, *April 7, 1943, p. 5. Courtesy, Library, University of California, Davis.*

food manufacturers and processors, and their advertising agencies, actually found their major purposes elsewhere.

The American advertising industry entered World War II disheartened by a decade of confinement in "the dog house of public opinion." Under attack from consumer activists and charged (along with the rest of big business) with a major share of responsibility for the depression, the industry had also been at war with itself over the decline of ethics and good taste in 1930s advertising.[17] The industry looked somewhat desperately to wartime conditions as an opportunity to gain redemption and prove itself "an adult medium of communication."[18] This was advertising's chance, as agency executive Walter Weir put it, to "justify its existence," to demonstrate its power "as it has never been demonstrated before." The war crisis provided advertising with an opportunity which "must never be lost," to gain public recognition for its contribution to national wartime goals and thus to gain the stature it needed to perform its most crucial function—safeguarding the free enterprise system in the postwar world.[19]

Arguing that a free press needed advertising support during wartime, and that it was only fair that corporations contributing heavily to war production be able to keep their brand names before the public, the advertising industry and business interests succeeded in gaining an exemption from wartime excess profits taxes for all advertising expenditures that were "ordinary and necessary and bear a reasonable relation to the business activities in which the enterprise is engaged."[20] This policy insured a high level of wartime advertising, even by companies now primarily producing military items. It also insured ample national advertising by food companies that sold a considerable portion of their output to the government and, because of food shortages, had no need to push current sales. Small retailers could take some comfort in knowing that manufacturers would keep national brand names prominently before the public so that these brands would not fade from customer consciousness. Because advertisers were anxious to prove that they were contributing to the war effort, they also constantly harangued retailers to play an enthusiastic role in carrying out the sometimes onerous duties of civilian mobilization.

Early in 1942, the advertising industry launched a War Advertising Council to prove its patriotism and to render expert service to federal civilian mobilization programs.[21] The War Advertising Council quickly established close ties with former industry executives within the federal government's Office of War Information (OWI); it offered the skills of agency copywriters and made contributions of newspaper and magazine space available from leading advertisers for messages crucial to home-front mobilization. Setting itself the patriotic goal of "A War Message in Every Ad," the Council sought to place advertising in the position of being able to claim major credit for the success of all wartime popular mobilization programs. It was through the War Advertising Council, then, that such massive mobilization drives as the "Fats Salvage" drive of 1942 and the "Food Fights for Freedom" campaign of 1943 were imparted simultaneously to the public and to grocery retailers, with each party assigned its own responsibilities.[22]

Through ads produced by such food giants as Del Monte Foods and General Foods, the War Advertising Council cooperated with the OWI and the WFA in explaining to the nation "the facts about the wartime food situation." With an emblem of Uncle Sam's Hand holding a market basket, and slogans such as "Produce and Conserve, Share and Play Square," the "Food Fights for Freedom" campaign mobilized citizens to plant Victory Gardens, to "pay no more than top legal prices," for food, and to shun black market operations. Retailers were urged to "*Serve your customers—serve your country*" by complying with ceiling prices on foods and distributing official kitchen posters. The Civilian Defense organizations of local communities were bombarded with "Tool Kits" (including materials to be used by volunteers in home visits) and instructions on "How to Mobilize your Community to make Food Fight for Freedom."[23]

Such mobilizations certainly allowed even the smallest grocery stores to view themselves as integral parts of a national war effort in which food was a "weapon" and every citizen could "shorten the war with food." But they also saddled retailers with additional burdens—materials to be posted and distributed and information to be acquired and promulgated. The more prosperous and "professional" grocers were assisted by trade journals and chain networks in acquiring the expertise necessary to participate more comfortably in such mobilizations. By contrast, the tiniest and least sophisticated Mom-and-Pop operations, like Bertha Abbott's "Little Corner Store," participated only marginally in these networks of information, often subscribed to no trade journal, and could not afford to make themselves a visible part of wartime campaigns through local advertising. While the large retailers could easily flaunt their patriotic cooperation, by using national messages such as "Food Fights for Freedom" as backdrops for their advertising, the corner grocer was likely to find more bother than benefit in these heavily exploited opportunities for "public service" by the national food industry.[24]

In yet another respect, national advertisers offered little more than psychic benefits to small retailers while pursuing their own political agendas. The war created optimum incentives for "educational" campaigns of advocacy and corporate image advertising. Many advertisers, including even food processors, could easily sell all of their limited production without any advertising stimulus. But government tax policies, which taxed excess profits at 90% and allowed a normal amount of advertising to be deducted as a nontaxable business expense, gave corporations a special incentive to invest their wartime profits in nonproduct advertising.

Corporate image ads often educated consumers in the wonders of the corporation's prospective contributions to postwar technologies; sometimes, corporations anticipated the political realities of the postwar period, and defended business interests by identifying free enterprise with American war goals. While small local grocers were unlikely to dissent from either of these goals, neither did they gain much from serving—as folksy, small-town, small-scale business often did—as the prototype through which big business made its case. For instance, Bertha Abbott and proprietors of other small grocery stores were unlikely to gain much satisfaction from Armour Company messages such as the one touting "Modern Business as a National Resource" that provided "Spiritual Dividends" to the American people, especially when Armour and other big wholesalers cut these same tiny retailers from their distribution system during the war (fig. 60).[25]

Large corporations confronted public relations problems, by seeking to associate themselves as closely as possible with small business. Again and again, they argued the case against government regulations by illustrating the stifling effects of such regulations on the "little guy" on the make. During World War II, in their enthusiasm to parlay their patriotic service into an ideological counterattack on the vestiges of New Deal thinking, many corporations turned even more resolutely to "Main Street" Norman Rockwell images as the optimum settings for "just folks" treatises on free enterprise as "the American Way." In the process, such figures as small shopkeepers, local barbers, and "Old Bill" of the small repair shop became the romanticized spokesmen for corporate values.[26]

Although this folksy imagery might be taken to heart by neighborhood grocers as an acknowledgment of the moral primacy of their traditional, personalized manner of conducting business, most wartime corporate appeals stopped far short of lauding the Mom-and-Pop grocery. Folksy corporate imagery entirely favored the small town, with its bustling-yet-friendly Main Street as the physical representation of what the nation was "fighting for." Urban, working-class neighborhoods, the sites of most surviving Mom-and-Pop groceries, enjoyed no presence in these "American pastoral" depictions of small-town America as the *true* America.[27] Moreover, advocacy ads for untram-

Fig. 60. *The Peoples Market at 62 Daniel Street, Portsmouth, N.H., ca. 1942. Photograph by Frank Hersey. On January 7, 1943,* The Portsmouth Herald *reported that Portsmouth's Peoples Market, one of five N.H. stores in a small chain, would be forced to close within the next few months because, according to store manager Rudolphe Blais (shown here), there was only enough meat allotted to the N.H. stores to keep two of them open—those in Laconia and Concord. Gift of Frank Hersey.*

meled free enterprise exalted the "little guy," who was lionized not for any intrinsic values that might be associated with conducting a small-scale operation, but for his potential to succeed through boundless expansion (as had the corporate giants who constructed him in the image of their own fancied origins).

Whether the setting for grocery-store tableaus in national advertisements was small town or nondescript, the gender of the grocer never varied. He was always male, and virtually always between 25 and 50 (see fig. 57). Ethnically, he was usually Anglo-Saxon but was occasionally presented stereotypically as Italian or as a member of another white ethnic group. A proprietor such as Bertha Abbott, or an assistant such as teenager Leslie Clough, almost never gained visual representation in national advertising. And the convention of the male grocer persisted throughout the war years, despite the fact that, by the end of 1943, the percentage of women working in grocery stores had increased since the beginning of the war from 21% to 30%.[28]

While articles and illustrations in the trade press did actively encourage the increased employment of women in groceries, and while some corporations even sought to ingratiate themselves with local retailers by providing them with "help wanted" appeals to housewives to join the retail grocery work force, the advertising stereotype of the authoritative male grocer persisted without interruption.[29] "Rosie" gained much attention from national advertising as riveter and factory production worker, but never the least recognition as grocer. It is possible that advertisers subconsciously presumed that the grocer's added responsibility for explaining complicated rationing and pricing procedures to housewives necessitated a male image (fig. 61). More plausibly, we might simply recall that advertising artists, except when an explicit and unusual selling strategy dictated otherwise, were in the business of trading upon stereotypes, not of overturning them. The naive, sentimental association of the giant corporation with the small tradesman called for an adherence to traditional roles, not their disruption.

If corporate imagery in the Norman Rockwell mode ignored the "Moms" of Mom-and-Pop stores and offered largely illusory comfort to the tiny retailer, the futuristic aura of the world-of-tomorrow strategy in corporate advertising can only be described as devastating. The bright, shining world of the future, which corporations envisioned as emerging from their wartime technologies, certainly envisaged no place for the tiny, quaint, congested neighborhood market. In the wondrous future created by new technologies, everything was spacious and streamlined. Even before the United States entered the war, Du Pont included images of a dark, crowded, old country store in its promotional films for Cellophane to emphasize, through a before-and-after contrast, the antiquated old times that were giving way to modern changes advanced by Du Pont's new technologies.[30] As American participation in the war brought producers of war weapons tax incentives for institutional advertising, they also heralded a technologically modernized future with unprecedented ardor. Du Pont, in its ads for Cellophane, even envisaged a future in which "Mrs. Kimble," and "Mrs. Peters," two typical housewives, traveled by their personal

Fig. 61. *Detail from "How to Shop with War Ration Book Two." Poster published by the Office of Price Administration, 1943 (see fig. 38). Gift of Charles E. Burden.*

helicopters to land in the parking lot of the "village market." Despite its name, obviously this grocery would bear no resemblance to existing neighborhood groceries—in size, in equipment, or in style of operations.[31]

In a sense, Du Pont's futurism merely exaggerated a tendency well established in the national product advertising of companies involved in food packaging and even, in some instances, in that of manufacturers of food and household products. When national advertisers chose a setting for their social tableaus of the lives and mores of typical consumers, they almost invariably selected a backdrop that conveyed a sense of the modern. The principle of favorable association dictated that the product should be seen in the "best company." The crowded, sometimes dark, and usually antiquated ambience of the tiny Mom-and-Pop grocery did not meet such criteria. If neighborhood grocers paid attention to the imagery promoted in national advertising, they could only lament the inevitable tendency of advertisers to connect the acclaimed products with spacious, liberally staffed supermarkets and modern, state-of-the-art equipment and fixtures.[32] As wartime ads moved toward exaggerating the modernistic styles of the future, small neighborhood grocers could expect little from the public influence of the giant elements of their industry except for vivid reminders of their impending obsolescence.

In the face of the slights and rebuffs from national advertising, however, and in defiance of the aggregated power of the chain stores and the bureaucratic burdens of wartime government controls, many of the tiniest of neighborhood groceries still found a socioeconomic niche in which to survive, and even to thrive, during the wartime interlude. Whereas the chain grocery stores had accounted for between 37% and 38% of all grocery sales in 1940 and 1941, they slipped to an average of only some 33% of such sales from 1943 to 1945. During the war years, moreover, the total retail sales in food markets increased in dollar amounts by some 70%. This constituted a very substantial increase, even when discounted for the concurrent increase in food prices. A number of grocery stores did go out of business during the war years. But, in contrast to previous decades, these were more likely to be larger independents or chain outlets than Mom-and-Pop groceries.[33]

Several conditions peculiar to wartime protected the neighborhood store. Before the war, the automobile had worked to the advantage of larger grocery stores because customers could easily and cheaply travel by car to take advantage of the wider selections and lower prices at chain stores.[34] But the severe wartime restrictions on automobile usage, particularly as they affected a lower- and working-class neighborhood such as that surrounding the Abbotts' Little Corner Store in Portsmouth, worked to the advantage of the nearby small store. "People stayed in their own neighborhood," Leslie Clough recalled. "We didn't have any automobiles to speak of."[35]

A leading OPA official had predicted in November 1942 that the war might bring "the renaissance of the village general store" because "consumers are now going to be doing their buying much nearer home than they used to."[36] *Modern Packaging* concluded that "with every mile of travel carefully considered by the consumer, it is evident that the neighborhood store is going to gain an advantage." Early in 1944, the editor of *Progressive Grocer* confirmed that gasoline shortages had influenced customer patterns in some 6% of national food sales.[37]

Another wartime shortage, that of new appliances such as mechanical refrigerators, also contributed to the viability of the corner store. Even those families who enjoyed substantial increases in income during the war could not move up from the ice box to the refrigerator. Thus, they could not respond to those helpful messages from food producers, aimed at the middle class, which called for women to shop only once a week. Puddle Dock families remained dependent upon frequent grocery shopping at a convenient neighborhood store.

Changes in American consumption patterns during the war also worked to the relative advantage of corner groceries in low-income neighborhoods. The war brought a temporary leveling of incomes, with the poorest families gaining dramatic percentage increases in household income. This shift brought decided changes in food purchases by working-class and lower-class families. Whereas in the mid-1930s the bottom half of American families by income had accounted for only 35% of all dollars spent for food, by mid-1942 that percentage had increased to 44.5%.[38] Not only were the families that initially made the greatest percentage gains from wartime prosperity those that had traditionally spent the largest portions of their money on food, but, throughout 1942, those families continued to spend the same high percentage of their income on food as their wages increased.[39] Moreover, the shortage of other consumer goods during World War II reinforced the tendency of lower-class families to channel their increased incomes disproportionately into purchases of food.

Mom-and-Pop grocery stores continued to occupy one niche in the retail food trade with some economic safety; they alone allowed customers to purchase on credit. The food chains did not accept credit; neither did the larger independents in food retailing. But groceries on credit had long been a necessity for poorer families.[40] Even during the more prosperous wartime years, uncertainties and fluctuations in lower-class incomes made the availability of credit an appreciated custom, if not a necessity, in neighborhoods such as the one where the Little Corner Store was located.

As one of six small grocery stores in this urban, working-class neighborhood, the Abbott store sold almost everything on credit to well-known local customers. Since Bertha Abbott also often cashed their paychecks, she was in a position to judge most families' ability to pay. Still, she was too close to these families and their children to be able to endure seeing them "go without." So, while the liberal granting of credit kept local customers loyal to the store, this practice could also erode profitability. Leslie Clough, Abbott's teenage assistant, ultimately stopped extending credit to new customers "for one simple reason." He had seen too many "hard times," as a result of families who "couldn't pay." Although occasionally one of these debtors would suddenly appear and announce that "I can pay you now," Clough more vividly recalled having a great deal of "money on the books we never could get."[41] Thus, although credit was an important element in preserving a protected economic niche for the corner grocery, it could also severely limit the possibilities for long-range profitability.[42]

In other respects, the special "services" provided by the tiny neighborhood grocery secured customer loyalty without these daunting financial consequences. As live-in businesses, such stores could often provide local residents with the convenience of extended hours. Jeannette Black who, with her husband, ran another tiny grocery store a few blocks away from the Little Corner Store, recalled that they stayed open "Seven days a week, Sundays, holidays, every day. . . . From six in the morning until 11:30 at night."[43] These long hours were important for war workers on the swing shift or the graveyard shift especially because during the war these workers included women, the traditional grocery store customers.[44]

A tiny neighborhood store like Bertha Abbott's also provided other personalized services. By all accounts, Bertha freely dispensed personal advice from across her small counter. Near the dinner hour, an entrant to the store might well encounter the aroma of stew on the stove in the adjoining kitchen.[45] Her special friends among the customers would be invited to cross the threshold into her living quarters and join her for tea or coffee.[46] Georgie Gould's neighborhood grocery (fig. 62), only a block away, also provided an important personal service—gossip. It was the "hangout" for a different local group—"The Gossip Gang."[47] Far from insignificant in the customer-bonding services of the Abbott store was a telephone available to all customers.[48] Bertha took messages for those without home telephones as well as providing

Fig. 62. *Gould's Market, 16 Charles Street, Portsmouth, N.H., ca. 1915, by an unidentified photographer. Following her husband's death in 1916, Georgie Gould became sole proprietor of this market, which was located only two blocks south of the store run by her half-sister, Bertha Abbott. Historic Photograph Collection.*

the opportunity for outgoing calls. In a neighborhood where only 26 of the 208 households had telephones in 1943, this service made visits to the Abbott store almost essential.[49]

The ambiance created by such services could, in itself, enhance the social functions of the neighborhood store and, despite its high prices, fortify its economic niche. In cities like Portsmouth, where war production created a new population boom and the social dislocations attendant upon new and transient residents, establishments such as the Little Corner Store could serve as refuges from social alienation. Portsmouth leaders, in appealing for federal financial assistance for community facilities, noted that the city had gained 10,000 additional residents in the two years since 1941. By comparison, the previous addition of 10,000 to its population required 150 years. For a community that had been relatively static, the "flood" of newcomers represented a psychological threat. The out-of-towners were "taking over," noted the *New York Times* in an article on Portsmouth's problems of adjustment.[50]

At neighborhood stores like the Abbotts', that would never be the case. Moreover, the comforting familiarity, reinforced by a deep sense of neighborhood loyalty, would be accompanied by special favors.[51] Regular customers could count on getting whatever scarce items were available. With sugar severely limited by rationing, families were often hard-pressed to come up with enough ration stamps for a full prepackaged bag. At Bertha Abbott's, however, sugar was repackaged and dispensed in smaller quantities to regular customers. Leslie Clough recalled that the store saved its small allotment of sugar "not only for our customers that charged with us, but [for] . . . some customers that came in and paid cash." If you "came just for the sugar," however, "and we weren't familiar with you, we didn't have it. It was out of sight. It was under the counter."[52] Such reversions to the practices of the old country store would hardly prove advantageous in postwar competition with chain stores and supermarkets. But during a time of war shortages, such flexibility and local favoritism proved to be a decided benefit that the Mom-and-Pop store could offer along with its reassuring, homey ambience. As the editor of *Progressive Grocer* would generalize, "consumers in these troublesome times find it more satisfactory to deal in a friendly neighborhood store where merchants can answer their questions, help them with their points and their buying, look after their welfare, and extend innumerable small courtesies to the harassed consumer."[53]

If attention to special needs and "small courtesies" gave the neighborhood store a slightly improved competitive position during World War II, another element of retailing that had previously placed it at a disadvantage proved less vital during wartime. This was the role of effective display in grocery merchandising. Experts had long castigated the small grocery retailers for their neglect of their store windows in cultivating consumers (fig. 63); the manufacturers of packaging materials and containers had also accentuated the display factor. People cared how the market *looked*, they emphasized; they were induced to increase their purchases by dramatic displays and were addicted to impulse buying of whatever caught their eye through point-of-purchase advertising. Everett Runyon of Del Monte Foods, in stressing the importance of "point of purchase" displays in the late 1930s, called attention to a survey that confirmed the power of impulse buying. Out of every 100 persons who

Fig. 63. *Ethel Smart on the steps of her grocery store at 160 Marcy Street, Portsmouth, N.H., ca. 1940, by an unidentified photographer. The photograph shows oversized product boxes in the display windows. Reproduced from a photograph in the collection of the late Leslie Clough.*

entered retail stores, according to the survey, 75 bought at least one item "on impulse."[54]

With the emergence of the self-service mode, it was the food *package* that bore the brunt of making the immediate sale. But the package had to be shown off to its best advantage. The small grocer who lacked the space, time, resources, and sophistication to create attractive displays, had little chance of meeting the standards of display promoted in the trade journals. Thus, even dramatic advances in attractive packaging did little to help the small retailer competitively. The best package would still display itself to best advantage in a spacious, well-lighted, newly equipped store; in the setting of the cramped Mom-and-Pop grocery, that same modern package might even induce customers to recognize just how outmoded and unstylish were its surroundings.

Wartime conditions, however, worked to reduce the display advantages of the larger grocery retailer. With some foods in short supply and consumers eager to buy, extra promotion was not as crucial to sales. If the undecorated window in urban groceries in working-class neighborhoods had long proclaimed "that trust and mutual aid should prevail over the cash nexus" in the "discourse of windows," as Keith Walden has argued, elaborate window displays during wartime might even invite criticism for an unpatriotic wastefulness.[55] Even *Modern Packaging*, ever a champion of modernity in display, acknowledged that with a war in progress, functionality was the theme of the moment and "glamour is on a compulsory leave of absence."[56] A grocery window that revealed nothing except the backs of shelves and stacks of supplies, as at the Abbotts' corner store, seemed appropriately functional and bereft of suspect lavishness.

What was more, paper and paperboard were declared in short supply. Food manufacturers shifted to substitute packages (see cats. 40–42, 46,50). The aura of the "wartime substitute" in packaging did not clash with the slightly antiquated ambience of the typical neighborhood store. Quite the contrary, it was likely to seem less out-of-place here than in the sleekest of modern supermarkets.

A final feature of the socioeconomic niche occupied by the neighborhood grocery stores was hardly new to wartime circumstances. But it did weigh more heavily between 1942 and 1945. This was the significant role of children in their clientele. Children were consumers in their own right, as purchasers of candy, soft drinks, and other snacks. Even more significantly, particularly for stores that offered credit, they were often the shoppers for their families. Where the store was close at hand, a child of eight or older was very likely to be assigned to "run to the store" to pick up a needed item or two for mother.[57] Even if a larger chain store or independent stood close by, the physical proportions and familiar faces of the corner grocery better suited children's dispositions. In this respect, as in several others such as extended hours and convenient access, the Mom-and-Pop grocery store prefigured the successful convenience stores of the postwar era. "Kids seemed to feel more at home in a 7-Eleven," observed an historian of that franchise chain, because it was close to their own size. It did not overwhelm them. . . . There was no high ceiling or numerous aisles where a child might become confused. The candy rack was handy and in easy sight of even the smallest youngster."[58]

Advisers to the grocery trade had long sought to persuade retailers to respect their youthful customers. "Be patient with the children," the author of a pamphlet of "pointers" implored them. "Wait upon them in their turn and be cheerful with them . . . . Remember, children will run errands to the store where they are treated best."[59] Food manufacturers also recognized children's frequent role as errand runners, occasionally depicting them in their ads and often worrying about how to insure that mothers would insist so vehemently upon the brand name that grocers could not induce the child shopper to accept "substitute" goods.[60] One minor example of the food manufacturer's consciousness of children's role appears in a board game produced and distributed by Libby, McNeill and Libby (fig. 64). The central object of the game was to go to the store for mother. Specific instructions for individual squares on the course of the trek included "Forgot 1 item, go back to store," and "Forgot what to get, go back home." (Other directions told the child players to tell mother to tune into Libby's radio program and to tell her to use Libby's products.)

World War II brought conditions that heightened the significance of the patronage of children at the neighborhood grocery store. Children had always been confined to local stores by lack of transportation to more distant chains and large independents. But now their parents were less mobile and, burdened by wartime work schedules, even more likely than before to send the

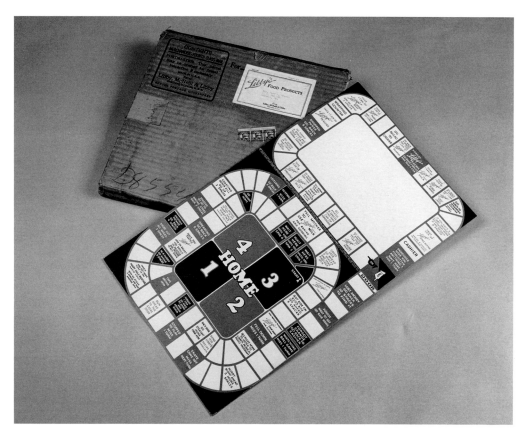

Fig. 64. *Supermarket Game. Distributed by Libby, McNeill and Libby, Chicago, Illinois, ca. 1923. Gift of Charles E. Burden.*

kids on store errands. More significantly, children grew in stature as both consumers and citizens during the war. They had been increasingly marginalized as superfluous people during the previous decades, but now they were called upon to carry out important wartime assignments—from participation in salvage drives to helping sell war savings stamps and bonds.[61] Their various contributions to the war effort and their more frequent employment in jobs in family businesses also marginally increased their discretionary spending money. Kids could sell tinfoil and other kinds of scrap to the nearby junk dealers in Puddle Dock and earn enough money to feed a substantial candy habit.[62] Grocers like Bertha Abbott devoted a very considerable space, proportionately, to the display of candy. Like others in the Mom-and-Pop grocery business, she recognized the crucial role that children played in the local community network that made the corner store viable.

The war ended in August 1945, and with it, burdensome work for the local grocer. But those conditions that had helped shelter the tiny neighborhood market in its protected socioeconomic niche also came to an end. New cars came into production; gasoline and rubber were no longer rationed. New refrigerators came on the market. People more frequently commuted to work by car and found it convenient to stop on their way home at the larger markets, with lower prices, modern furnishings, and wider selections. A tiny grocery such as Bertha Abbott's store would be hard-pressed to afford either the capital or the space to install the necessary facilities for selling frozen foods. Moreover, in the social and economic atmosphere of the postwar era, the appeal of nostalgia declined and the emphasis on modernity of style flourished. Advertisers found even less reason than before to adopt policies or cultivate images that would favor the antiquated Mom-and-Pop store.

Ironically, given the various contributions of the government's war mobilization to the temporary viability of the neighborhood store, it was a government publication—one inspired by recognition of the sacrifices made by military veterans—that most vividly foretold the jeopardy in which the tiny neighborhood grocery would be placed in the postwar world. Entitled simply *Grocery Store*, this volume appeared in a series of Department of Commerce publications that advised returning veterans on opportunities in establishing small businesses of their own. The authors drew upon information provided by the National Association of Retail Grocers to describe the requirements for success as an independent retail grocer in the months to come.[63]

No one contemplating the operation of a grocery like the Little Corner Store could have derived comfort or encouragement from reading *Grocery Store*. Although the authors acknowledged that there was still "a place for the very small store," they also noted that the earnings from such stores were "definitely limited" and that the proprietors often operated them as a side line to supplement other income. To establish a store that could be self-supporting as "a full-time commercial venture" and return "a comfortable living" the grocer should aim to start with an annual volume of $25,000 in sales and seek to grow to at least $50,000. Such a store would aim to supply at least 100 families with their groceries and to occupy a selling space of about 1080 square feet.[64] While we cannot document the annual sales of the Abbott grocery, we do know that it sought to survive in a neighborhood where 208 households were supplied by *six* neighborhood grocery stores as well as by the larger, somewhat-more-distant chains and independents. And, compared to the 1080 or more square feet recommended by *Grocery Store*, the Abbotts' store relied upon only 493 square feet of selling space, of which some 67 square feet was devoted to a bid for the "kid constitutency" in the form of a candy room.[65]

Further elements of the advice to prospective independent grocers in *Grocery Store* only magnified the disproportions confronted by the Mom-and-Pop operation. Illustrations conveyed the importance of attractive entrances and the "pleasing window display" (fig. 65). The authors of this guide warned against stores whose facades, although "once up to date," had become "outmoded and stodgy."[66] They observed that the sale of frozen foods "has increased rapidly" and concluded that "everything points to their growing popularity." The small grocer would already have been aware of the prominent national advertising of frozen foods by Birdseye and, as the authors of *Grocery Store* noted, any "decision to add a line of frozen foods" would require significantly more capital and more store space.[67]

The authors of *Grocery Store* emphasized the importance of selecting a neighborhood with a high- or middle-income level, one with an extended trade area, and one that was growing (fig. 66). This advice offered little comfort to Bertha Abbott and the survival of her Little Corner Store. Moreover, where in the Abbotts' store might any proprietor find room for piling up products in those "massed displays" so highly recommended for good sales results?[68] The early chain store, the authors of *Grocery Store* observed, had enjoyed the "advantage of being well lighted," making other stores look like "dingy caverns" by comparison (fig. 67). The Abbott grocery, with its single "hanging light . . . just a bare bulb" might surely have improved in this respect with a little investment. But the photographs of both interiors and exteriors in *Grocery Store* thrust upon any champion of the Mom-and-Pop store a devastating visual comparison.[69]

Fig. 65. (below left) *Illustration of a successful window display. From Nelson A. Miller, Harvey W. Huegy, and Associates,* Grocery Store *(Washington, D.C.: United States Department of Commerce, 1946), p. 40. Courtesy, Library, University of California, Davis.*

Fig. 66. (below right) *Illustration of "A modern corner store." From Miller et al.,* Grocery Store, *p. 6. This illustration makes it evident that the Little Corner Store fell far short of the standards that were assumed to be necessary for a successful corner store in the postwar era. Courtesy, Library, University of California, Davis.*

This small store has an attractive front. Notice the off-center entrance and the pleasing window display.

A modern corner store.

Fig. 67. *Illustration of attractive lighting and display techniques. From Miller et al.,* Grocery Store, *p. 44. This illustration shows that the Mom-and-Pop store could not hope to match modern standards in these areas. Courtesy, Library, University of California, Davis.*

Lighting helps to make this store and its merchandise attractive.

With many elements of the postwar economy favoring further competitive gains by the chain grocery stores and with new cars in production and tire and gasoline rationing at an end, it seemed clear that only an intense community loyalty to the corner store could insure its perpetuation. While there had been many positive elements in the allegiance it had commanded during the war and in previous times, the tiny grocery of the urban working-class neighborhood had also survived during wartime by reaping the advantages of a patronage enforced by deprivations—in transportation, in refrigeration, and in the degree of self-assurance attained by those in low income and urban ethnic groups. As those impediments faded in the prosperous, mobile, seemingly-classless American society of the postwar years, and as mobility and urban renewal disrupted the cohesion of poorer urban neighborhoods, the Mom-and-Pop grocery could only look back nostalgically upon the war years. Despite their onerous burdens, those had been the good old days.

NOTES

1. Oral History Interview, July 18, 1990, OH 2 SC 11, Strawbery Banke Museum, Portsmouth, N.H.

2. Oral History Interviews, July 18, 1990, OH 2 SC 11; February 13, 1992, OH 2 SC 33.

3. While the supermarket emerged in the 1930s as a distinct rival to established retail grocery chains, this distinction became less germane in the 1940s as chains such as A&P cut back on their smaller retail outlets and established more of their own supermarkets. On this and on the consistently lower prices in chain stores, see Richard Tedlow, *New and Improved: The Story of Mass Marketing in America* (New York: Basic Books, 1990), pp. 195–202, 226–230, 241–243.

4. Tedlow, *New and Improved*, pp. 217–225; Joseph Cornwall Palamountain, Jr., *The Politics of Distribution* (Cambridge, Mass.: Harvard University Press, 1955), pp. 78–81.

5. *American Grocer*, October 13, 1943, p. 3.

6. E. J. Soucy, Director, Salvage Division, to Frank W. Hollis, Chairman, Salvage Committee, Portsmouth, N.H., June 15, 1944. "SCD Salvage Committees by Towns (Portsmouth)," MS 96 Portsmouth War Records, Strawbery Banke Museum, box 2, folder 10; [hereafter, reports in this group are cited by the folder title, followed by PWR and, when first cited, the box and folder numbers in which the report may be found in the Cummings Library and Archives, Strawbery Banke Museum]. *Successful Grocer* 22 (August 1943): 14; (September 1943): 10; (October 1943): cover, p. 2; *American Grocer*, December 23, 1942, p. 41; November 3, 1943, p. 8.

7. Roy F. Hendrickson, *Food Crisis* (Garden City, N.Y.: Doubleday, Doran, 1943), pp. 95, 100–101; *American Grocer*, December 30, 1942, pp. 4, 13.

8. For a sense of the complexities involved, see *Successful Grocer* 22 (July 1943): 17–18.

9. On the complexities of figuring maximum prices under the price ceiling regulations, see *American Grocer*, November 11, 1942, pp. 4–5.

10. *American Grocer*, October 20, 1943, pp. 3–4. On the commitment to simplification, see *American Grocer*, November 4, 1942, p. 6. Marion Adams, who worked for a major local wholesaler in Portsmouth during the war, observed that for the small grocers the rationing regulations made "a lot of extra work. It was just like having another set of books." Oral History Interview, April 16, 1992, OH 2 SC 31.

11. *Advertising and Selling* 36 (June 1943): 15.

12. *The Portsmouth Herald*, April 1, 1943, p. 5.

13. Oral History Interview, February 13, 1992, OH 2 SC 33.

14. *Modern Packaging* 16 (July 1943): 63; *Successful Grocer* 21 (January 1943): 34; 22, (July 1943): 36; 22 (November 1943): 3; *The Progressive Grocer* 22 (July 1943): 17–19.

15. *Modern Packaging* 16 (January 1943): 77; *American Grocer*, November 4, 1942, p. 13, December 2, 1942, p. 6, January 6, 1943, p. 16, March 31, 1943, p. 7; *Good Housekeeping* 116 (January 1943): 75; 116 (February 1943): 77.

16. *American Grocer*, December 2, 1942, p. 5, December 1, 1943, p. 3; *Successful Grocer* 22 (April 1943): 3; *Good Housekeeping* 116 (January 1943): 75.

17. Roland Marchand, *Advertising the American Dream: Making Way for Modernity, 1920–1940* (Berkeley: University of California Press, 1985), pp. 300–317.

18. *Sales Management*, February 15, 1946, p. 129; *Advertising and Selling* 35 (June 1942): 14.

19. *Advertising and Selling* 35 (May 1942): 20; (November 1942): 32; Frank W. Fox, *Madison Avenue Goes to War: The Strange Military Career of American Advertising, 1941–1945* (Provo, Utah: Brigham Young University Press, 1975), pp. 38, 45–47, 56; Mark H. Leff, "The Politics of Sacrifice on the American Home Front in World War II," *Journal of American History* 77 (1991): 1307–1309.

20. Fox, *Madison Avenue Goes to War*, pp. 27, 40–41, 45.

21. A useful collection of documents on the origins of the War Advertising Council appears in Harold B. Thomas, "The Background and Beginning of the Advertising Council," in *The Promise of Advertising*, ed. C. H. Sandage (Homewood, Ill.: R. D. Irwin, 1961), pp. 15–58.

22. Minutes of the Meeting of the Board of Directors of the War Advertising Council, June 10, 1943, Thomas D'Arcy Brophy Papers, box 4, folder 8, State Historical Society of Wisconsin; Fox, *Madison Avenue*, pp. 49–53; Robert Griffith, "The Selling of America: The Advertising Council and American Politics, 1942–1960," *Business History Review* 52 (1983): 389–391; Theodore S. Repplier, "Advertising and 'The Forces of Righteousness,'" in *The Promise of Advertising*, ed. Sandage, pp. 61–62; *American Grocer*, August 18, 1943, p. 2.

23. *American Grocer*, October 6, 1943, p. 8, August 18, 1943, p. 2; "OCD [Office of Civilian Defense] 'Food Fights For Freedom,'" MS 96 PWR, box 3:2.

24. "Food Fights for Freedom," PWR.

25. *Good Housekeeping* 119 (August 1944): back cover; *Ladies' Home Journal* 61 (September 1944): 51.

26. For examples, see *Saturday Evening Post*, June 17, 1944, p. 60; *Advertising and Selling* 35 (September 1942):48; 36 (June 1943): 93; Hearst Newspapers, Untitled Oversized Brochure, n.d. (ca. 1942), Owen D. Young files, folder 15,4, General Electric Company Archives, Schenectady, New York.

27. Frank Fox has employed the term "American pastoral" to connote this predomi-

nate theme in wartime advertising in his *Madison Avenue Goes to War*, pp. 77–79.

28. Carl Dipman, "Wartime Changes in Food Distribution," *The Journal of Marketing* 8 (January 1944): 324.

29. For a few examples, among the thousands of such advertising stereotypes of the grocer as inevitably male, see *Time*, August 30, 1943, pp. 84, 85; *Ladies' Home Journal* 61 (October 1944): 55, (November 1944): 65; *Good Housekeeping* 116 (January 1943): 50. On the "help wanted" appeal, see *Successful Grocer* 22 (November 1943): 34.

30. *Successful Grocer* 19 (January 1941): 21.

31. *Time*, May 22, 1944, p. 92, November 20, 1944, p. 89; *Business Week*, August 25, 1943, p. 23. See also, *Newsweek*, April 24, 1944, p. 63 and *Business Week*, March 11, l944, p. 25.

32. For examples, prominent and minor, of such educating of the eye, see *Good Housekeeping* 119 (January 1943): 59, (March 1943): 65.

33. Willard F. Mueller and Leon Garoian, *Changes in the Market Structure of Grocery Retailing* (Madison: University of Wisconsin, 1961), p. 23; Nelson A. Miller, Harvey W. Huegy, and Associates, *Grocery Store* (Washington, D.C.: United States Department of Commerce, 1946), pp. 3–4; Dipman, "Wartime Changes in Food Distribution," pp. 321, 323; "Summary of Feb.–March Nielsen Report," attached to Bernard Angood to Thomas Brophy, June 8, 1944, Thomas D'Arcy Brophy Papers, box 40, folder 99, State Historical Society of Wisconsin. The First National Stores chain cut back its total number of stories from 1748 in 1942 to 1585 in 1943 and to 1463 in 1944. In New Hampshire, First National outlets declined from 114 in early 1943 to 108 in early 1944. First National Stores, Inc., *Annual Report, Year ending March 27, 1943*, n.p. and *Annual Report, Year ending April 1, 1944*, n.p.

34. Palamountain, *The Politics of Distribution*, p. 61; Tedlow, *New and Improved*, pp. 238, 256.

35. Oral History Interview, July 18, 1990, OH 2 SC 11.

36. *American Grocer*, November 4, 1942, p. 7.

37. *Modern Packaging* 16 (September 1942): 71; Dipman, "Wartime Changes in Food Distribution," p. 322.

38. Samuel G. Barton, "The Consumption Patterns of Different Economic Groups Un-

der War Changes," *The Journal of Marketing* 8 (July 1943): 52–53.

39. *Successful Grocer* 22 (December 1943): 19.

40. On the importance of groceries on credit to poorer ethnic families in Chicago during the two decades preceding World War II, see Lizabeth A. Cohen, "The Class Experience of Mass Consumption: Workers as Consumers in Interwar America," in *The Power of Culture: Critical Essay in American History*, ed. Richard Wightman Fox and T. J. Jackson Lears (Chicago: University of Chicago Press, 1993), pp. 140, 143.

41. Oral History Interviews, July 18, 1990, OH 2 SC 11, April 12, 1991, OH 2 SC 29.

42. Another partner in a Mom-and-Pop grocery store in the same neighborhood recalled that "We had customers that used to come in just on Saturday night, just before closing. 'Oh, I didn't get my paycheck.' And he'd (her husband) say, Well, I'm not gonna give 'em much, but they can have bread, and they can have milk, and a jar of jelly for the kids, so that they have something. At that time we allowed charging, Believe me, if I had the money that the people owed us!" Oral History Interview, December 12, 1988, OH 1 SC 1.

43. Oral History Interview, December 12, 1988, OH 1 SC 1. Long hours were typical for small urban stores and the emerging suburban "convenience" stores recognized the appeal of extended hours. See Mueller and Garoian, *Changes in the Market Structure of Grocery Retailing*, p. 26, and Allen Liles, *Oh Thank Heaven: The Story of the Southland Corporation* (Dallas: The Southland Corporation, 1976), p. 15.

44. *Advertising and Selling* 35 (August 1942): 13; 36 (January 1943): 48.

45. Oral History Interview, March 5, 1991, OH 2 SC 27.

46. Oral History Interviews, July 18, 1990, OH 2 SC 11; March 5, 1991, OH 2 SC 270.

47. Oral History Interview, July 18, 1990, OH 2 SC 11.

48. Oral History Interview, April 12, 1991, OH 2 SC 29.

49. *Manning's Portsmouth . . . Directory*, no. 42 (Boston: H. A. Manning, 1943). A Charles Street resident, who lived just one block from the Little Corner Store, recalled later that "we had a telephone and not many people around us did." Oral History Interview, March 29, 1990, OH 2 SC 6.

50. Franklin E. Jordan, *Portsmouth and*

National Defense, "SCD [State Council of Defense] Local Committees: Portsmouth," MS 96 PWR, box 2:1. "Portsmouth Tries to Adjust to an Influx of Men and Money," *New York Times*, October 5, 1942, pp. 1, 10.

51. Oral History Interview, March 29, 1990, OH 2 SC 6.

52. Oral History Interview, July 18, 1990, OH 2 SC 11.

53. Dipman, "Wartime Changes in Food Distribution," p. 322.

54. Everett M. Runyon, typescript of speech for "Canning Industry Day Program," November 9, 1938, box 2, p. 7, California League of Food Processors Archives, University of California, Davis. See also, *Modern Packaging* 15 (January 1942): 69–70.

55. Keith Walden, "Speaking Modern: Language, Culture and Hegemony in Grocery Window Displays, 1887–1920," *Canadian Historical Review* 7 (September 1989): 296; *Modern Packaging* 15 (May 1942): 104.

56. *Modern Packaging* 15 (April 1942): 112, 117.

57. For examples of children assigned to shop for their mothers at neighborhood grocery stores in the Puddle Dock area, see Oral History Interviews, March 28, 1990, OH 2 SC 3; April 12, 1991, OH 2 SC 29.

58. Liles, *Oh Thank Heaven*, p. 1.

59. Virtually all of the former residents of the Puddle Dock neighborhood interviewed by the Strawbery Banke project remembered clearly their many visits to tiny grocery stores as children. Only one informant dissented from the view that the Abbotts' store was comfortable for children: "It always seemed small and kind of creepy . . . probably the building was much older and it seemed darker and just unfamiliar. But I did go in from time to time with my friends . . . for candy." Oral History Interview, March 7, 1990, OH 2 SC 1; Alexander Todoroff, *Valuable Pointers for Grocery Store Salespeople* (Chicago: Grocery Trade Publishing House, 1931), p. 9. On the expected continuing importance of children to the small grocery, see Miller et al., *Grocery Store*, p. 22.

60. Roland Marchand, "Precocious Consumers and Junior Salesmen: Advertising to Children in the United States to 1940," in *Selling the Goods*, ed. Kathryn Grover (Rochester, N.Y.: Strong Museum, forthcoming).

61. Robert William Kirk, "Hey, Kids! Children in World War II" (Ph.D. dissertation, University of California, Davis, 1991), pp. 2, 6–8, 113–15, 130, 137–41, 176–77; Viviana A. Zelizer, *Pricing the Priceless Child: The Changing Social Value of Children* (New York: Basic Books, 1985).

62. Oral History Interviews, February 14, 1989, OH 1 SC 11; April 12, 1991, OH 2 SC 29.

63. Miller et al., *Grocery Store*.

64. Miller et al., *Grocery Store*, pp. 7–8, 27–29, 40. Although *Grocery Store* identified 1080 square feet as its benchmark size for the small grocery (p. 40), it also observed elsewhere (p. 36) that the "person starting out in a small way" should seek a location "at least 25 by 60 feet or 20 by 75 feet," and (p. 39) that the frontage "should be at least 20 feet, though 24 feet or wider is preferable, and the depth 60 feet or more." These dimensions indicated that between 1200 and 1500 square feet constituted a minimum desirable size.

65. Miller et al., *Grocery Store*, pp. 7–8, 29, 40.

66. Miller et al., *Grocery Store*, pp. 40–43, 53–59. On ideas about the coming standards for display, see also *Successful Grocer* 22 (July 1943): 15.

67. Miller et al., *Grocery Store*, p. 263. For examples of the Birdseye advertisement, see *Good Housekeeping* 116 (January 1943): 109, (February 1943): 93, (March 1943): 8.

68. For examples of the kinds of displays steadily promoted in the grocery trade journals but impossible to create in a space as small as the Abbotts' store, see *Successful Grocer* 22 (March 1943): 12, (November 1943): 23.

69. Miller et al., *Grocery Store*, pp. 6–7, 27–28, 40–44. On the single "bare bulb" which lit the Little Corner Store, see Oral History Interview, July 18, 1990, OH 2 SC 11.

From Corner Store to Convenience Mart:
A Footnote

by Gerald W. R. Ward

T HE "LITTLE CORNER STORE" exhibition and this accompanying book focus primarily on the latter years of World War II. Like a snapshot, the exhibition and book illuminate a significant time in the history of the store, as Bertha Abbott and her customers were forced to deal with rationing, wartime shortages, and other circumstances peculiar to the mid-1940s. But this brief period is just a thin slice in the long existence of the store, which was in operation from 1919 until 1950. For three decades, the Abbotts' store served its customers in a manner more or less typical of corner stores in New England, and thus represented in microcosm a tradition that, nearly half a century later, still continues in Portsmouth. Although often known today as convenience stores, these "corner stores" (no matter where they are located) are still a significant part of shopping in New England.

Today, most people in Portsmouth do their major grocery shopping in one of the large supermarkets that have come to dominate the food trade in this country since the 1930s. Only one of these supermarkets—Richardson's, a small, independent, venerable example on State Street—is located in the old downtown area. Another—an A&P—was situated in the North End until it closed early in 1993. Most of the operating supermarkets are located in shopping malls and centers and are available primarily by car. The principal stores in this category are the two large Super Shaw's Markets (one formerly located just across the town line in the Newington Mall and relocated to Durgin Square Plaza in April of 1993, and the other in the Southgate Plaza on Lafayette Road), the Market Basket in the Marshall's Mall on Woodbury Avenue, and the Pic 'N' Pay on Islington Street.

These stores represent a type of consumerism so different from the Abbott store as to constitute a difference of kind rather than of degree. The new Shaw's in Durgin Square, for example, is 48,000 square feet in size; the Little Corner Store was less than five hundred. Shaw's carries thousands and thousands of different items, as opposed to the four hundred or so stocked by the Abbotts. In the winter of 1992–93, two large wholesale food stores have opened up in Portsmouth—BJ's Wholesale Club and Costco—making a new level of grocery shopping—warehouse prices for warehouse quantities—available to the consumer. Enormous shopping carts, laser checkout scanners, computer directories, and vast quantities of foodstuffs and goods characterize these modern supermarkets, almost unbelievable testimonies to American abundance even during an extended recession.

But despite this type of competition, the Abbott store type of establishment still exists in Portsmouth, and in relatively large numbers. By my count, there are at least 28 such places within the city limits as of this writing, although many of them would technically be defined as modern convenience stores. Of these 28, a substantial percentage are not part of the chains or franchise operations often encountered in America (there are no 7-Elevens in Portsmouth, although Cumberland Farms stores have moved into the Hamptons, Exeter, and Rye), and even those affiliated with a large chain of stores or oil companies sometimes retain an air of individuality. The more typical store in Portsmouth is independently owned and operated and possesses its own character and ambience.

Many of these stores, like the supermarkets, are convenient only by car, which is perhaps the deciding factor in defining a modern convenience store. For example, there is a cluster of stores along Lafayette Road (U.S. Route 1), as one heads south from Portsmouth toward Rye and Hampton. Many of these are linked with gasoline service, in a revival of a tradition of the 1920s and 1930s. Going south one encounters the Food Mart and Citgo store; the Bread 'N' Butter (affiliated with Mobil gas); the Sunoco Mini Market; and the Elwyn Park Exxon Shop (my own corner store of choice, operated by Chuck and Linda George). Others may or may not have gasoline pumps, but still are most easily accessible by car: moving south again, one comes to the Chug-A-Lug, then to MacDonald's Meat Market and Convenience Store, which is located across from the Charter Food Store featuring Charter gas, and, finally, to the Maple Haven Beverage store at the corner of Lafayette and Ocean roads.

Other convenience stores are also strung out along well-traveled routes, including the classic group of six stores attached to gas stations located on the Route 1 Bypass between the Portsmouth traffic circle and the Sara Mildred Long Bridge over the Piscataqua River. While these stores are aimed primarily at passers-through, especially truck drivers, other examples within town gather a more local patronage, including The Bread Box and Beverage Barn, and The Store 24 on Islington Street; the Stop 'N' Go markets on Woodbury Avenue and Middle Street; and the Short Stop Market at the corner of Middle Road and Peverly Hill Road, ideally located not only at a major intersection, but also across from the National Little League field. The Little Goose on Sagamore Road (only as recently as 1992 a year-round operation, but now apparently to be only seasonal) is also located on a significant local thoroughfare.

But several stores still remain that are easily accessible to foot traffic and thus are more typical representations of the neighborhood store. Classic examples of these are the eponymously named Cabot Street and South Street markets, Izzy's Market on Dennett Street, and the Soda Pop Stop (formerly The Front Porch) on Richards Avenue. These are all located in parts of houses adapted for that purpose, just as the Abbotts' store occupied part of the early 18th-century Marden House in Puddle Dock.

In keeping with the Abbott store tradition, these stores still carry small quantities of a large variety of things. They feature some of the staples that were significant to the Abbotts: cigarettes, beer (carried in the Little Corner Store before Walter Abbott's death in 1938), soft drinks, candy, milk, bread, snacks, and so forth. Prices may be higher than in the supermarkets, but the hours are usually longer, items are easier to find, the lines are shorter, and service seems more personal.

But, of course, some things have changed. Lottery tickets and video rentals are now staple items at many of these stores. Condoms are displayed in a matter-of-fact manner. Prepared foods, including pizza and submarine sandwiches, are available at several of them, and hot coffee to go is more or less a standard feature. Plastic is everywhere. Newspapers and magazines, not stocked by the Abbotts, are almost universal. Self-service cash-and-carry is the invariable style. And the prices are higher.

Somehow, however, the changes seem less significant than the continuities. A visit to the re-created Little Corner Store is thus not so much a trip back to a time that is alien and vague, as it is a reaffirmation of a tradition that will seem familiar to many New Englanders. Some visitors may well look at the Abbotts' store through nostalgic eyes, but they should remember its links with our own time as much as its depiction of life on the home front during World War II. The restoration of the Abbott store—done with meticulous attention to detail and with an incredible array of surviving packaging and other objects—is perhaps a unique project in the museum world, especially noteworthy for its emphasis on using real (rather than reproduction) objects whenever possible. However, its greatest strengths to this observer are its celebration of the ordinary rather than the exceptional, its absolute fidelity to the everyday nature of urban life and its physical manifestations, and its testimony to the power of the prosaic. The restoration highlights a brief time during a momentous event in our nation's history, but it also invokes the importance of a longstanding 20th-century tradition that, at least for now, is still with us.

Much as it has ties with our own time, the Little Corner Store also reminds us of a tradition that moves backward in time. Many of the homes in the Puddle Dock neighborhood housed shops in one or more of their rooms, beginning in the late 17th century and continuing into the modern era. One of these small shops, a federal-period example in Drisco House, was re-created by Strawbery Banke Museum in 1988; another, operated by the widow Mary Rider in the first half of the 19th century, is evoked in the restoration of the Rider-Wood House, completed in 1990. The Abbott store installation thus bridges the gap between these earlier stores and our own time, reminding us of the continuities as well as the changes that have taken place within the narrow confines of the Strawbery Banke neighborhood.

PART 2

PLATE 4. *View of the front portion of the "Little Corner Store," looking south from the main entrance door, as restored to its 1943–45 appearance.*

PLATE 5. *View of the back section of the "Little Corner Store," looking east from the Mast Street door, as restored to its 1943–45 appearance.*

PLATE 6. *Candy Room of the "Little Corner Store" restored to its 1943–45 appearance .*

PLATE 7. *View of front portion of the "Little Corner Store," looking north toward the main entrance door, as restored to its 1943–45 appearance.*

PLATE 8. *Detergents and soap products ca. 1940–45, on display in the Little Corner Store, 1993.*

Fig. 68. *Exterior of the "Little Corner Store" as restored to its 1943–45 appearance.*

have taken record photographs (mostly slides) throughout the restoration process.

In putting together the store and kitchen installations, museum staff sought to explore life on the home front during World War II and the effects of wartime conditions—shortages, changes in foodways and food packaging and delivery, changing demographics, and the massive military buildup that resulted in full employment and changes in work patterns—on a blue-collar urban neighborhood of mixed ethnicity. The garage that had been built behind the house about 1930, and demolished in the 1960s, was reconstructed as a gallery space and has been installed with an exhibition entitled "The Home Front Battlefield: 1940–1945" (fig. 69) which places the Abbotts' grocery store, and the experiences of the people of Puddle Dock and Portsmouth, within a broader national and international context.

During the initial phase of the project (1984–1985) the plan was to restore the house and store to their appearance during the 1930s. When attempts to raise funds from a corporate sponsor were unsuccessful, the project was put on hold. It was not until Jane Nylander was appointed director of Strawbery Banke in 1986, that, with the help of collector and supporter Charles E. Burden, the project was resurrected. By this time it was clear that although the museum possessed excellent photographs of the store from the late 1930s, these were often difficult to interpret. We learned that the person with the best memory of what it was like to operate the store on a day-to-day basis was Leslie Clough. A frequent helper in the store when he was a young boy, Clough

Fig. 69. *"The Home Front Battlefield, 1940–1945," as installed in the reconstructed Marden-Abbott House garage, 1993.*

came to live with Bertha Abbott and became her full-time assistant in 1941, just three years after Walter Abbott's death. Clough lived and worked with Bertha Abbott until 1949, just before the store closed its doors for good.[1]

Leslie Clough (1925–1991) was a man with a remarkable memory. He shared his recollections of the Abbotts and their store with us on numerous occasions, and he was one of the first neighborhood residents to be interviewed as part of the museum's oral history project on life in Puddle Dock during the 1930s and 1940s. Leslie remembered many details about the operation of the store during the 1940s, and could even tell us what was kept on each shelf—by brand name. It was because of his keen recollections, and the surviving physical evidence of the store's appearance in the years just before it closed, that the museum ultimately decided to take the store back to the way it was in the 1940s. Not only did the museum possess an excellent source of information on the store during that period, but the story of food and packaging during the war was a fascinating one. The furnishing plan for the house and store was developed almost exclusively from the memories of the Abbotts' friends, neighbors, and relatives. All in all, staff members and research assistants interviewed 41 individuals, including several of the Abbotts' closest neighbors and four of their grandchildren—Joseph W. Hoyt, Arthur Hoyt, Dorothy Grace Holt Ober, and Herbert Holt.[2] The picture that arose from these interviews was a full and detailed one, and one which we hope our presentation in the store and family kitchen will do justice to.

The Abbotts' "Little Corner Store" is located in one of Strawbery Banke's oldest houses, built about 1722 by James Marden, a mastmaker, who owned a mast yard on the west side of Mast Lane (later named Mast Street). Shortly after Walter (1871–1938) and Bertha (1873–1959) purchased the house, they converted the lower west room into a small store, installing shelving and a pair of picture windows for display space. Sometime in the 1920s the Abbotts added a shed to the rear of the store, increasing its size by approximately 205 square feet (see PLATE 1).[3] The addition provided a second entrance into the store from Mast Street, and was the primary entrance through which supplies were delivered.

The lower east room of the house, and the entire second floor, became the Abbotts' living space. They used the downstairs room as their kitchen, and this became the room where they spent most of their time during the hours when the store was open for business. The family refrigerator, and the telephone for the house and store, were kept in the small room behind the stairs, known as the candy room, which also housed the cash register, the candy case, and the tobacco case.

The main entry to the domestic side of the house was through a formal doorway. Once inside, the visitor was confronted with a dainty oak halltree. The walls of the stairwell were papered frequently, with monochromatic designs, and later with colonial revival scenes.[4] Hanging in the stairhall, also in the colonial revival taste, were four Wallace Nutting photographs depicting the front doorways of various grand old Portsmouth homes, including the Langdon House, the Marvin House (fig. 70), and the Warner House.

Fig. 70. *"The Marvin Door,"*
Wallace Nutting, ca.1900–1915.
Hand-colored photographic
print; OH. 11⅞ in., OW. 9⅞ in.
Originally owned by Bertha Ab-
bott. Museum Purchase.

Fig. 71. (left) *Sewing Table, Imperial Company, Grand Rapids, Mich., ca. 1930. Mahogany; H. 29 in., W. 28³/₁₆ in., D. 14 in. Originally owned by Bertha Abbott. Museum Purchase.*

Fig. 72. (right) *Rocking chair, unknown maker, American, ca. 1910. Oak; H. 41 in., D. (seat) 19 in. Originally owned by Bertha Abbott. Gift of Joseph Hoyt and Arthur Hoyt.*

Fig. 73. (below) *Mixing Bowls and Custard Cups, unknown maker, ca. 1925. Earthenware; Largest bowl: H. 2⁵/₈ in., Diam. (rim) 3¹/₂ in. Originally owned by Bertha Abbott. Museum Purchase.*

Portrait photographs of Walter and Bertha Abbott also hung on the walls of the stairwell.

From the entrance hall visitors had direct access to the upper floor of the house. The west room over the store served as Walter and Bertha's living room. About 1919, they added a large bay window to the room to provide them with a commanding view of the street below. The bay window also signaled the room's use as a general living space, rather than as a bedroom, and allowed additional light to enter. A bathroom occupied the far southwest corner of the room; the room behind the staircase was a small bedroom; the east room was the large master bedroom.

The kitchen (PLATES 2, 3) contained two stoves—a gas stove and a large cast-iron stove (cat. 71) that burned both coal and oil. In the center of the room there was a large round table surrounded by four chairs (cats. 68, 69). Bertha Abbott's desk sat between the east window and the corner cupboard; her rocking chair sat in front of the window. At various times other pieces of furniture were kept in the room, including a small sewing table and a drop-leaf table. Leslie Clough recalled that the kitchen was "like kitchen/living room/dining room. . . . We *lived* in that kitchen. We had a nice parlor upstairs, but hardly ever used it."[5] Several original objects from the kitchen survive, including Bertha Abbott's desk, sewing table (fig. 71), and rocking chair (fig. 72). Because the chair sat directly in front of the built-in cupboard that held the family silverware, it was constantly dragged across the floor to allow access to the drawers. As a result, the rockers became so worn that they were completely flat; at some point these rockers were replaced with new ones. Fortunately, however, family members saved the old rockers, and they have now been restored. A number of smaller items associated with the Abbotts' kitchen have also "returned home," including a yellowware mixing bowl set (fig. 73), two blue and white Willowware platters (fig. 74), and a towel and towel rack.

Whenever a customer entered the main section of the store (PLATE 4), a bell would ring signaling their arrival. Once inside the store, customers saw a rack

Fig. 74. (left) *Blue Willowware Platters, unknown maker, ca. 1900. Transfer-printed earthenware; Large platter: H. 9¹¹/₁₆ in., W. 15¹/₁₆ in., D. 2¹/₄ in. Originally owned by Bertha Abbott. Museum Purchase.*

Fig. 75. (right) *Cash Register, National Cash Register Co., Dayton, Ohio, ca. 1910. Cast iron with brass finish, wood; H. 22¹/₂ in., W. 19⁷/₈ in., D. 16¹/₄ in. Museum collection.*

full of bulk and packaged cookies and crackers on their right, along the west wall, and open self-service shelves to their left, along the east wall. Straight ahead was a case full of cakes, pies, and pastries; bread and cereals filled the shelves above. Just to the right of the cake case there was a Coca-Cola cooler, and a glass case filled with medicine sat in a nearby window.

Large refrigeration units, an ice cream freezer, a butcher block and table, and a kerosene tank lined the walls of the back room (PLATES 1, 5). The shelves in the back portion of the store were filled with empty boxes for products that had already been shelved, as well as full boxes with contents waiting to be distributed to the proper places in the front of the store. A trap door led to additional storage in the basement.

The small room on the first floor behind the stairway was known as the "Candy Room" (PLATE 6). This room connected the domestic and business portions of the house, and contained the family telephone and refrigerator as well as store fixtures. The basic business functions of the store were carried on in this room. The cash register (fig. 75) stood on top of the large glass case filled with candy; credit slips, records, and ration coupons were kept on and above the shelves along the north wall. In order to assure limited access, tobacco products were kept in a glass case in the southeast corner of the room; cartons of cigarettes and boxes of candy filled the nearby shelves. A curtained doorway led to the adjacent family kitchen.

From numerous oral history interviews and extant photographs we were able to develop a detailed list of what was carried in the store. We used this inventory as our shopping list because we felt that it was important to limit our acquisition of period packaging. This way the finished store would better reflect the relatively limited variety of items available in a corner store of the period—approximately 400 name-brand items (PLATE 7) as opposed to the nearly 40,000 brands carried in the average supermarket today.

From the beginning, we were determined to collect as many examples of original packaging as we could and to acquire as many objects that carried special wartime messages, or reflected special wartime limitations on packaging materials, as possible. We were greatly assisted in our efforts by Charles Burden's diligence and energy. He not only found the great majority of the original products for the store, but he also began the laborious process of determining what 1940s packaging looked like by scouring popular magazines, collecting images for the notebook that would become our constant companion on collecting trips. An avid shopper—we came to call him "Shop-til-you-drop-Charlie"—we learned the wisdom of his two cardinal rules of antique shopping—1) Don't stop for more than ten minutes to eat lunch, and 2) If you pass a shop on the road, don't turn back, keep moving on. Museum staff members joined Burden on many of his shopping trips and searched through antique shops and flea markets from Pennsylvania to northern Vermont and rural Maine for 1940s packaging.

In addition to the images gleaned from popular magazine advertisements of the period, museum staff members also found a great deal of information on the appearance of packaging from trade journals such as *Progressive Grocer*, *Modern Packaging*, and the yearbook of the New Hampshire Retail Grocers' Association. Office of War Information and Farm Securities Administration photographs in the Library of Congress and National Archives; advertising ephemera in the N. W. Ayer and Warshaw collections of the National Museum of American History; and items in private collections also yielded a great deal of information. These sources were helpful in providing us with images of prevailing display techniques as well as data on wartime measures and their effects on producers and retailers. There is one source that contains an enormous amount of information that we did not tap: the original advertising and packaging on file in the United States Copyright Office. All items in these archives that date before 1940 have now been transferred to the National Park Service in Harper's Ferry, West Virginia, but post-1940 material in the Copyright Office is still expensive to access.

Staff members also compiled a list of all of the names and addresses of companies whose products were carried in the store, and contacted 40 different corporations for information about the appearance of their 1940s packaging. Although the archives of some of these companies had been lost in subsequent mergers, 24 generously provided us either with information on the histories of their companies, or on the appearance of their 1940s packaging.

The museum also issued numerous press releases publicizing the need for period packaging that yielded some interesting results. Although the calls often did not come until days or even weeks after a story appeared in the paper or on a television news program, we received many intriguing calls. The items were out there—in attics, basements, closets, and barns of old homes in the area, and rural camps in New Hampshire's lakes region and in southwestern Maine. Detergents and soap products were particularly abundant (PLATE 8). Some of the more interesting groups of objects that came to us as a result of these efforts were nearly 200 candy wrappers and can labels that one family had saved to turn in for various promotional offers; and several bread wrappers and Kool-Aid envelopes (fig. 76) that had been preserved by a woman

Fig. 76. *Kool-Aid Envelope, Perkins Products Co., Chicago, Ill., ca. 1942. Printed paper; H. 5 in., W. 3½ in. Gift of Charles E. Burden.*

who, because she lacked access to a landfill facility, wrapped them up, along with the rest of her paper trash, and stored the packages in a vacant camping trailer on her property. Other donations appeared, like abandoned children, literally on our doorstep. Sometimes we found that people who called us about giving objects of an earlier date, also had important objects needed for the Little Corner Store installation. One estate yielded little in the way of early 19th-century items, but included an impressive number of issues of *The Craftsman*, and a full and undisturbed Heinz ketchup bottle from 50 years ago (cat. 17).

Although we wrote and called dealers of ephemera and advertising, and all auctioneers whose notices included objects like the ones we were seeking, surprisingly few of the objects that we have collected came to us through these contacts. One Beverly Hills dealer, who specializes in providing packaging to studio producers for use as props in motion pictures, told us that she found most of her stock in New England—that we were already located in the best place for finding old packaging and advertising ephemera.

All in all the results of our search for period packaging have been astounding. We knew that, to be fully stocked, the store would require nearly 4000 objects. By the time the exhibition opens we will have collected approximately 2000 original items.[6] It is expected that more items will surface once the exhibition is open to the public and people better understand our needs. In the meantime, we have filled out the "holes" in the store stock with reproductions, most of them made from color photocopies of original packaging. Nearly 80 brands have been made from items in our own collection; other color photocopies and reproductions have come to us through the generosity of 24 different companies. Museum staff members and interns have assembled a great many of the reproduction objects, and we were particularly lucky that Jim McIntosh agreed to custom-make nearly 300 reproduction boxes for us. After experimenting with several different adhesives he came up with one that not only works well, but provides an authentic finish to the package surface. Because we were unable to find bread wrappers from the right period, these posed a special problem. Using images in period advertising Tracey Adkins, our project assistant and a talented fine artist, made full-scale drawings of bread wrappers which were photocopied and made into reproduction loaves.

In addition to the products sold in the store, there were also store furnishings, displays, and fixtures to be found. Fortunately, a number of the original contents still remained in the possession of family members and friends of the Abbotts. Two small display cases—for medicine and tobacco—survived, and have been presented to the museum as gifts. The old butcher block (fig. 77) which Walter and Bertha Abbott used for more than 30 years has come back to the store. The original store sign, from the early years of the store, also survived in excellent condition (fig. 78). This sign was replaced early in the history of the store by another exterior sign which has not survived, but which has been reproduced from old photographs. Some smaller items also survived, including a string holder, a group of small paper bags used for tea and sugar, and a Coca-Cola pretzel dish that was used to hold bottle caps.

Unfortunately, even after years of searching, some of the fixtures needed for

Fig. 77. *Butcher Block, unknown maker, ca. 1920. Oak; H. 29½ in., W. (top) 20 in., D. (top) 29½ in. Originally owned by Walter and Bertha Abbott. Gift of Leslie Clough.*

Fig. 78. *Original Store sign, 1919. Painted wood, H. 10 1/2 in., W. 46 in., D. 3/4 in. Gift of Leslie Clough.*

the store have not been located: we hope to add them as news of our needs spreads. The decision was made to build reproductions of the original oak and glass refrigeration units after it proved impossible to locate fixtures of the exact dimensions that were needed. The display cases for cakes and candy, and the rack for bulk cookies and crackers (see PLATE 26) came to the museum as gifts. Most of the reproduction cakes and pastries were purchased from commercial producers of imitation food. The bulk cookies and crackers were custom-made for the exhibition by Gary Hoyle of the Maine State Museum; museum staff members treated real candy with clear casting resin to make it suitable for display. Many of the candy bars were reconstructed using original wrappers; some are reproductions made from color photocopies.

In addition to providing details of the appearance of specific items in the store, the memories of oral history informants have made it possible for us to make the store "come alive" in a number of different ways. Museum staff recognized the need to make visitors aware, in the installation itself, that one of the features that made small Mom-and-Pop stores distinctive, and important to their customers, was that they extended credit. Leslie Clough described the Abbotts' method of keeping track of credit purchases in great detail. The Abbotts' accounting system consisted of pads of paper, each one with the name of a different customer on it (PLATE 7). A running list of purchases was kept on each pad; these were totaled at the end of each week. Customers were supplied with a duplicate pad as a means of helping them to keep track of their accounts. Credit was extended to individuals who frequented the store on a regular basis. Because the Abbotts often cashed their customers' paychecks, they knew how much customers could afford to charge on their accounts. In addition to their extension of credit to local residents, which allowed the consumer a certain amount of flexibility on a shoestring budget, the Abbotts regulated their customers' purchases. During the war, when commodities, such as sugar, were scarce, they reserved them for their regular customers.[7]

The Candy Room also housed the Abbotts' telephone—a candlestick type (see cat. 65). For many years the telephone number was 1515. As one of only 26 telephones in a neighborhood with 208 households, it served not only as a private telephone for the Abbotts, but as a public telephone for their neighbors and regular customers.[8] Many individuals received and relayed messages through the store, and the telephone was always surrounded by slips of paper.

According to oral history informants, many of the store's customers were children. Although some children went to the store on family errands, many others went to the store on their own, returning bottles for cash to purchase candy and soda. One woman who grew up in the neighborhood especially remembered that if they were outside playing "kick the can" or "hide and seek," she and her friends would often go into the Abbott store for a cold drink. The "big cooler" filled with Coca-Cola and other soft drinks made a particular impression on her:

> they'd stand the bottles up, in the bottom of this and, they had a cover, and they filled it with ice, so the ice kept them cold. Only it seems to me that every time *I* went in the ice had all melted. There was no longer just ice holding these bottles up. . . . Half of them would be laying down in the water. . . and I'd have to reach my hand into this freezing cold, usually kind of, almost slimy at that point—water to get whatever cold drink I wanted.[9]

Children played a vital role in the dynamics of the Little Corner Store. They were drawn into the store, not only to purchase goods, but also to work. Leslie Clough and other neighborhood children who frequented the store were often enlisted as helpers. One informant, who lived next door as a young girl, remembered that "Nana" Abbott taught her to help around the store. She cleaned off the shelves, and put canned goods away, always carefully putting the new stock at the back of the shelf, so that the older items would sell first. She also learned to slice bologna, and to weigh potatoes on the large scale. Bertha Abbott insisted on keeping a spotless store, and many people who shopped there remember how clean it was. She refused to sell beer or wine in her store, although when her husband was alive, the store did carry these alcoholic beverages. Former customers also remember Bertha Abbott as a quiet woman who, although she could sometimes be stern with children who dawdled over their purchases of penny candy, had a special wisdom. She was not afraid to speak her mind, and often did so when giving advice to young visitors. She was also kind, often inviting her special young helpers to join her for stew in the kitchen.[10] The Abbotts' grandchildren also spent many hours tending the store, and remember the special tricks that their grandparents had for stocking the shelves, tying bundles so that they would remain secure, and doing a host of other daily tasks.[11]

The Little Corner Store is an innovative and provocative museum exhibition that will, hopefully, touch people from all walks of life. It is characteristic of a new type of historic house restoration that portrays common, ordinary people, rather than the elite and unusual. Regardless of where, when, or how often each of us has frequented a corner grocery store, these small vanishing vestiges of enterprise and neighborhood unity remain a shared experience for nearly all Americans. The Abbott grocery store exhibition supports and enrichs Strawbery Banke's mission to interpret 350 years of history in the Puddle Dock neighborhood, and carries us forward into a fuller understanding of, and appreciation for, the history of the 20th century.

NOTES

1. Oral History Interviews, March 26, 1990, OH2 SC2; January 22, 1990, OH2 SC2A. Strawbery Banke Museum, Portsmouth, N.H.

2. Dorothy Holt Ober died in the winter of 1992–93.

3. The exact date of the addition is unclear. It is not shown on the map published by the Sanborn Insurance Company in 1920, but it does appear on the 1939 map, and is visible in photographs of the house taken ca. 1937.

4. Because we had only verbal descriptions of the wallpapers in the kitchen and hall, and no surviving remnants, we decided to search for period papers and match the recollections of neighbors and family as well as we could. We finally found an incredible source of authentic wallcoverings in New York City—Second Hand Rose, at 270 Lafayette Street— where we were able to purchase appropriate period wallpapers.

5. Oral History Interview, July 18, 1990, OH2 SC11.

6. At the time this catalogue goes to press, approximately 1100 of these original objects are on view in the store; the remainder are archival examples which remain in storage.

7. Oral History Interview, July 18, 1990, OH2 SC11.

8. *Manning's Portsmouth . . . Directory*, no. 42 (Boston: H. A. Manning Co., 1943).

9. Oral History Interview, March 28, 1990, OH2 SC3.

10. Oral History Interviews, March 25, 1990, OH2 SC2; January 22, 1990, OH2 SC2A; February 15, 1991, OH2 SC26; March 5, 1991, OH2 SC27.

11. Oral History Interviews, October 2, 1990, OH2 SC14; October 2, 1990, OH2 SC15A, OH2 SC15B; October 12, 1990, OH2 SC17.

Preparing the Collection for Display

by Rodney D. Rowland

WHEN Strawbery Banke first approached the question of how best to preserve the objects collected for the installation of the Abbotts' "Little Corner Store," two problems came quickly to the forefront. First, the task of preparing approximately 3000 to 4000 objects was enormous both in terms of time and in terms of funding. Second, preservation of 20th-century mixed-media packaging, which includes metal, paper, and glass, was almost unheard of in the museum community, and it was therefore difficult to find good models to follow.

Before we began, we established a clear set of preservation goals that would guide us through the entire process. To determine these goals we asked ourselves three basic questions. How much treatment was necessary to prevent the objects from further deterioration? What did the product packages look like originally? And, how much of this original appearance could we realistically expect to achieve? It was obvious that 50-year-old boxes of detergent were not going to be made to look new. Therefore, the project staff decided that packages should be made to look clean (insofar as possible) and unopened. Other issues, we believed, could only be resolved with the assistance of a conservation consultant. This was the beginning of Strawbery Banke's relationship with Elizabeth Morse, associate conservator of paper at the Harvard University Library Conservation Laboratory and formerly conservator of paper at the Strong Museum in Rochester, New York.

The museum staff was committed to including as many authentic objects in the Abbott grocery store exhibition as possible. However, doing so meant placing objects on long-term display in a historic house that would not be climate controlled. Because visitors would be constantly opening and shutting the door, we knew that it would not be possible to prevent flies and other insects from entering the exhibition area. We knew that the objects could be vulnerable to dampness and heat, and that there was a danger that their contents might attract insects and rodents. In addition, it was evident that the contents, over the 50-year history of some of the objects, were having an adverse effect on the structure of the packages themselves. Some powdered detergents, for example, had absorbed water and expanded to such a degree that increased pressure was placed on the walls of the package. Two boxes of Twenty Mule Team Borax had expanded outward so much that only one seam remained intact (fig. 79). A few cigarette packs and flour boxes displayed signs of insect damage. We discussed all of these matters with Elizabeth Morse, and

Fig. 79. *Twenty Mule Team Borax box, Pacific Coast Borax Company, New York, N.Y., ca. 1945, prior to conservation.*

she helped us to arrive at the decision to remove the contents of all objects placed on display, unless those contents were completely inert.

Our goals for preservation of the objects were to stabilize them for long term exhibition, to clean them to look as new as period packages could, and to preserve them using currently acceptable, completely reversible, preservation techniques. As a safeguard, we decided to retain "archival" examples of all package types, both with contents and without. These untouched examples are stored in climate-controlled conditions in the museum's curatorial center.

In the best of all possible worlds, Strawbery Banke would have delivered all of the approximately 2000 original objects to be displayed in the Little Corner Store to professional conservators for treatment. To see if this course of action would be economically feasible, staff members selected one object—a box of 1940s Oxydol detergent—that we deemed to be in good condition, and took it to a professional conservation center for an estimate. A short time later the museum received a letter from the center stating that the object had presented the center's staff with a unique problem and that everyone had come together to decide on a course of action. In the final analysis the center recommended a treatment costing between $400 and $600. Since even the most expensive objects collected for the project had been purchased for less than one fourth of this amount, it seemed unwarranted to spend such huge sums on preservation.[1]

Having identified our preservation objectives, project staff decided that it would be possible to do the work "in house" in consultation with Elizabeth Morse. Morse agreed to train staff members in basic techniques, and to assist us in selecting the proper tools and materials with which to equip a small conservation laboratory. We were very lucky to find a conservator who could teach us how to prepare a wide variety of objects in a short time (we gave her only five to ten business days to do so) without compromising the Code of Ethics and Standards of Practice of her field. She taught us basic cleaning, repairing, and exhibition preparation techniques, and cautioned us against doing any work that was outside of our capabilities and knowledge. Morse demonstrated several examples of each technique, performed work on a few of the more difficult examples, and compiled a list of the equipment we would need.

The basic list of conservation materials acquired for the project included Mars Stadtler erasers, scalpels, microspatulas, tweezers, brushes, wheat-starch paste, acid-free mat board, blotter paper, canvas duck, and Japanese tissue.[2] Morse also recommended that the museum acquire a steam pencil to make it easier to remove labels from badly deteriorated cans, for opening boxes, and for removing old tape repairs. But most of all, she recommended that we set aside one room as a conservation laboratory (fig. 80). This room was used solely for the conservation of materials going into the Little Corner Store. The importance of having our own space for this work became evident quickly. First, the materials we used were always located in one place and were not difficult to find. Second, records of work performed on each object could be easily stored in the same area as the objects themselves. Last, the lab was a secure, climate-controlled space that could be devoted to this project. The lab was not always a place of pure cleanliness, but it was a space free from outside distraction and mess that would interfere with our work.

Prior to cleaning, museum staff compared all the objects of a set with one another and designated the best ones as "archival" examples for study purposes only. These objects retained their original contents, were not faded, and had

Fig. 80. *View of Strawbery Banke's Conservation Lab showing preservation equipment used throughout the project. The variety of product packages shown indicates the diversity of mediums encountered during the preservation process.*

very little structural damage. Each object was numbered and placed in our storage facility. Museum staff will monitor these objects for the effects of age and regularly compare them with the objects on display.

Except for the study pieces, most objects were treated in a step-by-step process according to the project goals. During World War II, manufacturers altered the composition of packaging because of government restrictions on the use of certain materials. As a result, many of the objects in the Abbott store collection are made of inferior, unrefined wood pulp, and have degraded faster than other packages of similar age. The variety of ingredients that we encountered in wartime paper and adhesives made it difficult for us to find a standard way to treat every item. The technique or materials used in the preservation process changed according to the medium.

In order to decide on a course of treatment, each object was studied for structural integrity and assessed for overall cleanliness. Every artifact was lightly dusted to remove loose surface dirt, and then, assuming the object walls were strong enough, each was lightly cleaned with an eraser to remove more stubborn dirt. We used Mars Statler erasers because their unique composition allows them to pick up surface dirt and hold it within the eraser material; the eraser material can then be easily brushed away. Starting in the corner, each side of the object was cleaned using a circular motion from left to right. The eraser surface was checked frequently to make sure none of the artifact's color was being removed. Other media were cleaned with a cotton swab and distilled water once it was determined that the surface was not water soluble.

The next step in preparing the objects for display was to remove package contents (fig. 81). The process for emptying the contents was often difficult. The most awkward packages were those made of paper wrapped around paperboard, such as Palmolive Beads, Elastic Starch, Bisquick, and Aunt Jemima Pancake Mix. These packages are made up of an inner cardboard box

Fig. 81. *Dill's Best Smoking Tobacco box, J. G. Dill Co., Richmond, Va., ca. 1945, with contents removed. Note the decay of the interior liner.*

wrapped with a soft tissue paper covering that has the product information printed on it. To access the contents it was necessary to open the paper wrap before opening the box underneath it. Unfortunately, the paper often was so weak that it had a tendency to tear rather than to unfold; steam only weakened the structure of the paper fibers further. After several unsuccessful attempts with steam, we discovered that methyl cellulose would break down the adhesive bond, but not the paper fibers, allowing us to make some progress toward opening the package. However, this process takes three to four hours per box, and so the conservation of these products was put on hold until the majority of the other objects were ready for installation.

Another item that proved to be a test of our ingenuity was Old Dutch Cleanser. Most of our examples were strong, intact, and unopened when examined by staff. Old Dutch Cleanser containers of this period are paper-wrapped cardboard cylinders with metal ends. The sides of the container can not be disturbed without irreversible damage to the label. The only way to remove the contents without ruining the appearance or integrity of the package was to make a small hole in the bottom and literally drain or shake out the cleanser. This process is not reversible, but it was a compromise we had to make to achieve our preservation and exhibition goals. Fortunately, all the other packages were fairly easy to open using either steam to break down the adhesive, or a sharp scalpel or microspatula to break the bond between the adhesive and the paper. Once a package had been emptied, we brushed out the interior to prepare the object for the next phase of the process.

What happened to the now empty object was dependent on its condition and make-up. Objects that were found to be structurally unstable or weak, we furnished with an interior frame or "armature" made of acid-free mat board. A strip of mat board was cut to within an eighth of an inch of the total depth of the object. Pencil marks were made on this strip to indicate the length of the bottom, side, top, opposite side, and bottom of the object, in this order. We then scored the mat board at these marks so that it could be bent without breaking the strips. The scored lines became the joints of the frame supporting the corners of the object. We found that making a finger notch in the section of the frame that formed the bottom allowed for easy removal of the frame once it was installed. When in place this frame acted as a substructure to support the walls of the artifact and to keep it in its proper shape.

Once structurally stable, any object that we felt was light enough to be blown off the shelf in the store was also fitted with a weight. The weight consisted of an inert canvas duck shell cut to twice the depth and slightly less than the length of the object. The fabric was then folded in half to fit the box, sewn to form a pouch, filled with washed sand, and sewn closed. The result was a weight which was heavy enough to hold the package on the shelf, but light enough to avoid crushing the bottom of the object. Once the weight was in place the object was resealed along the original fold lines using wheat-starch paste as a bonding agent (fig. 82).[3] It is worth noting that objects which required a stronger bond to keep them closed were treated with an adhesive consisting of methyl cellulose, wheat-starch paste, and polyvinyl acetate

Fig. 82. *Quick Elastic Starch box, The Hubinger Co., Keokuk, Iowa, ca. 1945, with acid-free mat-board armature and sand-filled canvas duck weight.*

Fig. 83. *Fig. 79 after conservation*

(PVA) in equal amounts. The methyl cellulose extends the drying time of the mixture and the PVA adds to the bonding strength.

Tears, weak folds, and small holes—if they compromised the integrity of an area of an object—were repaired using wheat-starch paste and Japanese tissue (fig. 83). Like wheat paste, Japanese tissue has been used for a very long time because of its known properties and its strength. The process for these repairs was quite simple. A section of tissue slightly larger than the tear was outlined using a fine tipped artist's brush moistened with water. This allowed us to remove the desired piece from the larger sheet in a way that retained the tissue fibers which add to its strength and bonding capabilities. We lined up the tear edges as close to their original position as possible and then applied the tissue, which we had coated with paste, to the tear. Each repair was allowed to dry for 20 to 30 minutes, under a light amount of pressure, before any edges were trimmed. We discovered, through experience, that large repairs should be made with several small pieces of tissue rather than with a large strip. One of the first repairs we made was to a World War II–era poster that had been repeatedly folded and was in danger of tearing in half. Initially we applied one long strip of tissue across an entire fold. However, when the tissue dried, the tissue fibers that ran opposite to those of the poster caused the repair to buckle. Because the process was reversible, the repair was removed and redone correctly.

Throughout the process, unforeseen problems caused us to make variations in the procedures outlined above that are worth noting. For instance, cellophane outer wrappers on cigarette packages, which were opened for removal of the contents, were resealed using gelatin because wheat-starch paste proved to be ineffective on cellophane. For these objects and others whose only surface was constructed of cellophane, accession numbers were written on acid-free paper and placed against the bottom of the object inside the cellophane.

Occasionally the museum acquired posters and other objects that had been repaired by previous owners. Repairs that used pressure sensitive tapes, rubber cement, and other modern forms of adhesive destructive to the objects, were very difficult to reverse. The process for removing these adhesives varied according to the type of tape or glue used. We found that we could sometimes remove modern pressure tape, if it had been recently applied, by carefully pulling it off with tweezers. The most successful way to remove older tape repairs was by applying hot steam to the tape and then slowly lifting the tape off with tweezers. Before this was done we tested the object's inks to make sure they were not water soluble. We frequently used blotter paper during this process to absorb excess moisture. For glue or rubber cement the procedure was much more time-consuming, and often we were not entirely successful. Elizabeth Morse spent almost two days removing the backing from a poster that had been mounted on cardboard with rubber cement. She pulled away all of the cardboard except the layer actually attached to the poster. She then detached the last layer by applying methyl cellulose to the paper and then painstakingly scraping away the weakened paper fibers. The remaining rubber cement was removed with rubber cement pick ups (square blocks of synthetic rubber). The old cement adheres more readily to the pick ups than to the paper fibers, and thus can be pulled from the poster.

Another problem we faced was how to remove paper labels from bottles and cans. Although this was not always necessary, in some cases it had to be done so that we could color photocopy labels of brands that were hard to find. In other cases it had to be done to preserve labels, usually on cans, that were in danger of deteriorating because of corrosive reaction between the labels and the materials on which they were originally mounted. We found that most of our bottle labels could be safely removed with steam. Again, blotter paper should be used frequently to absorb excess moisture, but cautiously so that the wet, and now delicate, label does not tear.

Can labels are a little more perplexing. Morse told us that in the conservation field there is a principle known as "acceptable loss," which means that when an object is in terrible condition it may be necessary to lose a portion of the object in order to retain most of it in good condition. Many of the cans we worked on were rusted and corroded, and the paper labels had become permanently affixed to the corroded areas of the cans. Using a sharp scalpel placed against the can, we tried to scrape the rust loose in order to leave the label intact. When this did not work, it was necessary to cut the damaged area away in order to free the majority of the label from the can. Fortunately, this problem usually occurred at the seam, where one end of the label overlapped the other, and we could cut the label free underneath the top edge. In reattaching the label to a new can, we were able to conceal the loss by overlapping the edges (fig. 84).

One of the decisions made by the project staff was whether or not an object should be conserved using reversible techniques or whether it should undergo a thorough restoration that would return it to its 1940s appearance. All the packaging could be cleaned and preserved by the museum staff and made to look aesthetically pleasing. However, the cast-iron cookstove, the refrigerator,

Fig. 84. *Armour's Star Vienna Sausage can, Armour and Co., Chicago, Ill., ca. 1945; and Heinz Tomato Ketchup bottle, H. J. Heinz Co., Pittsburgh, Penn., ca. 1940, with labels removed.*

and the kerosene pump were all in very poor condition. The stove, for example, was found out-of-doors, in several inches of mud, where it had been slowly rusting for several years. The iron surface was badly pitted, the chrome corroded, and the interior was full of decayed leaves. Because it was our aim to present the store as a "time-capsule"—to give it the look of having been closed for 50 years and suddenly reopened—we hoped to return these appliances to their 1940s appearance. Strawbery Banke does not have the equipment necessary for such extensive work, and so these three objects were sent out to different repair shops. Following the practices often used in the treatment of antique cars, planes, trains, and machinery, these objects were thoroughly restored. Rust was cleaned from the surfaces in order to preserve them from further deterioration, and the objects were repainted.

Bertha Abbott's original desk and rocking chair were also restored. The Strawbery Banke carpentry shop tightened the legs and rebuilt the sides and back of one of the drawers of the desk and fitted new, appropriate brass knobs to the drawer fronts, as most of the originals were missing. The rocking chair was treated in a similar manner. Although the chair's original rockers were replaced with new ones many years ago, the owner saved the original rockers, and these were replaced.

Coca-Cola, Moxie, and Model Tobacco signs, all of which were originally displayed on the exterior of the store, were not restored, but reproduced. For security reasons the originals will remain in collections' storage, while the reproductions have been placed on the exterior of the store. The Old Dutch Cleanser "Groceries" decal was reproduced because the original example in the museum's collection had been mounted on plexiglas and could not be successfully removed.

In the case of some labels in the collection, we have only fragmentary examples. We had an opportunity to send one label in this category to the Rochester Institute of Technology's Center for Imaging Science for digital reproduction. We selected a Marshmallow Fluff label that was too fragile and deteriorated to be reproduced or used in its present state (fig. 85). Adam Hansen, an R.I.T graduate student working under the supervision of faculty member Dr. Jonathan Arney, undertook the task of digitizing the label using a high resolution color scanner and personal-computer-based image manipulation software. Areas of the label that had been torn and physically separated or deformed were moved, geometrically manipulated, and reinserted into their original position in the label. Correspondingly, color reconstruction was achieved by selecting one area of the label for each color, and placing this color into the appropriate areas (fig. 86).[4]

Although many of the objects were conserved and are original, a number of the packages that visitors will see in the Little Corner Store installation are reproductions. Original candy bar wrappers, canned food labels, pasta boxes, and other products from the 1940s were particularly hard to find in significant numbers. For this reason, we made color photocopies of examples in the collection so that we could present ten to twelve examples of each product that

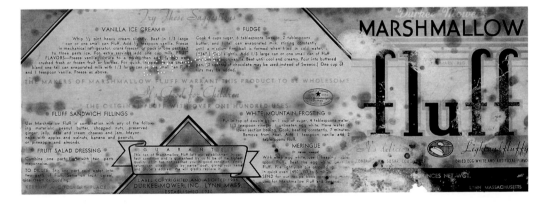

Fig. 85. *Marshmallow Fluff label, Durkee-Mowers, Inc., Lynn, Mass., ca. 1935.*

Fig. 86. *Digital reproduction of Fig. 85 performed by the Rochester Institute of Technology's Center for Imaging Science.*

Fig. 87. *Color photocopies made from originals in the collection of the Strawbery Banke Museum, and subsequent reproduction objects.*

Bertha Abbott kept in stock. Where we did not have examples of the desired packages, we often were able to obtain color photocopies from the companies that manufactured the products. Approximately 72 original labels from the collection, and 32 original packages from company archives were reproduced several times so that the shelves of the store would be suitably stocked. The copies were then wrapped around new cans, stuffed with polyester fiber, or folded into boxes to re-create an object whose appearance was as close to the original as possible (fig. 87). Some boxes were made by mounting the color photocopies onto paperboard which was then scored and folded. Glass jars proved to be more difficult because, although we could easily photocopy the labels, original jars are scarce. We used some modern substitutes, but the majority of the jars on view are period examples.

Once a package was fully preserved or reproduced, whether at Strawbery Banke or elsewhere, it was given an accession number, and stored in a polyethylene bag until its installation in the store. Different types of accession numbers are used to indicate original objects and reproductions. Each object's file contains a catalogue sheet describing in detail the object and its history. Files also contain a photograph or photocopied image of the object, a copy of the deed of gift or sales receipt, and a conservation sheet. The conservation sheet records the specific course of treatment used for the object, the date of treatment, and the name of the person who performed the work.

It is plain to see that the task of preparing the objects for exhibition in the Abbotts' grocery store was time consuming and complex. The result, however, is a display of 2000 to 3000 objects that we feel look the best they can and will present an appearance which closely approximates 1940s' aesthetics. The museum achieved this by following a set of reasonable goals and expectations. The sheer volume of objects to be treated necessitated on-site treatment of the artifacts, but clearly it is always advisable to send work of this type to qualified conservators. The conservation field is constantly changing; some techniques commonly used ten years ago are now known to be detrimental to the long-term life of historical works, and so it is important for museums to seek out the most up-to-date information. Performing permanent repairs on objects is irresponsible and can cause more harm than originally anticipated. Strawbery Banke undertook the preservation of the objects for the Little Corner Store installation under the guidance of an experienced conservation consultant, and staff members took care to make sure that every treatment was thoroughly documented and fully reversible.

NOTES

1. The total would have come to nearly $1.5 million (3000 objects times $500).

2. Museum staff initially considered the use of deacidification spray as an easy way to lower the pH of paper objects. Elizabeth Morse, however, informed us that the use of these products was controversial and would not be appropriate for our collection. Tests with deacidification spray by other conservators demonstrated that they sometimes cause paper to yellow over time. We decided that since there were concerns about the use of this spray, and because objects in our collection had several other more serious problems, we would not use any deacidification methods. If, in the years to come, conservators develop an appropriate method of deacidification that can safely be used on objects in the Abbott store collection, they can be treated at that time.

3. Wheat-starch paste has been used by conservators for many years because it is a reversible, long-lasting bonding agent, its drawback is that it has a very short shelf life. It takes 45 minutes of stirring and straining to prepare a batch of paste, and the resulting nasty white mass will spoil in less than two weeks. Fortunately for us, our conservation consultant was able to package our paste in aluminum tubes (similar to toothpaste tubes) which keep the paste fresh for more than a year.

4. Adam Hansen's final report describing the details of the image digitization, reconstruction, and final printing of the reconstructed label is in the curatorial files of the Strawbery Banke Musuem.

Selected Catalogue

1

"Keep the Home Front Pledge," 1942

Office of War Information, Washington, D.C.
Printed poster
H. 40 in., W. 29 in.
Gift of Richard Cheek

"FOOD FIGHTS FOR FREEDOM is more than a slogan. It is a statement of grim wartime reality." So began a War Food Administration (WFA) directive introducing the "Food Fights for Freedom" campaign. Organized in military fashion with "mobilization" schedules, "drives," "Land Armies," and "Crop Corps," the campaign's goal was to make food a "vital weapon of war." Local Citizens' Food Information Committees urged women to sign pledge cards committing them to "pay no

more than top legal prices" and "accept no rationed goods without giving up ration stamps."

The WFA endlessly repeated the same slogans and graphic images to mobilize support for the program. The emblem of Uncle Sam's hand holding a market basket and the woman taking the pledge were two of the most ubiquitous. The circular "Basic 7" food chart with a happy, healthy family at its center (see fig. 55) was also featured on official posters and in newspaper and magazine ads. The slogan "Produce and Conserve, Share and Play Square" also was used, in whole or in part, in a wide variety of media.

The organizers of the Food Fights for Freedom campaign carefully timed aspects of the program to coincide with seasons of the year. "Produce and Conserve" were the themes for the summer months when the campaign emphasized victory gardens, home food preservation, and nutrition education. "Share and Play Square" and "Keep the Home Front Pledge" were the themes during the winter months when the campaign emphasized compliance with rationing and ceiling prices, and cooking with low-point foods.

The WFA produced a "Tool Kit" for local committees that included posters, booklets, radio materials, speech notes, a "Food Quiz," newspaper advertising copy, background material crammed with statistics, and month-by-month guidelines for implementing the program.

This poster incorporates many elements of the campaign. The woman taking the pledge, the basket emblem, and various slogans are used to promote the message that everyone could help to "shorten the war with food."   GCC

SOURCE:

Portsmouth, N.H., Strawbery Banke Museum, MS 96 Portsmouth War Records, "Food Fights For Freedom," "Home Front Pledge Campaign."

2

"Save Waste Fats for Explosives," 1943

Signed H. Koerner
Office of War Information, Washington, D.C.
Printed poster
H. 28 in., W. 20 in.
Gift of Richard Cheek

Portsmouth citizens, inspired by posters such as this one encouraging people to "Save Waste Fats for Explosives," led the state of New Hampshire in fat collection in September 1943. Collecting an average of 21.1 pounds per 100 persons, New Hampshire ranked third in New England and eighth in the nation in the salvage of waste fats. As the war continued, used household fats became increasingly important in the production of

glycerine for explosives, medicines, and drugs. Fats were also needed to forestall threatened shortages of necessary home-front items such as soaps, synthetic rubber, and prepared poultry feed. The Salvage Division of the State Council of Defense maintained a system of monthly awards to the New Hampshire cities and towns collecting the largest amounts of used fats per capita.

During World War II, posters designed to visually communicate a message in six seconds or less were everywhere—from small "car cards" mounted on subway and trolley cars to huge roadside billboards. They were displayed in stores, schools, government buildings, on sidewalks, and in other public areas. These "weapons on the walls" were produced by numerous federal bureaus, boards, and agencies in average press runs of 75,000 to 170,000.

The Office of War Information (OWI) and the Treasury Department's War Finance Division (WFD) were the two largest single poster producers. The OWI produced posters on a variety of subjects; the WFD issued war bond posters. H. Koerner, the artist who created this poster, may have been one of the more than 8000 artists involved in "Artists for Victory," an organization of 24 artists' associations throughout the United States, which designed posters for the OWI.

The abstract, flat, "European" style characteristic of World War I posters was replaced during World War II with realistic three-dimensional images. Instead of the crusading rhetoric of fear and hatred so common in World War I propaganda, President Roosevelt favored positive imagery that engaged home front citizens in the war effort. In this poster, a well-manicured female hand, gripping the handle of a frying pan, pours a thin stream of fat into a white-hot, explosive center from which a variety of bombs, shells, and bullets are propelled outward, thus creating a dynamic link between the housewife and the battlefield. To reinforce the message of posters produced for the waste-fats salvage campaign, Walt Disney produced his third wartime film "Out of the Frying Pan into the Firing Line," for the Conservation Division of the War Production Board.   CPR

SOURCES:

"Portsmouth Leads State in Fat Salvage Collection." *The Portsmouth Herald*, November 18, 1943, p. 1.

Blum, John Morton. *V Was for Victory: Politics and American Culture During World War II*. New York: Harcourt Brace Jovanovich, 1976.

Crawford, Anthony R., ed. *Posters of World War I and World War II in the George C. Marshall Research Foundation*. Charlottesville: University Press of Virginia, 1979.

Nelson, Derek. *The Posters That Won The War*. Osceola, Wis.: Motorbooks International, 1991.

3

"I'm Out To Lick Runaway Prices," 1943

(See plate 11)

Office of Economic Stabilization, Washington, D.C.
Printed poster
H. 28 in., W. 20 in.
Gift of Calvin P. Otto

4

"We'll Take Care of the Rising Sun," 1943

Office of Economic Stabilization, Washington, D.C.
Printed poster
H. 22 in., W. 16 in.
Gift of Richard Cheek

The goal of the "Seven Keys to Victory" campaign was to combat inflation by admonishing people to support government price controls. By the end of 1942 wartime conditions—high wages coupled with shortages—had resulted in 12% inflation.

Unlike the many posters designed to inspire a simple emotional response through visual effect, the Seven Keys posters were textual and lecturing. Messages always included some reference to controlling prices, and emphasized that inflation threatened the Allied cause. "Pay willingly our share of taxes" is not designed to motivate but to instruct.

Both of these posters feature a single subject with a grimly set expression and either a pointing finger or clenched fist. The thumbs-up gesture and set chin of the soldier in "We'll Take Care of the Rising Sun," mirror the expression and body language of the housewife in "I'm Out to Lick Runaway Prices." The wording of the soldier's slogan plays upon anti-Japanese sentiment and further suggests that the Allies could defeat Japan only if the people at home continued to do their part—both civilians and soldiers were essential to victory.

Like many World War II posters, these two examples personalize the war effort. The home-front consumer can directly relate to a specific soldier fighting to win the war. "I'm Out to Lick Runaway Prices" may have been illustrated by the prolific James Montgomery Flagg, an artist who produced posters during both world wars.   GCC

SOURCE:

Nelson, Derek. *The Posters That Won the War*. Osceola, Wis.: Motorbooks International, 1991.

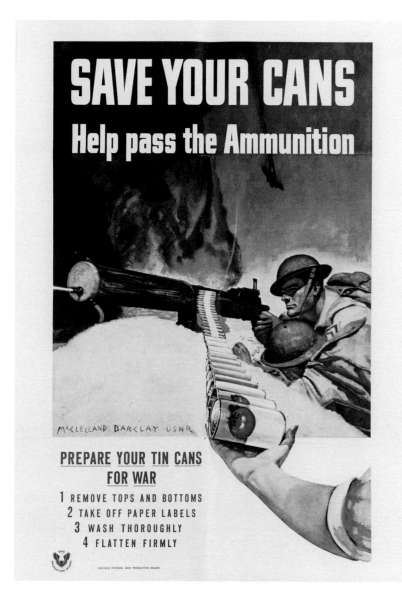

5

"Save Your Cans," 1941–42 (See plate 13)

Signed McClelland Barclay
War Production Board, Salvage Division,
  Washington, D.C.
Printed poster
H. 40 in., W. 22 in.
Gift of Richard Cheek

One effective means of impressing upon civilians the connection between their support of home-front programs and victory on the battlefield, was to show how salvaged household products were converted into weapons of war. Posters showing tin cans, waste fats (see cat. 2), and old tires being transformed into bullets, bombs, and tanks were especially useful in promoting nationwide scrap drives.

This example shows what is clearly a female arm holding a tin can that forms part of a long line of cans which, about halfway along, turns into an ammunition belt for a machine gun manned by two determined-looking soldiers. Thus the connection between home front and battlefront is physical and direct. The poster's design highlights a crashing enemy aircraft and a fire—the ultimate result of the collaboration between civilians and soldiers.

A member of the Naval Reserve, McClelland Barclay designed posters during both the First and Second World Wars. Barclay traveled to field hospitals sketching wounded soldiers; he was lost in action in the South Pacific in 1943.   GCC

SOURCE:

Nelson, Derek. *The Posters That Won the War.* Osceola, Wis.: Motorbooks International, 1991.

6

"Your Victory Garden Counts More Than Ever," 1945 (See plate 12)

Signed Morley
War Food Administration, Washington, D.C.
Printed poster
H. 26 in., W. 19 in.
Gift of Charles E. Burden

Although there were few shortages of fresh vegetables, Victory Gardens were an amazingly successful way to give people on the home front a sense of contributing to the war effort. By the 1945 date of this poster there were more than 80,000 private or municipally sponsored Victory Gardens registered in New Hampshire. The U.S. Department of Agriculture estimated that the more than 18 million gardens nationwide produced enough food for home canners to put up more than 3 billion quarts of food by 1944.

The Department of Agriculture encouraged wide display of this poster throughout the country in late winter and early spring, when people were preparing to plant their gardens. The slogan on this poster urges people to continue planting gardens because they "count more than ever." With the war obviously nearing its end there was a well-founded fear that support for government programs would diminish, especially in the area of food conservation.

This poster, signed just "Morley," has an unusual design and color scheme. While most war posters personalized the home-front effort, this one is impersonal and abstract. The faceless people working in the garden are dwarfed by the giant, geometric vegetable shapes floating in the air.   GCC

SOURCES:

Guyol, Philip. *Democracy Fights: A History of New Hampshire in World War II*. Hanover, N.H.: Dartmouth Publications, 1951.
Levenstein, Harvey. *Paradox of Plenty*. New York: Oxford University Press, 1993.
"Your Victory Garden Counts More Than Ever." *Poster Facts*, January-March 1945, n.p.

7

Pocket Books' Editions, 1940–45

Pocket Books, New York, N.Y.
Printed and coated paper
H. 6½ in., W. 4½ in.
Museum Collection

Robert de Graff started Pocket Books in partnership with Simon & Schuster in 1939. By reprinting classic and popular novels as well as self-help books in a new format, the company became the first successful paperback publisher in the United States. The precursors of today's mass-market paperbacks, Pocket Books were designed to fit into a pocket or handbag and sold for only $.25. By the mid-1940s, Pocket Book became almost a generic term for any paperback.

The wartime paper shortages caused significant problems for the publishing industry. Pocket Books sought to solve the problem and expand its market at the same time. Although the covers of these books are made of heavy paper, the text block paper is thinner than standard book paper and, according to the publishers, was "in full compliance with the government's regulations for conserving paper and other essential materials." To save even more paper, margins were cut to a minimum (often making it impossible to read the book without breaking the binding), and text was set in smaller-than-usual type. The books were designed to be inexpensive and disposable.

A statement near the front of each of these books urges the reader to donate it to the "Victory Book Campaign." This program, sponsored by the USO, the American Library Association, and the Red Cross, sent used books overseas to American soldiers.

Ethel Vance's *Escape* is typical of the titles produced by Pocket Books. A bestseller in hardcover when it was published in 1939, its publication in paperback was timed to coincide with the release of the movie starring Robert Taylor and Norma Shearer.

Prelude to Victory, by James B. Reston, and *The Pocket Book of the War*, edited by Quincy Howe, were two of the company's "war series" books, some of which were written especially for Pocket Books. Although these two titles are serious, the series also included *The Pocket Book of War Humor* (about army life), and *The Pocket Book of Cartoons*.

The Atomic Age Opens, compiled by the editors of Pocket Books, was published in August 1945. One of many so-called "instant books" published about timely events, it contains detailed information about the destructive effects of the strike on Hiroshima, most of it taken from newspaper reports. It also extolls the peacetime uses of U-235 ("marvelously compact and incredibly easy to manage") in automobiles, home heating and lighting, and agriculture. Its authors predicted that "the power behind the atomic bomb could be harnessed to produce the Utopia that men have dreamed of." The book sold 265,000 copies in its first three months of publication.   GCC

SOURCE:

Davis, Kenneth. *Two Bit Culture: The Paperbacking of America.* Boston, Mass.: Houghton Mifflin, 1984.

8

Young Americans Paint Book, ca. 1942

Whitman Publishing Co., Racine, Wis.
Printed paper
H. 14 in., W. 11 in.
Gift of Charles E. Burden

In 1916, the Hamming-Whitman Publishing Company of Chicago was absorbed by Western Printing Company, of Racine, Wisconsin, to form the Western Publishing Company. Western Publishing is probably most famous for developing "Little Golden Books" for children in 1942. Whitman, a subsidiary of Western, still prints children's material.

During the war, children were bombarded with toys, games, and advertising designed to indoctrinate them with a sense of patriotic duty and to reinforce role models and gender stereotypes. The *Young Americans Paint Book* hits all of the notes in this tune. The cover design is red, white, and blue, reminiscent of the American flag, and incorporates a war-bond advertisement at left center. The main characters of the book symbolize the acceptable wartime aspirations of 1940s children: boys are coast watchers, gunners, and pilots; girls are nurses and ambulance drivers.

This book may have been based on a British model. A gunner in one interior illustration sits in a plane with Royal Air Force markings, biplanes land on aircraft carriers, and the field uniforms are more consistent with World War I and interwar styles than with World War II styles.

Designed for young children, the drawings are simple, with few details, and with large areas to color. Everyone, invariably, has a smile. These pictures allowed very young children to make some sense out of the war news they must have heard and seen each day.   GCC

SOURCE:

Santi, Steve. *Collecting Little Golden Books: A Collector's Identification Guide*. Florence, Ala.: Books Americana, 1985.

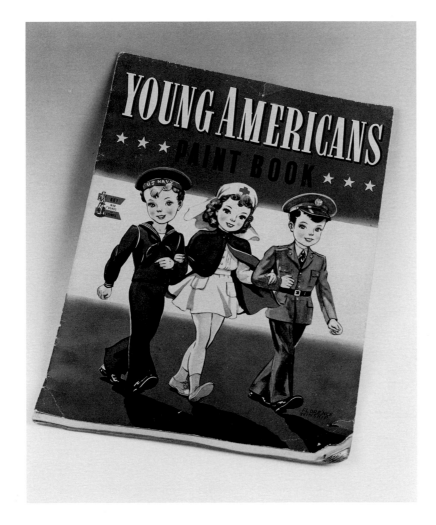

9

Official Kit: Jr. Aircraft Warning Service,
1943

Leo Hart Co., Inc., Rochester, N.Y.
Printed paper and paperboard
Envelope: H. 7½ in., W. 10½ in.
Gift of Charles E. Burden

Like today's merchandising tie-ins with popular movies or television shows, producers capitalized on the major media event of children's lives: World War II. This kit appealed to children's desire to imitate grown-ups through imaginative play. The handbook explains that "the material contained in the Jr. Aircraft Warning Kit . . . will give you the opportunity of gaining practical experience so that when you reach the proper age, you will be qualified to become a full fledged member of the regular Aircraft Warning Service." The Aircraft Warning Service (AWS) was a volunteer network of ground observers organized and staffed by the American Legion and operated under the ultimate authority of the Army Air Corps. Unlike *How You Can Defend Your Home* (cat. 10) which illustrated Axis as well as Allied aircraft, all planes illustrated in this kit were Ameri-

can—the only planes that American children were likely to spot.

The design of the envelope in which the kit is contained uses a red, white, and blue color scheme and incorporates a pseudomilitary insignia of a red plane inside a black circle. (The insignia of the real AWS was a blue armband with yellow wings.) The words "OFFICIAL KIT" neglect to specify by what authority, if any, it was produced. Four boys and a girl are perched on a hilltop overlooking a rural town—with the requisite church steeple—observing and recording passing aircraft using their kit. The boys do the work of identifying the planes while the girl dutifully acts as secretary.

This kit came with everything a Jr. Observer needed to start an observation post just like a real one: a sign, plane identification chart, flight direction indicator, altimeter, handbook, arm band, and identification card. The handbook also urges young observers to "WEAR YOUR ARM-BAND—CARRY YOUR IDENTIFICATION CARD."

GCC

SOURCE:

Guyol, Philip. *Democracy Fights: A History of New Hampshire in World War II.* Hanover, N.H.: Dartmouth Publications, 1951.

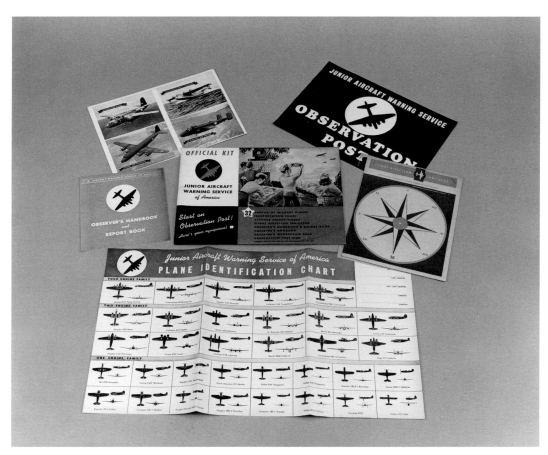

10

How You Can Defend Your Home, 1942

Jolaine Publications, Inc., New York, N.Y.
Printed paper
H. 10 in., W. 8 in.
Gift of Charles E. Burden

Capitalizing on the air-raid hysteria that existed just after Pearl Harbor, Jolaine Publications combined sensationalism and real information in this booklet which was designed to be hung on a string or hooked on the wall using the hole in the upper-left corner. The cover is designed in red, white, and blue, and the text mimics newsreel headline graphics and style. Inside are pictures and specifications for 50 Allied and Axis planes, air-raid advice from the Office of Civilian Defense, thumb-nail sketches of aviation innovators, and encouraging messages from the Mayor of New York and First Lady Eleanor Roosevelt. Unlike the more upscale Jr. Aircraft Warning Service Kit (cat. 9), its comic-book format appealed to a mass-market urban consumer.

Patriotic appeals became a staple of war-time advertising. Although publishers disseminated useful information, they obviously expected to make a profit from the sale of pamphlets of this kind. Through the use of inflammatory phrases such as "WHEN [not if] THE ENEMY STRIKES," the publisher plays upon public fear of the virtually nonexistent threat of enemy air attacks. The back cover urges consumers to purchase Defense Savings Bonds.   GCC

11

V-Mail examples, 1945

Photographic prints
H. 2½ in., W. 3½ in.
Museum Collection

12

V-Mail Stationery, ca. 1942

Stanley Wessel and Co., Chicago, Ill.
Printed paper
Envelope: H. 10 in., W. 6½ in.
Gift of Charles E. Burden

13

*"Reach Your Boy Overseas By
V-Mail,"* 1942

Office of War Information, Washington, D.C.
Signed Schlaiki
Printed poster
H. 28 in., W. 22 in.
Gift of Calvin P. Otto

The United States government was eager to encourage people to write letters to soldiers overseas to build morale both at home and abroad. The sheer bulk of the correspondence, however, made transporting and processing this mail a daunting task. One solution to these problems was V-Mail. The correspondent purchased a V-Mail blank, wrote his or her message on the inside area, and then folded and mailed it like any other letter. The letter was entirely self-contained on one sheet; anything written outside the lines was cut off in the final printing process. The Army Post Office system opened the letters and photographed them using a process similar to microfilming. As the poster (cat. 13) illustrates, rather than the bulky paper, the exposed and developed reels of film were sent across the ocean. The letters were read by government censors, printed, and put into special window envelopes. Installations that lacked photographic capabilities sent the original letters.

Until stationery manufacturers caught up with the demand, all official blanks were sold through United States Post Offices. In this commercial example (cat. 12) the "V" motif runs throughout the stationery. The lines on the outside of the blank even formed a "V" when folded correctly. Patriotic names for the packages such as "The Bomber" (with 22 blank sheets) and "The Pursuit" (with 12 blanks), further promoted the wartime message.

These examples (cat. 11) were mailed from Europe and the Pacific by friends and relatives of the Burch family of 144 Washington St., in the Puddle Dock neighborhood of Portsmouth, N.H. One is addressed from "Somewhere in Germany," another from Paris, France. The third, a Christmas card, comes from Hawaii. The letters carry the censor's stamp in the upper left corner and are the end result of the V-Mail process.   GCC

SOURCE:

Portsmouth, N.H., Strawbery Banke Museum, MS 96 Portsmouth
War Records, "Health and Welfare Survey."

14

Skrip ink box and bottle, 1942–44

(See plate 17)

W. A. Sheaffer Pen Co., Fort Madison, Iowa
Printed paper and paperboard, glass, metal
Box: H. 2⅞ in., W. 2 in., D. 2 in.
Gift of Charles E. Burden

Skrip ink was first introduced in 1922 and is still being manufactured today by the Sheaffer Company. Walter Sheaffer, the company's founder, devised this dependable ink for his pens so that customers would not have to rely "on the unpredictable quality of the inks being produced by others." His formula for Skrip ink proved to be dependable, but wartime conditions necessitated changes.

Beginning in 1942, most of the pens and pencils made by Sheaffer were sent abroad for use by the military—few were available for civilian use. This was not the case, however, with ink. Sheaffer developed V-Black specially for use on V-mail. According to the box, this permanent black ink "Photographs Best / For V . . . – Mail / " (". . . –" is the Morse code symbol for "V"). This innovation

and others like it meant that the company actually tripled ink production during the war.

To further lure consumers, the eye-catching yellow and black box was outlined with a red strip which contained the V-Mail message. The glass bottle has a label of similar color and is equipped with a top-well for filling a fountain pen.

During the war, when the Sheaffer Company nearly ceased manufacturing writing instruments in favor of "high precision items needed for the war effort," they joined a long list of companies in adapting current packaging and products to meet wartime needs. Craig Sheaffer, who became president of the company in 1938, gave two reasons for the shift in production: 1) producing needed war materials allowed the company to maintain a high level of employment in the Fort Madison area; and 2) "Unless we lick the Axis, nothing else will be worthwhile." This latter sentiment was shared by businesses throughout the United States.   RDR

SOURCES:

Casey, Robert S. *Writing Ink*. Fort Madison, Iowa: W. A. Sheaffer Pen Co., 1961.

Sheaffer Eaton, Inc. *A History of the Sheaffer Pen Company and Walter A. Sheaffer, Its Founder*. Fort Madison, Iowa: W. A. Sheaffer Pen Co., 1990.

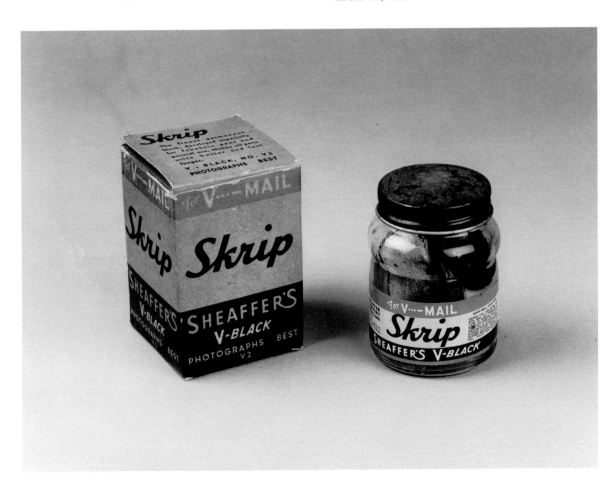

15
Meal Planning Guide, 1944

Home Economics Institute, Westinghouse
   Electric & Manufacturing Co., Mansfield, Ohio
Printed paper
H. 9 in., W. 6⅛ in.
Gift of David Rutherford

This cookbook is full of solid information to help members of the "Health for Victory Club" buy, cook, and plan "point-thrifty" meals. The smiling soldier in uniform on the front cover is a visual clue to the wartime content. Inside the front cover, the purpose of the publication is clearly stated: to "help Food Fight for Freedom." The back cover is more serious, and features a battleship, airplane, tank, and artillery gun accompanied by the legend "Food is the mightiest weapon of them all." The text reads, in part: "Food can lighten the task of our soldiers. . . can win victories without a shot being fired . . . can shorten the war and help win the peace. There's still plenty of food for the home front . . . if each and every one of us will avoid waste, clean the plate, do our share." Below this is the familiar "Food Fights for Freedom" emblem with Uncle Sam's hand, drawn to appear like the stripes on the American flag, gripping the handle of a market basket. The American flag and the words "Produce and Conserve / Share and Play Square" are also printed on the back cover.

The pamphlet contains useful information making it "A Helping Hand in Planning Wartime Meals," according to Mrs. Julia Kiene, national director of the Health-for-Victory campaign. Kiene covers such topics as the importance of good nutrition, how to plan meals that are economical in terms of dollars *and* ration points, as well as marketing, food preservation, and cooking tips. All of the recipes were prepared and tasted by test families of varying sizes and lifestyles. The average cost per person per meal was $.18.

Most recipes in the book are straightforward "American" dishes. Daily menus provide suggestions for a balanced diet. The food groups from the "Basic 7" (see fig. 55) are noted beside each recipe to aid in planning nutritionally sound meals. The recipes encourage readers to make use of game and less desirable cuts of meat; several dishes include tame or wild rabbit. In addition, the text reminds consumers to check meat for the purple government stamp, their insurance "against Black Market meat" which might "cause disease."

CPR

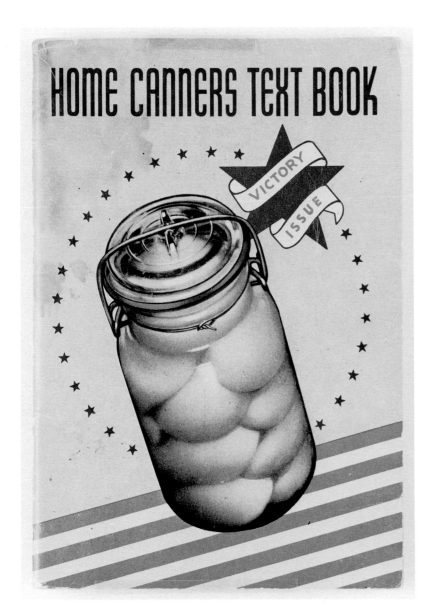

16

Home Canners Text Book, 1943

Boston Woven Hose and Rubber Co.,
  Cambridge, Mass.
Printed and coated paper
H. 8 in., W. 5½ in.
Museum Collection

The "Victory Issue" of the *Home Canners Text Book* opens with a quotation from War Food Administrator, Claude R. Wickard: "Food will win the war and write the peace." Written as an advertising vehicle for canning supplies produced by the Boston Woven Hose and Rubber Company, this booklet features Good Luck Jar Rubbers and the company's wartime substitute—Bull Dog Jar Rubbers (see fig. 52), which were touted as being made to conform with government restrictions on the use of rubber.

Unlike victory editions of similar booklets, which often feature only a special cover with no change to the inside text, the *Home Canners Text Book* is permeated with wartime messages. The book's authors appeal to a "citizen army of growers and canners" who, by growing and processing countless quarts and pints of vegetables and fruits, are "helping the United States of America and its allies to win this war," and remind readers of the "almost forgotten thrill of thrift and self-sufficiency" that accompanies home canning. The authors go on to praise citizen canners for embodying "the 'old-fashioned' American virtues" that "the national emergency calls . . . to arms again."

The book warns readers that they must follow directions precisely to avoid mistakes for, when the country is at war, spoilage is worse than uneconomical, it is unpatriotic. There must be no waste. Because of restrictions on metals being used "for tools of war," the authors caution that new water-bath canners and steam pressure cookers may be difficult to obtain. The booklet suggests, therefore, that readers rent or borrow equipment and organize "canning bees" at their local church or parish house as one solution to the problem. A canning bee, the authors claimed, could be "more fun than the old-fashioned quilting bee, really."

Several pages of canning recipes and advice are included in the book; most show no evidence of having been adapted for wartime shortages and rationing. It was advised, however, that fruit juices be "put up" in 1943 "because the proportion of sugar is low . . . and you will find many uses for them." The pamphlet also contains perforated gummed labels preprinted with the names of various foodstuffs for the convenience of the home canner.   CPR

17

Heinz Tomato Ketchup bottle and label, ca. 1939–45 (See plate 9)

H. J. Heinz Co., Pittsburgh, Penn.
Glass, metal, printed paper
H. 9¼ in., Diam. base 2½ in., Diam. top 1⅛ in.
Bequest of Edith Chase

H. J. Heinz founded the Heinz Company in 1869. First noted for its pickles and relishes, the Heinz Company soon became famous for its 57 varieties, one of the most popular of which was tomato ketchup.

During World War II, ketchup was rationed—in 1943 it averaged 5 points for a 14-ounce bottle. As a result, many home canners added ketchup to their repertoire.

The Heinz ketchup bottle is perhaps one of the most familiar objects in modern American culture. Its basic components have changed relatively little over the years. The design elements of this example from the early 1940s—the octagonal base, tapering neck, screw-on cap, and applied paper label in the shape of a keystone, the symbol of the state of Pennsylvania—are repeated in today's examples with only subtle changes. One reason for the bottle's persistence is that it is well-suited to its function. The faceted base allows the user to grip the bottle more easily, while the tapering neck facilitates pouring the viscous tomato sauce onto hamburgers, French fries, or (as Americans are wont to do) almost anything.

Heinz products were one of the national brands well represented in the stock of the Abbotts' Little Corner Store. In addition to ketchup, the store carried Heinz pickles (sweet gherkins and fresh cucumber), horseradish, relishes, and white vinegar.

The bottle illustrated here was found in a cupboard beneath the stairs of the summer home in Pittsfield, New Hampshire, of the late Edith Chase of Boston. It had never been opened. Such is the ubiquity of Heinz ketchup in 20th-century America, however, that it could as well have been found in Chase's Beacon Hill home.   GWRW

SOURCE:

Alberts, Robert C. *The Good Provider: H. J. Heinz and his 57 Varieties*. Boston: Houghton Mifflin, 1973.

18

Del Monte Brand Peas and Carrots label and can, ca. 1940–45 (See plate 9)

California Packing Corp., Oakland, Calif.
Paper, tin-plated metal
H. 4⅛ in., Diam. 3⅛ in.
Gift of Charles E. Burden

19

Del Monte Foods Advertisement, 1944

California Packing Corp., Oakland, Calif., as printed in
    the January issue of *Good Housekeeping*
Printed paper
H. 11 in., W. 8½ in.
Museum Collection

During the first three decades of the 20th century, The California Fruit Canning Association (CFCA), and the Tillman and Bendel Company of Oakland, California, shared the Del Monte brand in association with the prestigious Hotel Del Monte in Monterey, California. CFCA used the label for fruits and vegetables, Tillman and Bendel used it for coffee.

In 1916 the CFCA, along with three other prominent companies, merged to form the California Packing Corporation (Calpak). Like CFCA, Calpak used the Del Monte label for its premium fruits and vegetables, thus establishing a national market under one label. After a long legal battle, Calpak won exclusive rights to the Del Monte name in 1933.

In the 1920s and 1930s, Calpak expanded its packing operation to include fish products such as tuna, sardines, and salmon. During World War II, one half of Calpak products were sent to Allied armed forces; civilian supplies of canned fruits and vegetables were limited. The company introduced glass packs in 1940, and these were used increasingly during the war years as supplies of tin-plated metal diminished.

Because of fighting in the Pacific, Calpak's production of fish and pineapple waned considerably. In 1942, the United States Coast Guard commandeered Calpak's tuna and salmon fleets for the war effort, and Calpak was forced to close its San Diego tuna cannery and curtail its salmon operations. Philpak, Calpak's pineapple packing plant in the Phillipines, leased land to the United States for an airfield. When the airfield was bombed by the Japanese on December 8, 1941, the plant sustained considerable damage. The airfield served as an outpost and supply depot for Allied forces in the Phillipines and was used as a shelter for General Douglas MacArthur and his family after the fall of Bataan in April 1942. When the

Japanese gained control of the Islands, many Philpak employees were interned as prisoners of war.

Back on the home front, Calpak suffered more from labor shortages than from supply shortages. Intense recruitment of housewives, students, office and sales staff, and even prisoners of war kept the company in business. In fact, Calpak enjoyed record sales between 1942 and 1944; 1943 was the best year in the company's history. In 1944, the War Food Administration awarded 27 achievement awards to Calpak plants.

Calpak was particularly concerned with keeping the Del Monte name before the public during the war years. Advertisements, such as this one (see also fig. 59), contain a variety of wartime messages—menu suggestions, tire and gas rationing conservation pleas, information on home canning and nutrition, and ideas on how to make the most of rationed foods.

Sales of Del Monte products boomed in the postwar period. In 1967, Calpak became the Del Monte Corporation in honor of its most famous brand. The company's packaging has changed little; a slightly more streamlined version of the shield was introduced in the 1970s. In 1979, Del Monte merged with R. J. Reynolds, but continues to operate independently as the Del Monte Corporation.

TEA

SOURCE:

Braznell, William. *California's Finest: The History of Del Monte Corporation and the Del Monte Brand.* San Francisco, Calif.: Del Monte Corp., 1982.

20

B & M Baked Beans jar and label, ca. 1940

Burnham and Morrill Co., Portland, Maine
Printed paper, metal, glass
H. 4⅜ in., Diam. 4¼ in.
Gift of Charles E. Burden

21

B & M Dehydrated Baked Beans container, ca. 1942–45 (See plate 9)

Burnham and Morrill Co., Portland, Maine
Paperboard, tin-plated metal, printed paper
H. 5 in., W. 3⅛ in., D. 2⅛ in.
Gift of Charles E. Burden

The production of certain food items, such as processed "convenience" foods for which the consumer could find other substitutes, was greatly restricted by War Production Board (WPB) and Office of Price Administration (OPA) regulations. Less metal was available for packaging these products because the WPB reasoned that homemakers could make these dishes from other ingredients. In addition, many processed foods were purchased for military and lend-lease use. B & M

Baked Beans were unavailable to American consumers during much of the war. Dehydrated beans, a nonrationed substitute, were not generally advertised by the manufacturer, and probably only appealed to consumers who were attempting to furnish air-raid shelters or to stockpile emergency supplies at home. The "duration" package utilized paperboard supported by tin-plated metal ends. The message on the back of the package explained to the consumer that the product was a "temporary wartime replacement."

The makers of Friend's Baked Beans turned to another expedient. Finding themselves unable to obtain tin-plate for canning their beans, they developed a frozen substitute that could be packaged in a cellophane bag and placed inside a cylindrical paperboard container.

Many consumers missed familiar convenience foods, and *Progressive Grocer* recommended that grocers answer the customer's question "Why haven't you any pork and beans?" in the following way:

> Grocer: As you know the war has caused a shortage of tin in this country. To assure a supply of essential canned foods to the peo-

ple, the government has issued a list of nonessential foods for which no tin can be obtained. Canned beans were naturally placed on this list because you can often buy them in glass or cook dry beans yourself. It means a little more work preparing some of our food, but after all, we still have plenty of food.

The Burnham and Morrill Company seconded the recommendation that consumers buy dry beans and cook them themselves by advertising the availability of their own recipe for B & M Baked Beans to anyone who wrote to the company asking for it. The same advertisements let consumers know that although their beans had gone to war, they would soon be available again.

BMW

SOURCES:

"Here's Help on Five Wartime Problems." *Progressive Grocer* 21 (1942):84.

B & M Baked Beans advertisement. *Good Housekeeping*, February 1944.

"Design Histories." *Modern Packaging* 16 (March 1943): 65ff.

22

Old Colony Black Pepper Substitute container, ca. 1943

Old Colony Packing Co., Boston, Mass.
Paperboard, printed paper, tin-plated metal
H. 3⁹/₁₆ in., W. 2⁵/₁₆ in., D. 1¹/₄ in.
Gift of Charles E. Burden

23

Victory Brand Imitation Chocolate Concentrated Extract bottle and label, ca. 1943
(See plate 9)

Victory Extract Manufacturing Co.,
   Rochester, N.Y.
Glass, printed paper
H. 6 in., W. 2 in., D. 1³/₈ in.
Gift of Charles E. Burden

The curtailment of ocean shipping during the war reduced the available supplies of popular imported food items such as pepper and chocolate. Black pepper, indigenous to the Malabar Coast of India, was widely cultivated in East India and tropical regions of Africa and the Western Hemisphere. Chocolate was primarily imported from South America. Spice companies extended their supplies of these commodities by creating substitutes to supplement their regular products.

Old Colony's Black Pepper Substitute was made from a cereal base, to which capsicum—a pepper derivative—and pepper hulls and pepper oil (which would normally have been discarded) were added to make a suitable product for the dining room table. A survey of randomly selected recipes published in *The Portsmouth Herald* during 1943 indicates that the vast majority of nondessert recipes included pepper as an ingredient. Pepper was one of the few widely used spices during the 1940s, yet Leah Widtsoe, author of *How to Be Well, A Handbook and Cook-book Based on The Newer Knowledge of Nutrition* recommended abstinence from pepper altogether:

> While salt is relatively a harmless substance, unless taken in excessive amounts, the same cannot be said of pepper. Few people realize how exceedingly irritating pepper is to the mucous membrane lining of the stomach and intestines, and especially to the kidneys. Since the body has no need for this substance, it would seem wiser to eliminate it entirely from the diet and avoid the irritation resulting from its use.

Chocolate, on the other hand, was recognized as a stimulant, and, when combined with sugar, as a source of quick energy. The Victory Extract Company produced Victory Brand Imitation Chocolate Concentrated Extract from chocolate oil, propylene, alcohol, glycol, ketone, and imitation colors and flavors. Enriched with Vitamin B complex, including thiamine and riboflavin, the extract was recommended as a substitute for use in all recipes calling for cocoa or chocolate. Because it was "highly concentrated" the housewife only needed to use a small amount to simulate the flavor of chocolate.   SVLM & BMW

SOURCES:
Encyclopedia Britannica (1987), s.v. "black pepper," "chocolate."
Widtsoe, Leah. *How to Be Well, A Handbook and Cook-book Based on The Newer Knowledge of Nutrition.* Salt Lake City, Utah: Desert Books, 1943.

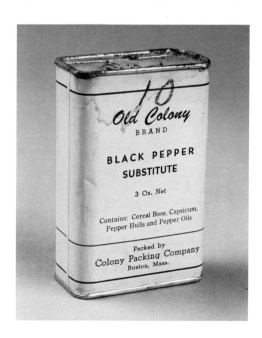

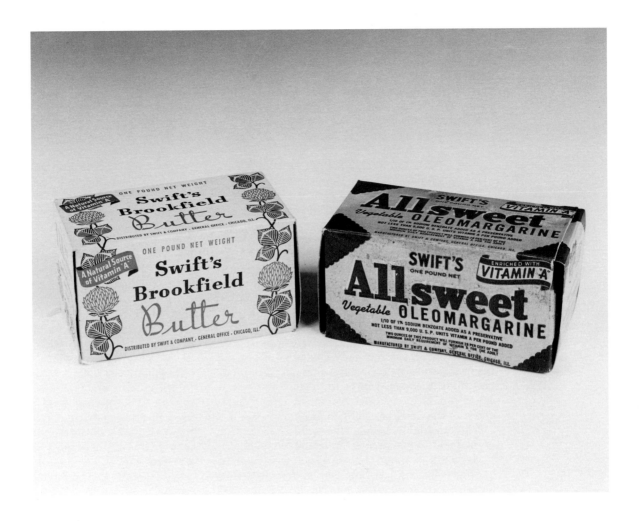

24

Swift's Brookfield Butter package,
ca. 1940–50 (left) (See plate 9)

Distributed by Swift & Co., Chicago, Ill.
Printed paperboard with waxed coating
H. 2⅝ in., W. 4¾ in., D. 2¹¹/₁₆ in.
Gift of Charles E. Burden

25

Swift's Allsweet Vegetable Oleomargarine
package, ca. 1940–50 (right) (See plate 9)

Manufactured by Swift & Co., Chicago, Ill.
Printed paperboard with waxed coating
H. 2⅝ in., W. 5¹/₁₆ in., D. 2⅜ in.
Gift of Charles E. Burden

Butter is made by churning pasteurized sweet or
soured cream until the particles of butterfat cling
to each other; the buttermilk is then washed
away, and the resulting substance "worked" to remove air and most of the water. Margarine can be
made from either vegetable or animal fats and is
churned in pasturized milk during processing
taking up milk solids and a corresponding "butter" flavor.

Butter was marketed as a "natural" product; its
only ingredient was pasteurized cream. The
graphic images of clover flowers and leaves on the
package, as well as Swift's choice of the name
"Brookfield," emphasized the freshness of the familiar product as well as its origins in the mead-
ows of America. A scrolled banner printed in red
in the upper left corner immediately draws attention to the message that butter is "A Natural
Source of Vitamin 'A'."

Butter is naturally high in vitamin A which
keeps the body's skin and mucous membranes in
good condition and bolsters the immune system.
It is especially helpful in preventing certain res-
piratory and eye diseases, maintaining tooth
enamel, and helping to prevent degenerative
changes in nerves. When fortified with vitamin A,
margarine (oleomargarine) is nutritionally equiv-
alent to butter.

Margarine manufacturers, without the benefit of generations of consumers behind them, had to find ways to appeal to the public. Although Swift's indicated on the package of its Allsweet margarine that it was "Made from American Vegetable Oils From Products of American Farms," the package design does not attempt to link the product with nature. The banner in the upper right corner proclaims that the product was enriched with vitamin A, "ENRICHED WITH" appears in smaller type size than the bold lettering of "VITAMIN 'A'." The front and back panels advise that two ounces of the product furnish 28% of the minimum daily adult requirement of the nutient. The product was awarded the seal of acceptance of the American Medical Association Council on Foods and the *Good Housekeeping* guarantee.

During the same period, Kraft's marketing message for its Parkay brand margarine attempted to appeal to consumers with an interesting blend of modern quasi-scientific technology and the romance of traditional labor. Parkay's quality and delicate flavor, the company explained, were the result of careful selection of American farm products, and its manufacture in modern, "spic and span" plants by "skilled craftsmen long experienced in the processing of fine foods."

When available, people who could afford butter preferred it to margarine. On December 24, 1942, Portsmouth resident Louise Grant recorded in her diary, for the first time, not being able to find butter. Over the next few months she documented the uncertainty of the local butter supply and her family's response to the situation. For example, on New Year's Day 1943 they were able to purchase a half pound of butter; they continued to buy that amount approximately every two weeks until February 27, when her jubilant entry reads "Ma got a whole lb of butter! First whole lb for a long time." The diary is then silent on the subject

of butter until August 22, 1943, when Grant indicated that butter was so scarce and expensive (10 ration points per pound) "that you can't afford to use it on corn, etc." Eventually she recorded the elimination of butter from the family diet in two telling entries. On September 29, 1943, she wrote "Butter is going up to 16 points & that would be a whole week's points for one person. We haven't bot any for a long while," and on October 7, 1943, "No butter of course but then we don't use it now."

Louise Grant's family made their own butter substitutes during 1943 and 1944, which she referred to as "oleo-butter" and "Dixie butter." She did not elaborate on "Dixie butter" other than to mention that it took about a half an hour to make. On August 25, 1943, Grant wrote about making oleo-butter: "Thinned out one row of beets & had greens. Made oleo-butter . . . My hands are a sight. As tho beet greens weren't enough I got oleo color on them then bean stain & tonite I worked on the tomatoe vines." Because of a Federal tax on artificially colored margarine it was usually sold in its "pure natural white" form and colored "a rich appetizing yellow by adding the vegetable coloring that accompanies each package." Although the coloring used was similar to that used in coloring butter, to this day many people remember the performance of this unpleasant task as one of their most vivid memories of the war years.   CPR

SOURCES:

Given, Meta. *Modern Encyclopedia of Cooking.* 2 vols. Chicago: J. G. Ferguson and Associates, 1949.

Kraft Parkay Oleomargarine advertisement. *Woman's Home Companion,* February 1944.

Portsmouth, N.H., Strawbery Banke Museum. S. Louise Grant Papers. Louise Grant Diary.

Russell, Judith, and Renee Fantin. *Studies in Food Rationing.* Washington, D.C.: Office of Temporary Controls, Office of Price Administration, 1947.

26

Minute Plain Unflavored Gelatin box and inner envelopes, 1943 (See plate 9)

Minute Tapioca Co., Inc., Orange, Mass.
Printed paperboard and paper
H. 3⅝ in., W. 2⅞ in., D. ¾ in.
Gift of Charles E. Burden

Gelatin was a popular and versatile food product that appeared in many wartime dishes. One cookbook placed the steps in making gelatin desserts with the rudimentary cooking techniques of stirring, beating, creaming, whipping, and frying. In another, nine out of the 22 salad recipes included were based on gelatin. Unflavored gelatin, originally developed by Charles B. Knox in the 1890s for making aspic, was marketed during World War II as an effective extender for many different rationed products. This package of Minute Gelatin includes recipes for 22 different items ranging from "Minute Mayonnaise Spread," to "Coconut Snow Pudding," and the famous "Minute Butter-Saver Spread."

By February 1943 butter was so scarce in Portsmouth, New Hampshire, that a police detail was assigned to regulate traffic in and out of a store on the city's main thoroughfare that had received a shipment of the "goldbrick." Gelatin was heavily publicized as a butter extender, although the results tended to be more crumbly than butter and margarine, or butter and milk, combinations. Cream—today's heavy cream—was replaced with "wartime cream," or what we now call half-and-half, serviceable for coffee perhaps, but not for the perennial New England favorite, ice cream. One of the recipes enclosed in this package of Minute Gelatin shows the homemaker how to make an ice cream that called for milk and light cream, and a sherbert that called for no dairy products at all.

SVLM

SOURCES:

Heseltine, Marjorie, and Ula Dow. *The Hood Basic Cook Book.* Boston: Houghton Mifflin, 1947.
"Portsmouth Hunts Butter in Rain Downpour." *The Portsmouth Herald,* February 5, 1943, p. 9.
Robertson, Helen, Sarah MacLeod, and Francis Preston. *What Do We Eat Now?* Philadelphia: J. B. Lippincott, 1942.

27

Maxwell House Coffee jar and label, ca.
1943–45 (left) (See plate 9)

Maxwell House Div., General Foods Corp.,
    Battle Creek, Mich.
Glass, metal, paper
H. 6⅛ in., Diam. (top) 2½ in., Diam. (base) 4¹/₁₆ in.
Museum Purchase

28

Maxwell House Coffee can, 1940–45
(right)

Maxwell House Div., General Foods Corp.,
    Battle Creek, Mich.
Tin-plated metal
H. 3⅜ in., Diam. 5 in.
Museum Purchase

The Can Manufacturers' Institute of New York
noted in 1944–45 that "Cans Fight for Victory,"
and that during the war "vacuum-packed coffee
and other favorite products in cans are missing
from dealer's shelves." In addition, the War Production Board limited the supply of coffee to civilian consumers because of reductions in the inventory of green coffee available to roasters. Consumer coffee rationing began in November of
1942, with individual consumers being allotted
approximately five pounds of coffee per month.
For this reason the one-pound container became
the most popular size.

Although the glass jar became a familiar
wartime substitute for the metal can, both were
sold in stores simultaneously. The paper label applied to the glass jar retains the same colors and
design, and nearly the same text, as that appearing on the metal tin, providing continuity for the
consumer's eye. The jar is made of Owens-Illinois
"Duraglas," and is in a standardized shape used
by many coffee producers during the war. It has a
smooth midsection, where the label is glued, and
pebbled glass (which requires less material)
above and below. Although it was not possible to
vacuum pack coffee in glass jars, originally the
screw-on lid, made of metal (as here) or sometimes of fibreboard, was protected by a Cel-O-Seal
cellulose band made by DuPont.

The American Can Company also offered another "war substitute" package for coffee made
entirely of fibre but in the same shape as the
metal can. This package ensured that "the housewife w[ould] instantly recognize the same familiar package she used to know in metal." GWRW

SOURCES:

American Can Company advertisements. *Modern Packaging* 16
    (June 1943); 19 (July 1944).
Can Manufacturer's Institute advertisements. *Good Housekeeping*
    (November 1944; January 1945).
Johnson, Laura. "Advertising During the War Years, 1941–1945."
    Unpublished seminar paper, Tufts University, 1991.
Russell, Judith, and Renee Fantin. *Studies in Food Rationing.*
    Washington, D.C.: Office of Temporary Controls, Office of Price
    Administration, 1947.
DuPont Cel-O-Seal Bands advertisement. *Modern Packaging* 16
    (June 1943).

29

M & M Cream Doughnuts box, ca.
1940–45 (See plate 9)

M & M Bakeries, Dover, N.H.
Printed paperboard, cellophane
H. 3¼ in., W. 7½ in., D. 3 in.
Museum Purchase

30

Sign, ca. 1939–46 (p. 196; also see plate 19)

M & M Bakeries, Dover, N.H.
Metal
H. 13⅛ in., W. 24¾ in.
Gift of Charles E. Burden

Joseph Marquette and Patrick H. McManus established M & M Bakeries in a small shop on Central Avenue in Dover, New Hampshire, in 1913.
Originally a small operation, by 1927 it had
grown enough to warrant the construction of a
three-story plant on Third Street. M & M Bakeries eventually distributed its bread and baked
goods in approximately 100 trucks to more than
1000 wholesale customers from Portland, Maine,
to the north; Lake Winnipesaukee, to the west;
and Portsmouth, New Hampshire, to the south.

Patrick H. McManus, an innovative business-
man who was always seeking out new ways to appeal to consumer needs, became sole owner of the
company sometime before 1923. He marketed his
whole grain breads as health breads as early as
the 1930s, and experimented with new
recipes—including carrot bread and potato
bread—during the same period. McManus was always anxious to learn new approaches to nutrition and regularly attended educational seminars
offered by Fleishman's Yeast and Standard
Brands in New York City. He also made annual
trips to visit the large cereal companies located in
Battle Creek, Michigan.

During the 1930s McManus entered into an
arrangement with a mill in Hillsdale, Michigan
(whose owners summered on Lake Winnipesaukee), to obtain flour milled to his precise
specifications. The flour, packaged in 98-pound
bags, arrived by the freight-car load on railroad
tracks that led directly to the bakery's loading
docks. Wartime conditions put a temporary end to
this arrangement. Nonetheless, the mill's owner,
Frederic W. Stock, remained impressed with M &
M Bakeries, and in 1946 he purchased the company from McManus. Stock served as president of
M & M Bakeries until the company went bank-
rupt in 1962.

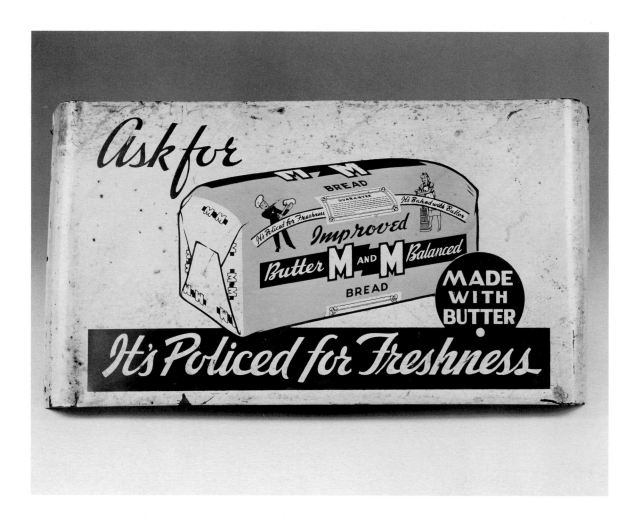

Like most manufacturing concerns, M & M Bakeries was touched by labor shortages during the war. Robert McManus, who worked for his father at M & M, remembers that many women who had worked in the textile mills in Dover came to work at the bakery during the war. Many of these new female employees were put to work in the cake decorating department—in jobs that had previously been considered prestigious by male employees. Women were considered to be fit for nearly all jobs in the plant—only jobs hauling large flour bags and acting as driver-salesmen were off-limits to them. Men released from the Navy Prison at the Portsmouth Naval Shipyard were regarded as particularly "prime" employees because they were strong men who could not be drafted. Few, however, stayed on the job for long periods of time.

During the war M & M experienced some difficulty in packaging their bread; cellophane was not available, and Robert McManus remembers that the bread they delivered to military installations was not wrapped at all. This sign shows the waxed-paper wrapping used during and after World War II. In addition to signs, the company produced a number of other promotional materials, including painted screens (such as the one provided to the Abbotts' "Little Corner Store," see frontispiece), and similarly printed rubber door-mats.

M & M made a variety of products—doughnuts, fruit cakes, pies, and "fancy" rolls—as well as bread. In addition to their machine-cut plain "Cream Doughnuts," M & M also made honey-dipped doughnuts that were wrapped in plain bakery cartons; only the Cream Doughnuts were packaged in printed paperboard boxes.   BMW

SOURCES:

Norman Badger. "Shoreline Industries: M & M Bakeries Incorporated, Dover, New Hampshire." Reprinted from *Shoreliner Magazine*, July 1951. Strawbery Banke Museum.
"M. & M. Bakeries Constitute Large and Growing Dover Enterprise." Clipping from *Foster's Daily Democrat*, ca. 1923. Strawbery Banke Museum.
Oral History Interview. October 19, 1992, OH2 SC38, Strawbery Banke Museum.

PLATE 9. *Group of products sold in the "Little Corner Store" with Victory Carry-All, ca. 1943–45.*
For further information on individual products see cats. 17, 18, 21, 23, 24, 25, 26, 27, 29, 31, 34, 36,
37, 42, 44, 45, 46, 50, 52, 53, 54, 57, 60, 62, 63, 70, and 72.

PLATE 10. *"Grow More Can More in '44."* See also fig. 54.

PLATE 11 (left). *"I'm Out to Lick Runaway Prices."* See also cat. 3.

PLATE 12 (right). *"Your Victory Garden Counts More than Ever."* See also cat. 6.

PLATE 13. *"Save Your Cans—Help Pass the Ammunition." See also cat. 5.*

PLATE 14. *"Use it Up, Wear it Out." See also fig. 35.*

PLATE 15. *"I'll Carry Mine Too." See also fig. 36.*

PLATE 16. *"Food is a Weapon—Don't Waste It." See also fig. 48.*

PLATE 17. *Skrip Ink bottle and box, ca. 1942–44. See cat. 14.*

PLATE 18. *Vicks VapoRub jar and box, and Vicks Va-tro-nol box. See cats. 48 and 49.*

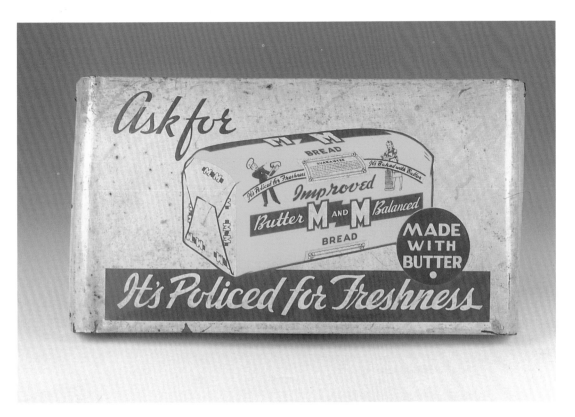

PLATE 19. *"Ask for M & M Bread—It's Policed for Freshness." See also cat. 30.*

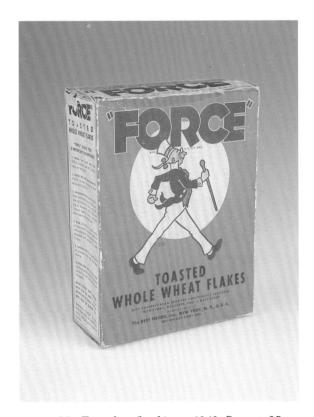

PLATE 20. *Force box (back), ca. 1942. See cat. 35.*

PLATE 21. *Force box (front), ca. 1942. See cat. 35.*

PLATE 22. *Pall Mall Cigarettes, carton and packs, ca. 1942–45. See cat. 52.*

PLATE 23. *Wings Cigarettes, King Size pack, 1941 and regular pack, 1943. See cats. 53 & 54.*

PLATE 24. *Jell-O packages, ca. 1941–45. See cat. 39.*

PLATE 25. *Bolster box, 1942–45 and Bolster wrapper, ca. 1947. See cats. 58 and 59.*

PLATE 26. *Uneeda Bakers Cookie and Cracker Display Rack with original overlays and boxes, and reproduction cookies and crackers. See cat. 64.*

31

Badger Farms Creameries milk bottle,
1943 (See plate 9)

Badger Farms Creameries, Portsmouth, N.H.
Printed and embossed glass
H. 9½ in., Diam. (top) 2³/₁₆ in., Diam. (base) 3¾ in.
Museum Purchase

32

Badger Farms sign, ca. 1930–40

Badger Farms Creameries, Portsmouth, N.H.
Painted metal, paperboard
H. 32³/₈ in., W. 20½ in., D. 22 in.
Gift of Charles E. Burden

33

Badger's Ice Cream tub, ca. 1940–50 (p. 206)

Badger Farms Creameries, Portsmouth, N.H.
Printed paperboard, metal
H. 9 in., Diam. 9½ in.
Gift of Charles E. Burden

Charles A. Badger and Daniel W. Badger each
owned dairy farms in Portsmouth, New Hampshire, and delivered milk to customers in the sur-

rounding community. In the late 19th century
they combined their efforts and established Badger Farms Creameries. As Norman Badger wrote
in 1951, "These two young brothers developed a
door-to-door dairy business in the days of horse-
drawn wagons and galvanized milk cans."

In 1917, Badger Farms Creameries moved their
bottling plant to Bow Street near the waterfront
in downtown Portsmouth. Moving to this location
gave the company an advantage over its local
competitors. The move put them in close proximity to the Portsmouth Naval Shipyard which "was
in need of a ready milk supply for its employees
and was prepared to grant a contract," and gave
them the room necessary to upgrade their equipment so that they could pasteurize their milk as
the Shipyard required. The company continued to
expand throughout the 1920s adding employees
and new products.

During both world wars, dairy products were an
essential part of the war effort and were in constant demand in the United States and abroad.
Production of dairy products increased dramatically between 1941 and 1945, but labor was often
a problem. The *Saturday Evening Post* summed it
up best in a cartoon depicting a cow entering the

lar publication. The government did, however, make an effort to make "real" ice cream available to the fighting men abroad. Ice cream was difficult to ship because there was no way to keep it frozen, so in 1945 the Navy "built, at the cost of one million dollars, a floating ice cream parlor. A concrete barge was outfitted to produce ten gallons of ice cream a second."

Except for the date embossed on its base, this bottle (cat. 31) is identical to the examples used by Badger Farms before and after the war. It is made of Owens-Illinois's "Duraglas" and is embossed with the unit price and net weight on the side; and the date, manufacturer, bottle use, and patent number on the bottom. This example, made in 1943, held one quart for retail sale costing the customer $.05. It is unclear where the bottle was printed with the company name and product line.

Badger Farms prospered during the postwar period, and although control shifted to Daniel Badger's sons, the company continued under the same name until the 1970s.   RDR

SOURCES:

Badger, Norman. "Shoreline Industries: The Badger Farms Creameries." *Shoreliner Magazine*, June 1, 1951.

deSarro, Rodney. Cartoon. *The Saturday Evening Post*, May 20, 1944, p. 67.

Portsmouth, N.H., Strawbery Banke Museum. S. Louise Grant Papers. Louise Grant Diary.

Russell, Judith, and Renee Fantin. *Studies in Food Rationing*. Washington, D.C.: Office of Temporary Controls, Office of Price Administration, 1947.

Selitzer, Ralph. *The Dairy Industry in America*. New York: Books for Industry, 1976.

office of the War Manpower Commission with a milk bucket on one horn and a milking stool in its mouth.

Because it could be easily stored and transported, the production of cheese skyrocketed during World War II, rising from from 54 million pounds annually before the war to 292 million pounds in 1944. In addition, dried milk production went from one million pounds annually to 67 million in the same period. Wartime nutrition messages emphasized the importance of milk and dairy products in the daily diet, but milk was in relatively short supply because of the large amounts needed to make cheese for overseas shipment. The government gave careful consideration to the possibility of fluid milk rationing, and although a plan was developed, it was never put into effect.

Ice cream was extremely popular, but shortages of heavy cream made it necessary for the average home-front citizen to turn to special recipes during wartime. Louise Grant, a Portsmouth schoolteacher, complained to her diary about "wartime ice cream," a concoction undoubtedly made using one of the recipes provided in the Health for Victory *Meal Planning Guide* (cat. 15) or other simi-

34

Wheaties box, 1944 (See plate 9)

General Mills, Inc., Minneapolis, Minn.
Printed paperboard
H. 8³/₈ in., W. 6¹/₂ in., D. 2³/₈ in.
Gift of Charles E. Burden

Wheaties was first introduced in 1924 by the Washburn Crosby Company, one of the several mills that joined together in 1928 to form General Mills. In 1933, the "Breakfast of Champions" motto was adopted, beginning the product's long and continuing exploitation of an association with sports as an advertising tool. As is the case here, Wheaties advertising often featured various premiums as well. These premiums were designed to build customer loyalty among young consumers.

This eight-ounce package, boldly designed in blue, white, and orange, enticed the young consumer (and his or her mother) with an ad for the "Future Champions of America Sports Library"

on the back. By redeeming one Breakfast of Champions star, cut from the lid of the box, accompanied by a dime, the youngster could order two of the 14 titles in the series, which included books on football, baseball, softball, golf, tennis, swimming, basketball, track and field, bowling, and "home and neighborhood games." Featured on this package is *Want to be a Softball Champion?* by Ty Gleason and Arnie Simpson.

Pseudo-scientific advertising on one side of the package is addressed to "Mother," and emphasizes the nutritional value of *"three square meals every day,"* beginning with "a big bowlful of Wheaties with plenty of milk and fruit." This would provide "full Whole Wheat amounts" of thiamine, niacin, riboflavin, iron, phosphorus, and "Food Energy, for which Whole Wheat is famous."

GWRW

SOURCES:

Gray, James. *Business without Boundary: The Story of General Mills*. Minneapolis, Minn., 1954.
Kovel, Ralph, and Terry Kovel. *Kovels' Advertising Collectibles Price List*. N.Y.: Crown Publishers, 1986.

35

Force box, 1941–43 (See plates 20 and 21)

The Best Foods, Inc., New York, N.Y.
Printed paperboard
H. 8½ in., W. 6½ in., D. 2½ in.
Gift of Charles E. Burden

One of the first cold cereals on the market, Force Toasted Whole Wheat Flakes was introduced to the American consumer market in 1901 by the Force Foods Company. Force Foods was purchased by H-O Cereals in 1909. H-O merged with Hecker Products in 1936, and in 1942 Hecker bought Best Foods–Hellmanns from General Foods and became The Best Foods, Incorporated. In 1958, Best Foods became a subsidiary of what is now CPC International.

Force cereal was on the forefront of advertising and package design in 1941. The patriotic red, white, and blue design features "Sunny Jim," the company salesman, who was first introduced in 1903. The product name, a convenient coincidence during wartime, was printed on all sides of the box in large blue letters.

Force marketing depended heavily on premiums such as trading cards, stamps, presidential coins, Sunny Jim dolls, silk stockings, balloons, and so on. This particular package offered "FREE! WAR PLANES of the WORLD STAMP COLLECTION." Every box of Force contained four war plane stamps. A total of 32 in all were available

and a stamp album could be purchased from the company. In addition to this appeal to child consumers, Best Foods offered mothers "6 IMPORTANT ADVANTAGES" including "ENERGY," "IRON," "PROTEIN," and "DELICIOUS MALTED FLAVOR." Because of the success of these messages, it was not until 1943 that a reorganization of Best Foods brought about a change in the Force package.

Force cereal was particularly popular in England, but because the British government stopped the importation of all cereals and many other commodities in March 1940, during the war most Force cereal was sold to American consumers. The situation was only temporary however, because after the war, the rights to Force were sold to an English manufacturing firm, and the cereal ceased to be available in the United States. RDR

SOURCES:

CPC International. In, *International Directory of Company Histories*, ed. Paula Kepos. Detroit, Mich.: St. James Press, 1990–92.
Opie, Robert. *Packaging Source Book*. N.J.: Chartwell Books, Inc., 1989.
Personal Communication with Thomas DiPiazza, Corporate Communications Manager, CPC International.
Rothman, Dorothy M. *The History of CPC International*. Englewood, N.J.: CPC International, 1984.

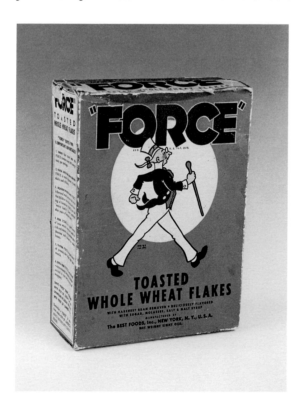

36

Grape-Nuts Flakes box, ca. 1942–45

(See plate 9)

Post Products Div., General Foods Corp.,
  Battle Creek, Mich.
Printed paperboard
H. 7³⁄₈ in., W. 5³⁄₈ in., D. 2¹⁄₂ in.
Gift of Charles E. Burden

37

Postum Cereal Beverage box, ca. 1943

(p. 210, also see plate 9)

Post Products Div., General Foods Corp.,
  Battle Creek, Mich.
Printed paperboard
H. 7 in., W. 4 in., D. 2³⁄₄ in.
Gift of Joan Pearson Watkins

An example of packaging with a straightforward wartime message, this box of Grape-Nuts Flakes was printed in red and blue on an off-white ground. Both front and back are designed alike with the exception of a dynamic broad arrow on either side which directs the consumer's eye to important nutritional information on one side panel. The essence of the message, found on many other products of the period, was that the war effort demanded more and more strength and energy from its citizens: "To keep well and strong, make sure that you and your family eat nutritional foods. Your government urges you to 'eat the Basic 7'" (see fig. 55). Of course, Grape-Nuts Flakes provided "essential nutritive elements in the form of crisp, delicious flakes with that grand Grape-Nuts flavor that everyone loves." The nutritional benefits were not an exaggerated claim for Post Products—the manufacturer of Grape-Nuts Flakes had its origins in a late 19th-century health cereal.

Charles W. Post traveled to the Kellogg brothers' renowned sanitarium in Battle Creek, Michigan, in 1891, in hope of improving his health. While there, he became a health-food enthusiast, and decided to stay, opening the La Vit Inn, where he experimented with healing by mental suggestion and special diets. In 1895, he began marketing Postum, a caffeine-free drink made from wheat, bran, and molasses, which he hoped would become the beverage of choice for the country's coffee drinkers. He incorporated the Postum Cereal Company the next year. This example is a special wartime package; just prior to and following the war, Postum was packaged in tin-plated metal cans.

In 1897 the company introduced Grape-Nuts, a cereal made from whole wheat and malted barley flour. Baked for 20 hours to turn starch into dextrose, Grape-Nuts was promoted as a partially

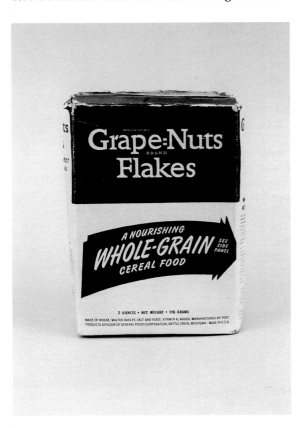

39

Jell-O packages, ca. 1941–45 (See plate 24)

General Foods Corp., Battle Creek, Mich.
Printed paperboard
H. 3 in., W. 3¼ in., D. 1 in.
Gift of Nancy and Robert Withington

In 1897, Orator Francis Woodward of the Genesee Pure Food Company bought a company that produced packaged flavored gelatin from Pearl B. Wait of LeRoy, New York. Although Wait's product had not been very successful, Woodward believed that it had potential, and renamed it "Jell-O," marketing it as "America's most famous dessert." The company advertised that the powdered mix was sealed inside a "safety bag" that would keep the contents "as pure and sweet as on the day it was made." In 1925 the Jell-O Company joined with the Postum Company to become General Foods (see cats. 36, 37).

During World War II, General Foods advertised Jell-O as a "quick wartime dessert" for busy mothers on-the-go. Advertising messages also pointed out that Jell-O provided a portion of the recommended daily requirements for protein, and that it was a quick and easy way to turn fruit into dessert when the sugar and lard for heavier baked desserts—especially pies—was in short supply.   BMW

SOURCE:

Stern, Jane, and Michael Stern. *The Encyclopedia of Bad Taste.* New York: HarperCollins, 1990.

40

Crisco label, ca. 1943 (left)

Procter and Gamble Co., Cincinnati, Ohio
Printed paper
H. 2¾ in., W. 12¼ in.
Gift of Mr. and Mrs. Clayton Tenney

41

Crisco jar and lid, ca. 1943 (center)

Procter and Gamble Co., Cincinnati, Ohio
Glass, metal
H. 8½ in., Diam. 8 in.
Gift of Charles E. Burden

42

Crisco wrapper, ca. 1942 (right, and p. 214)

(See plate 9)

Procter and Gamble Co., Cincinnati, Ohio
Printed paper
H. 8½ in., W. 6 in.
Gift of Mr. and Mrs. Clayton Tenney

The Procter and Gamble Company was founded in 1837 by two British businessmen—William Procter and James Gamble—to manufacture and sell candles and soap in Cincinnati, Ohio. As a by-product of its candle-making operation, the company began producing lard in the 1860s, and later developed Crisco as the first all-vegetable short-ening.

Producers of fats and shortenings for home consumption found themselves limited by War Production Board (WPB) and Office of Price Administration (OPA) regulations in two ways: although government agencies restricted supplies of animal fat available to home-front consumers because the glycerine in fat was needed to make explosives, the OPA recognized the need to increase the amount of vegetable fat available for home cooking as supplies of dairy products—butter in particular—became increasingly scarce. Producers were also restricted in the amount of metal that they could use in packaging, and therefore the producers of fats developed a variety of "duration" packages to replace the old cans.

In October 1943, the editors of *Modern Packaging* pointed to Crisco as a "fine example" of experimentation with different types of packaging. "This product has undergone a complete change

in its outer garment as a consequence of wartime emergencies," they noted. The familiar tin, which at one time had been wrapped in paper, "shook off its outer garment" as a consequence of wartime emergencies. When tin became a critical material, the package was replaced by a glass container with a metal cap. Later, when the WPB eliminated even this small amount of tin from use in shortening containers, the company adopted a paper cap of the milk-bottle type.

Procter and Gamble used glass containers for the one- and three-pound sizes of Crisco, but found it necessary to augment their supply of glass containers with new package types—"the glass-with-paper-top unit, a fibre can and a butter type carton." The illustrations for the article show glass jars such as this one (cat. 41) packed in paperboard boxes that are similar in design to this paper wrapper (cat. 42).

Although the *Modern Packaging* article mentions that Procter and Gamble was testing consumer acceptance of their new containers, it does not indicate the relative popularity of the different types of packaging, but does note that the butter-type cartons had been used in Canada for some time prior to their introduction in the United States. BMW

SOURCES:

Russell, Judith, and Renee Fantin. *Studies in Food Rationing*. Washington, D.C.: Office of Temporary Controls, Office of Price Administration, 1947.

Procter and Gamble. In, *International Directory of Company Histories*, ed. Paula Kepos. Detroit, Mich.: St. James Press, 1990–92.

"You Will See Favorite Brands in More Than One Container." *Modern Packaging* 17 (October 1943).

43

P AND G White Naphtha Soap wrappers, 1940–42, 1946–50 (left)

Procter and Gamble Co., Cincinnati, Ohio
Printed and waxed paper
H. 2³/₄ in., W. 4¹/₈ in., D. 1¹/₂ in.
Gift of Charles E. Burden

44

P AND G White Laundry Soap wrappers, 1942–45 (right)

(See plates 8 and 9)

Procter and Gamble Co., Cincinnati, Ohio
Printed and waxed paper
H. 2³/₄ in., W. 4¹/₈ in., D. 1¹/₂ in.
Gift of Charles E. Burden

During World War II, soaps were used as lubricants for the production of ammunition, wire, cables, springs, and steel blanks because they are clean, easy to handle, concentrated, and adaptable to a variety of conditions. The successful use of soap in these applications, and limitations placed on supplies of soap oils available to manufacturers in 1942, reduced the quality and quantity of soap products available to consumers.

Eventually the War Food Administration (WFA) eased these restrictions by making 100 million pounds of lard available to soap manufacturers. Soap builders, such as sodium, phosphates, soda ashes, and increasing amounts of rosin, were also added as fillers. The wartime increase in the use of rosin—which had previously been considered too harsh on the skin, was sticky, and often turned clothing yellow—prompted consumer concern. In conjunction with the WFA, soap manufacturers conducted research to assure consumers that a small proportion of rosin, when combined with other ingredients, would actually increase the quality of available soaps.

Naphtha, another element used in soap products, particularly laundry soap, was first introduced as an ingredient in Fels-Naphtha bar soap and soap chips. In 1905, Procter and Gamble introduced its own variety—P AND G White Naphtha Soap. Procter and Gamble made P AND G white because Fels-Naptha was yellow; reasoning that white would be associated with clean. P AND G claimed to "keep more clothes white than any other soap in the world." Apparently consumers agreed.

Naphtha, a petroleum-based element, was needed for fuel during World War II, and in 1942 the government implemented a moratorium on naphtha soaps. After the naphtha was removed from their soap, Procter and Gamble had to do

some quick remarketing. Keeping the blue-and-white package design essentially the same, to ensure product recognition, the company changed the name of the soap from P AND G White Naphtha Soap to P AND G White Laundry Soap. The company's famous moon-and-stars emblem, copyrighted in 1882 and refined to its final design about 1930, was printed on the back of the Naphtha version of P AND G. (The moon is meant to represent the man-in-the-moon; the stars represent the original 13 British colonies that joined to make up the United States.)

Instead of bearing the moon-and-stars symbol, the back of the wartime version of P AND G contained the following message:

> This is the new P and G White Laundry Soap. Because of conditions caused by the war, we are producing it in place of P and G The White Naphtha Soap. P and G's many friends will find this new soap as safe for washable colors as ever, and still easier on hands. It has all the cleansing power which has made P and G the largest selling bar soap in the world.

Procter and Gamble's aim was to keep consumer confidence in the quality of the product. Mentioning the contribution of naphtha toward the war effort was also good for the company's public image.

After 1945, Procter and Gamble put the naphtha back into P AND G White Naphtha Soap. The soap remained on the market until the early 1950s.   TEA

SOURCES:

"Household Cleaning Solvents." *Consumers' Research Bulletin*, August 1944.

Merck and Co. *The Merck Index: An Encyclopedia for the Chemist, Pharmacist, Physician, Dentist and Veterinarian*. Rahway, N.J.: Merck, 1940.

Personal communication with Edward M. Rider, Corporate Archivist, Procter and Gamble Co., Cincinnati, Ohio, 1993.

Procter and Gamble. In, *International Directory of Company Histories*, ed. Paula Kepos. Detroit, Mich.: St. James Press, 1990–92.

"Soap in Lubricants." *Scientific American*, February 1944.

"Wartime Laundry Soaps." *Consumers' Research Bulletin*, December 1944.

45

Oxydol box, 1930–50 (See plates 8 and 9)

Procter and Gamble Co., Cincinnati, Ohio
Printed paperboard
H. 8½ in., W. 6 in., D. 2⅛ in.
Gift of Charles E. Burden

One of Procter and Gamble's many successful products was Oxydol Soap. Developed as an all-purpose cleaner for the laundry and kitchen, Oxydol was originally the property of the William Walthe Company of St. Louis, Missouri. In 1928 Procter and Gamble bought the Walthe Company and their two most prominent products—Oxydol and Lava soaps.

The original packaging design for Oxydol incorporated an angel with lightning bolts emanating from the tip of its left hand and a wand with a star at the top in its right hand. In 1930, Procter and Gamble marketed Oxydol as strictly laundry soap and redesigned the package. The colorful bull's-eye pattern was designed to enhance the pack-

age's effectiveness as a marketing tool. However, Procter and Gamble kept a scaled-down image of the angel on the package with the bullseye so that established customers would recognize the soap. Once the new package design became familiar, the angel was removed permanently. In a 1930 issue of "Moonbeams," the company newsletter, the new design for Oxydol was heralded as "Dashing! Dazzling! Dynamic!" The new package resulted in a 35% to 75% increase in sales nationwide.

In 1933, Oxydol was the first soap to sponsor a daytime radio drama—Ma Perkins, starring Virginia Payne, "Oxydol's own Ma"—which ran from 1933 to 1956, and became the country's first "soap opera."

During World War II, Procter and Gamble filled government contracts for 60-millimeter mortar shells and glycerine. Procter and Gamble was one of the largest manufacturers of glycerine, a component found in fats which was important in the production of explosives (see cat. 2). The packaging for Procter and Gamble products, including Oxydol, remained almost unchanged during the war. The only additions to the designs were small notices urging consumers to buy war bonds.

TEA

SOURCES:

Moonbeams, July 1930.
Personal communication with E. M. Rider, Corporate Archivist, Proctor and Gamble Co., Cincinnati, Ohio, 1993.
Procter and Gamble. In, *International Directory of Company Histories*, ed. Paula Kepos. Detroit, Mich.: St. James Press, 1990–92.
Terrace, Vincent. *Radio's Golden Age, The Encylopedia of Radio Programs*. N.Y.: Tantivy Press, 1981.

46

Cashmere Bouquet Talcum Powder container, 1942–45 (left) (See plate 9)

Colgate-Palmolive-Peet Co., Jersey City, N.J.
Printed paperboard
H. 5⅝ in., Diam. (base) 2¾ in., Diam. (top) 1 in.
Gift of Charles E. Burden

47

Cashmere Bouquet Talc Powder container, ca. 1925 (right)

Colgate and Co., Jersey City, N.J.
Printed metal
H. 4½ in., W. 2⅜ in., D. 1 in.
Gift of Charles E. Burden

Because of war production demands, the United States began to experience shortages of tin and steel even before the attack on Pearl Harbor. War Production Board limitations reduced the amount of tin and steel for domestic consumer use by 44% in 1942. One of the biggest reasons for the shortage of cans on the domestic front was that they were the most reliable containers available for shipping foods and other supplies to troops and civilians overseas.

The Colgate Company was founded in 1806 by William Colgate, and originally produced starch, soap, and candles. Colgate and Company merged with Palmolive-Peet, a midwestern company, in 1928. Although headquartered in Jersey City, New Jersey, the new company was originally controlled by Palmolive management; the Colgate family was able to regain control of the company after the stock market crash in 1929. In 1953 the company simplified its name to Colgate-Palmolive, and in 1956 moved its main offices to New York City.

Modern Packaging, the trade journal for the packaging industry, presented one of its annual design awards to this paperboard cone (cat. 46). Designed for Colgate-Palmolive-Peet by William A. Troy, and produced for the company by Sonoco Products, it was heralded as one of the most successful "conversion" packages developed during 1943 to save metal for wartime use. Much of this same technology would find a ready market after the war as paperboard cylinders became the favored containers for a whole series of dry foodstuffs including baking powder, cocoa, and salt. The paperboard cone, however, did not enjoy a lasting popularity and the shape is distinctive to wartime packaging.   BMW

SOURCES:

Annual Design Awards. *Modern Packaging* 16 (April 1943): 96ff.
"Canners Face Grim Year with Determination." *Modern Packaging* 14 (March 1942): 60ff.
Colgate-Palmolive Company. In, *International Directory of Company Histories*, ed. Paula Kepos. Detroit, Mich.: St. James Press, 1990–92.
Mansfield, Harvey. *A Short History of OPA*. Washington, D.C.: Office of Temporary Controls, Office of Price Administration, 1947.

48

Vicks VapoRub jar, label, and lid,
ca. 1930–50 (left) (See plate 18)

Vick Chemical Co., Greensboro, N.C.
Glass, metal, printed paper
H. 3¼ in., Diam. 1⅞ in.
Gift of Charles E. Burden

49

Vicks Va-tro-nol box, ca. 1930–50 (right)
(See plate 18)

Vick Chemical Co., Greensboro, N.C.
Printed paperboard
H. 3½ in., W. 2¼ in., D. 2¼ in.
Gift of Charles E. Burden

During World War II, one recurring theme in government messages and product advertising was the need to keep one's self and family healthy as a contribution to the war effort. Proper nutrition was one part of the program; timely medication and proper medical care was another.

The "Vicks Plan," developed by Vick Company scientists and medical advisors, purported to eliminate 50% of all common colds. The plan asked people to: 1) Observe simple health rules—avoid excesses, drink plenty of water, keep elimination regular, get needed rest and sleep, avoid crowds, and avoid people who have colds; 2) Use Vicks Va-tro-nol at the first warning sign of a cold "to aid nature's own defenses against colds"; and 3) Rub on Vicks VapoRub at bedtime if all other precautions failed.

Vicks VapoRub was intended for external use. It also could be liquified in a vaporizer or bowl of steaming water and inhaled, however, or a small lump could be melted in the throat. The active ingredients included camphor, menthol, steam-distilled wood turpentine, and oils of eucalyptus, cedar leaf, nutmeg, and thymol in a "specially balanced" formula. Va-tro-nol, a nasal medication, was a "scientifically balanced combination of menthol, camphor, eucalyptol, and other aromatics, with the alkaloid, ephedrine." According to this package, Vick chemists tested the medication for nine years before perfecting it in 1931.

The Vick Chemical Company advised that customers call a doctor promptly if cold symptoms persisted. Getting a doctor, however, was another matter, as a public service advertisement produced by Wyeth Incorporated—makers of pharmaceuticals, biologicals, and nutritional products—pointed out in the same issue of *Good Housekeeping*. Wyeth stressed that almost half of the country's physicians were in the armed forces and that those still at home each had to care for an average of 1700 people. Harry Anderson's illustration for the ad shows a doctor's wife anxiously peering out the window of her Georgian-style home—"The House the Doctor always comes to last"—and the ad ends by reminding people to "Save your Doctor's time in Wartime!"   CPR

SOURCES:

Vicks VapoRub and Va-tro-nol advertisement. *Good Housekeeping*, February 1944.
Wyeth Inc., advertisement. *Good Housekeeping*, February 1944.

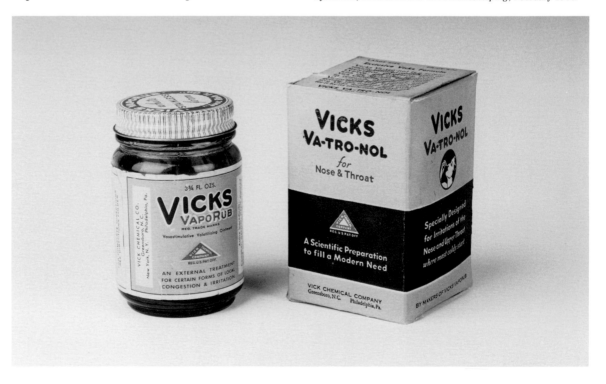

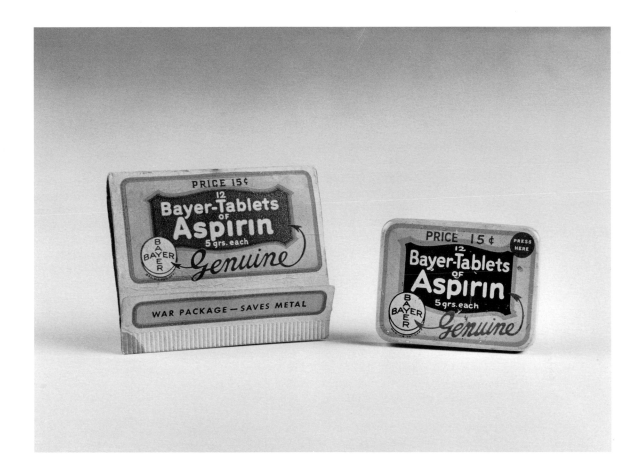

50

Bayer-Tablets of Aspirin container, ca.
1943 (left) (See plate 9)

The Bayer Co., Inc., New York, N.Y.
Printed paperboard
H. 1⅝ in., W. 2⅜ in., D. ¼ in.
Gift of Charles E. Burden

51

Bayer-Tablets of Aspirin container, ca.
1939 (right)

The Bayer Co., Inc., New York, N.Y.
Tin-plated metal
H. 1¼ in., W. 1¼ in., D. ⅜ in.
Gift of Charles E. Burden

Like many other consumer goods, Bayer Aspirin
had been packaged in a tin-plated container prior
to the war. Conversion packaging helped to alleviate the shortage of scarce tin and tin-plated
steel, but as the war continued, paper pulp became scarce as well. In November 1943, the Ox-

ford Paper Company declared, in an advertisement placed in the trade magazine *Modern Packaging*, that

> Wood pulp today is a vital material of war. It
> is used in producing hand grenades, gas
> tanks, camouflage, ammunition boxes, and
> hundreds of other fighting aids. It is molded
> into airplane wing tips. It is impregnated
> with resins and pressed into metal bearings
> and gears.

Oxford Paper further urged consumers to understand that salvaging waste paper and paperboard
would help "enormously to supply paper fiber and
to make up for steady deficits in virgin pulp."
Manufacturers experimented with increasingly
economical means of making packaging from limited supplies, with the result that many containers were flimsy, and contained paper of very high
acidity.   BMW

SOURCE:

Oxford Paper Co. advertisement. *Modern Packaging* 17 (November
    1943).

52

Pall Mall Cigarettes packs and carton,
ca. 1942–45 (See plates 9 and 22)

American Cigarette and Cigar Co., Inc.,
    Durham, N.C.
Printed paper, paperboard
H. 1¾ in., W. 10⅞ in., D. 3½ in.
Gift of Charles E. Burden

The Abbotts' "Little Corner Store" carried a dozen types of cigarettes, including Pall Malls in their bright red package. Although cigarettes were not affected by government rationing, by the end of the war they were in short supply. Stores coped with the shortage by selling only to long-time customers or reducing the hours when cigarettes were sold. Wartime restrictions also altered cigarette manufacturing. Here, for example, the usual cellophane wrapper around each pack is absent; as the DuPont Company noted, "in addition to protecting U.S. Army food ration units, . . . the Government is finding many other vital wartime uses for Cellophane." By the end of the war, each individual pack in this carton of ten probably cost $.20, although the black market price might be as high as $.50.

The design, and the message on each pack, indicate a desire to appeal to many potential markets. Although the pack is identified as a "Modern Design" in text on the reverse, the name of the cigarette refers to an obsolete 17th-century English game and a London street, and it has an 18th-century style coat of arms, complete with Latin phrases, on the front. The relationship of the phrases IN HOC SIGNO VINCES ("By this sign [the Cross] you will conquer") and PER ASPERA AD ASTRA ("To the stars through hardships"), to cigarettes is not clear. The "V" for "Victory" on the back of each pack, along with the dot-dot-dot-dash Morse code symbol for the letter V, identifies these cigarettes as wartime products and reflects the manufacturer's desire to link patriotism with the habit of smoking. The text "Wherever Particular People Congregate" attempts to lay a veneer of sophistication and distinction upon the Pall Mall smoker. Today, the Pall Mall design remains virtually unchanged, except for the deletion of the wartime content, and the addition of the Surgeon General's warning and a computer bar code.

GWRW

SOURCES:

Encyclopedia Britannica (1987), s.v. "pall mall."
Jesoraldo, Philip. "The American Tobacco Industry during World War II." Unpublished seminar paper, Tufts University, 1991.
"New Cellophane Restrictions: Limitation Order L-20 as Amended Jan. 4, 1943." *Modern Packaging* 16 (Jan. 1943).
Smith, Jane Webb. *Smoke Signals: Cigarettes, Advertising, and the American Way of Life.* Richmond, Va.: Valentine Museum, 1990.
Woodcock, Thomas, and John Martin Robinson. *The Oxford Guide to Heraldry.* New York: Oxford University Press, 1988.

53

Wings Cigarettes King Size pack, 1941
(left) (See plates 9 and 23)

Brown and Williamson Tobacco Corp.,
    Louisville, Ky.
Printed paper, foil, cellophane
H. 3⅜ in., W. 2⅛ in., D. ⅞ in.
Gift of Charles E. Burden

54

Wings Cigarettes pack, 1943 (right)
(See plates 9 and 23)

Brown and Williamson Tobacco Corp.,
    Louisville, Ky.
Printed paper, foil, cellophane
H. 2¾ in., W. 2⅛ in., D. ⅞ in.
Museum Purchase

The Brown and Williamson Corporation first introduced Wings cigarettes in the early 1930s. The Wings name was adopted to make the brand attractive to the growing number of smokers in the armed forces, and Brown and Williamson's Bugler Rolling Paper was decorated with the image of a bugler on the front for the same reason. Wings, an economy-brand of cigarette, was manufactured until the late 1960s, but was most popular during World War II.

Most bargain cigarette brands sold well only for a short period of time. Brown and Williamson kept the cost of Wings down by using inexpensive wrapping and advertising. The back of the 1943 pack reads "No costly wrappings. No costly ballyhoo. Just 15¢ Quality Turkish and domestic tobacco for 10¢. 'A perfect blend from end to end.'" Both packs use plain three-color labels with brand name, trade mark, and a short product description to sell the cigarettes. The low cost, and war associated name and package, made this brand particularly popular and long-lived.

The sale of the Wings brand was further increased by the introduction of trade cards. In 1939 Brown and Williamson introduced series A, B, and C trade cards illustrating 150 types of aircraft. To further increase sales, the company sponsored a 1940 radio show on Friday evenings called "Wings of Destiny." During the show, listeners were told how to enter a contest to win a Piper Cub Trainer airplane. Every Friday the company would draw one of these cards and the individual who had that card won a brand new airplane. The success of the contest made Wings exceptionally popular. The company gave away a plane a week for more than a year, but discontinued the contest when the United States entered the war.	RDR

SOURCE:

Personal communication with Roberta Ashe, Communications Coordinator, Brown and Williamson Corp., Louisville, Ky.

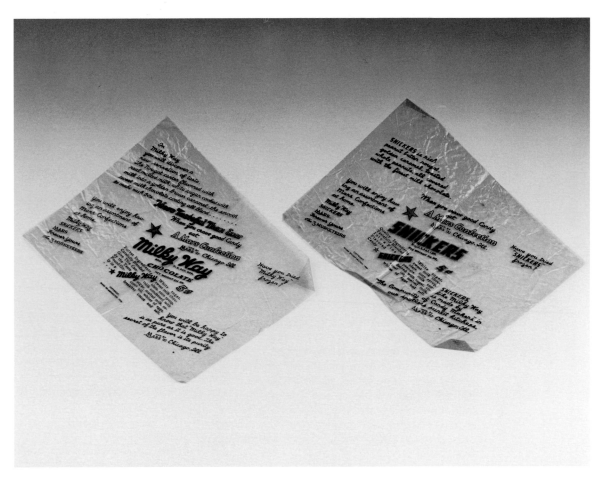

55

Milky Way wrapper, 1939–45 (left)

Mars, Inc., Chicago, Ill.
Printed waxed paper
H. 5³⁄₈ in., W. 8¹⁄₄ in.
Gift of Charles E. Burden

56

Snickers wrapper, 1939–45 (right)

Mars, Inc., Chicago, Ill.
Printed waxed paper
H. 5³⁄₈ in., W. 8¹⁄₄ in.
Gift of Charles E. Burden

Franklin C. Mars made his first piece of candy in his home kitchen in 1911. In less than 20 years the company moved from that kitchen in Washington State to Minneapolis and finally to a new and larger plant in Chicago in 1929. Product diversity and superior quality were the trademarks that allowed the company to grow rapidly.

Mars communicated the diversity of its products to consumers through "short memorable themes or propositions," designed to convey a particular brand's unique consumer benefit. The Milky Way bar was introduced in 1923, with the "purest ingredients." A motto printed in red claims that the bar is now "More Tasteful Than Ever." Snickers, introduced in 1930, was sold as a source of energy to satisfy one's hunger until mealtime—a sales pitch still used by the company today.

The war affected the Mars Company's product development. M&M candies were introduced in 1940 "as a neat, convenient treat that would be easy to eat in almost any climate." Because of this, when the United States entered the war one year later, M&Ms became a staple in military rations. Mars introduced its first food brand—Uncle Ben's Converted Rice—in 1943. A rice that would not spoil and that was easy to make, Uncle Ben's was specifically developed for use by the military.

The candy division of Mars, including Snickers and Milky Way, did not significantly change during the war. Rationing and shipping problems plagued the company as they did all food producers, but the package design and the dedication to quality remained unchanged.   RDR

SOURCE:

Consumer Affairs, M&M/Mars, Inc. *A Little Illustrated Encyclopedia of M&M/Mars*. Hackettstown, N.J.: M&M/Mars, 1992.

57

Hershey's Milk Chocolate Bar labels,
1936–51 (See plate 9)

Hershey Chocolate Corp., Hershey, Penn.
Printed paper
H. 5 in., W. 4³/₄ in.
Gift of Mr. and Mrs. Clayton Tenney

Milton S. Hershey started his candy business in 1876, but after a series of setbacks and failures he decided that if his company was to survive, he would have to find a new, more modern, product to manufacture. In 1893 Hershey traveled to Europe and was introduced to the process of making milk chocolate. Although he purchased his first chocolate-making machines upon his return home, his milk-chocolate-making process took time to perfect and it was not until 1900 that Hershey introduced his first chocolate bar to the public.

World War II caused a drastic shift in the type and variety of confections produced by the Hershey Company. A joint venture between the United States Government and the Hershey Corporation saw the creation of the "Field Ration D" bar and the "Tropical Bar." Both were developed in 1937 and their production took over most of the space in Hershey's factories. The field ration bars were designed to taste worse than regular chocolate bars so that soldiers would only eat them when necessary. The Tropical bar was formulated so that it would not melt in soldiers' pockets while they were fighting in "tropical" locations. About 500,000 of these bars were turned out each hour, 24 hours a day, at the Hershey factory. Hershey received five Army/Navy "E" awards for its production efforts. Great quantities of regular Hershey bars were also sent to the troops.

The production of these three products left little room for Hershey to manufacture other bars during the war, and "Crackle" bars and other newer Hershey products were temporarily discontinued. Because of the lack of metal for foil wrap, the production of Hershey Kisses was also suspended until after the war. The foil shortage caused Hershey to begin making the inner wrappers of Hershey Bars out of a glycine or wax-like paper, a material that the company continued to use until the 1980s.

Hershey Bars are still wrapped in the dark reddish-brown and silver label that the company introduced in 1906. At first the lettering was gold, but a lawsuit by another company brought about the change from gold letters to silver. Block lettering was introduced in 1936 and the company began printing the words "MILK CHOCOLATE" in a silver rectangle in 1938; the label remained essentially the same until 1968.   RDR

SOURCE:

Broekel, Ray. *The Great American Candy Bar Book*. Boston: Houghton Mifflin Co., 1982.

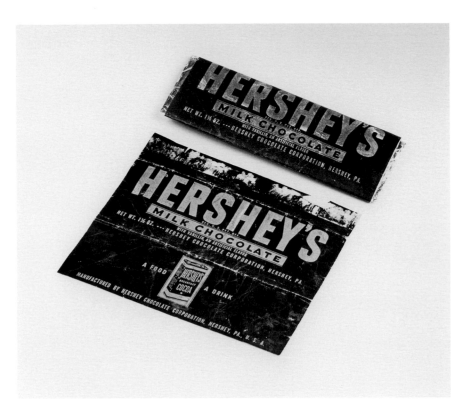

58

Bolsters box, 1942–45 (See plate 25)

New England Confectionery Co.,
    Cambridge, Mass.
Printed paperboard
H. 2½ in., W. 8⅞ in., D. 7⅝ in.
Gift of Charles E. Burden

59

Bolster wrapper, copyright 1947

(See plate 25)

New England Confectionery Co.,
    Cambridge, Mass.
Printed waxed paper
W. 7 in., D. 4¾ in.
Gift of Pam and Donald Bruce

The New England Confectionery Company, or NECCO, was established with the merger of three confectionery companies in 1901. "Bolster, a peanut crunch bar covered with milk chocolate," first appeared on the market in 1930. Named Bolster because its shape resembled a soft, round, pillow, it was one of many new products the company introduced during the first half of the 20th century.

In response to wartime sugar shortages, NECCO changed its distribution policies. The Bolster bar was one of the company's gourmet items, and therefore was not cut from production, but instead was sold to a limited market. Orders from "the military received highest priority, after that the remaining bars would be sold in an area east of the Hudson River."

Even this was not enough to ease production and distribution problems caused by the war. In 1941, NECCO *News*, a company newsletter published for wholesalers, recommended:

> Three Ways to Ease The Shipping Problem In The Months To Come.
> 1. Save all old Paper.
> 2. Order Merchandise Earlier.
> 3. Order in larger quantities when practical.

These suggestions were meant to help NECCO streamline its shipping operations and to ease the shortage of shipping cardboard.

The Bolster box was a perfect way for retailers to purchase bars in the large quantity recommended by NECCO. Each box held 120 "Penny Bolsters," a smaller version of the regular 1½ ounce size. This wartime box includes a "Buy War Bonds" message, and is completely covered with the "NECCO Candies" logo. The bottom of the box features a picture of the NECCO factory in Cambridge, Massachusetts, which covered 600,000 square feet and was the envy of the confectionery industry when it was built in 1926.

NECCO Wafers, Bolster, Sky Bar, and many other NECCO products were carried in the Abbotts' "Little Corner Store" and are still available today.   RDR

SOURCES:

Broekel, Ray. *The Great American Candy Bar Book*. Boston: Houghton Mifflin, 1982.

New England Confectionery Co. *A Capsule History of New England Confectionery Company*. Cambridge, Mass.: New England Confectionary Co., n.d.

New England Confectionary Co., *NECCO News* 4, no. 8 (1941).

Personal communication with Tom McNaulty, New Business Development Manager, NECCO.

60

Canada Dry Pale Ginger Ale bottles, ca.
1925–47 (See plate 9)

Canada Dry Ginger Ale, Inc., New York, N.Y.
Printed paper, green glass, metal foil
H. 9¾ in., Diam. (base) 2⅝ in.
Museum Purchase

In 1890, J. J. McLaughlin began making and selling plain soda-water for soda fountains. "Observing his soda-water being used in the drugstore to mix fruit extracts and juices and the end product favorably accepted by patrons, he promptly had notions of expansion." McLaughlin diversified his product base with his Pale Dry Ginger Ale in 1904.

The bottle label, referred to by company personnel as "the map label," was designed to exploit the "aura about the word 'Canada' that excites the imagination of people everywhere." The map, which highlights Canada in bright pink and the United States in bright yellow, is meant to illustrate the connection between the soft drink's main ingredient—water from the "cool, pure, wholesome climate of Canada"—and the manufacturing plant in New York City. Canada Dry wrapped the necks and caps of its "Champagne of Ginger Ales" with gold foil to enhance the product's connection with champagne.

During the 1920s and 1930s Canada Dry was portrayed as a drink for the elite that "would eliminate barriers to upward mobility." This message was quickly cast aside during World War II as images of patriotic individuals and wartime messages took over Canada Dry advertising. A 1943 ad in *The Saturday Evening Post*, for instance, encouraged readers to

> Grow green things . . . red things. Grow 'em big and tall and can them right, so the boy at the front can get the food his fighting heart deserves.

And a 1944 ad praised the American working woman for putting "every penny she can spare" toward "extra purchases of War Bonds" with "Bravo . . . keep up the good work!" No direct connection was made between these messages and the product itself, but the campaign did keep the Canada Dry name in people's minds at a time when wartime restrictions caused product shortages. One ad apologetically explained that Canda Dry Ginger Ale would be available "in the handy 5 cent individual bottle . . . as soon as conditions permit." Wartime limitations on packaging and shipping materials encouraged manufacturers to bottle soft drinks in larger containers. Canada Dry was no exception. Unlike some companies, Canada Dry did not increase its sales during the war.   RDR

SOURCES:

Canada Dry advertisement. *The Saturday Evening Post*, August 19, 1943.
Canada Dry advertisement. *Woman's Day*, November 1944.
Canada Dry advertisement. *Woman's Home Companion*, February 1944.
Manwarring, T. E. "WPB Member Explains Glass Order Amendments." *Modern Packaging* 17 (October 1943): 95.
Marchand, Roland. *Advertising the American Dream.* Berkeley: University of California Press, 1985.
Moore, Roy W. *Down From Canada Came Tales of a Wonderful Beverage.* New York: The Newcomen Society in North America, 1961.

61

Standard Coca-Cola Ice Cooler, 1934–39
(See plate 4)

Westinghouse for the Coca-Cola Co., Atlanta, Ga.
Painted metal
H. 35½ in., W. 31 in., D. 25 in.
Museum Purchase

62

Coca-Cola Six-Pack Bottle Carrier, 1939
(See plate 9)

The Coca-Cola Co., Atlanta, Ga.
Printed paperboard
H. 9⅝ in., W. 7⅜ in., D. 4⅝ in.
Gift of Charles E. Burden

63

Three Coca-Cola bottles, (left to right)
1951–59; 1923–37; 1937–51 (See plate 9)

The Coca-Cola Co., Atlanta, Ga.
Glass
H. 7¾ in., Diam. (base) 2¼ in., Diam. (top) 1 in.
(Left to right) Museum Purchase; Gift of Marion Fuller
Brown; Gift of Barbara Widen

Dr. John Styth Pemberton started his own patent medicine business in 1885. In his efforts to create a cure-all, Pemberton stumbled on to the formula for Coca-Cola. The original recipe combined sugar and water with extracts of the coca leaf and the kola nut, to which Pemberton added caffeine so that he could market the syrup as a headache remedy. At first, Coke was advertised as a cure-all and as a beverage with a great taste. Coca-Cola is one of only a few companies that prospered and grew through wars and depressions by selling just one product.

Throughout the years, Coke's aggressive advertising has made the company's famous red-and-white trademark perhaps the best-known trademark on earth. The trademark is embossed on the bottles, and appears in white lettering on a red background on both the six-pack carrier and the cooler.

In addition to package design similarities, both the bottle carrier and the cooler were introduced by the Coca-Cola Company to enhance consumer convenience, to optimize product flavor, and to increase domestic sales. In an effort to encourage customers to buy Coca-Cola and take it home, the company first introduced a closed paperboard box, called a six-box, that made transporting the bottles easier. Introduced in the 1920s, this carton never achieved customer acceptance. Claude Kieth developed this design for the six-pack bottle carrier in 1934 (cat. 62). The new carrier was better looking, easier to carry, and, most importantly, cheaper to construct (allowing for a cheaper price per bottle) than its predecessor. "At a cost of about one cent each, the new carton was one-fourth the cost of the old."

To make sure the company's new item and its benefits reached the public, the carrier was advertised in *Better Homes and Gardens* as the convenient way to bring Coke home. An ad in *House and Garden* even included an illustration showing bottles of coke in a bowl full of ice with opener, glasses, ice tongs, and cocktail napkins nearby.

In spite of company efforts to increase carton sales, such sales fell off during the war when Coke was sometimes in short supply. Most Coke was still sold by the individual bottle. A metal cooler provided additional point-of-sale advertising for the product, and allowed store owners to chill

large numbers of Coke bottles, thus making "the famous 'Pause' truly refreshing." Both this type of cooler (cat. 61), which cools with ice, and the "Master Electric" cooler, were introduced in 1934. For added convenience this cooler has a lower shelf on which to store empty crates and bottles and is equipped with a bottle opener. The Abbotts used a Coke pretzel dish, situated on the cooler top, to hold bottle caps (see PLATE 4).

As effectively as Coke used advertising, "It was World War II that catapulted Coca-Cola into the world market and made it one of America's first multinational companies." The company was determined to supply Coke to every soldier throughout the world. Magazine advertisements in *The Saturday Evening Post* and *Good Housekeeping* equated Coke with patriotism and the American way of life. Copy such as "Welcome, Friends" and "You're invited to our house" was accompanied by illustrations of visiting soldiers being served Coke in home gatherings. These ads, and a specific "request by General Eisenhower" prompted Coke to establish plants wherever American troops were fighting in Europe and North Africa. These plants

continued in operation throughout the war, and made Coke a truly international product.

Astute marketing and an acute understanding of what the public wanted made the war years productive ones for Coca-Cola, and the market value of its stock increased rapidly. Postwar consumers could truly follow the advice incorporated in a company advertising slogan adopted in 1942, "Wherever you are, whatever you do, wherever you may be, when you think of refreshment, think of ice-cold Coca-Cola"   RDR

SOURCES:

Bateman, William, and Randy Schaffer. *The Coca-Cola Collectors News*, 1988.

Coca-Cola advertisement. *Good Houskeeping*, May 1944.

Coca-Cola advertisement. *House and Garden*, June 1940.

Coca-Cola advertisement. *The Saturday Evening Post*, September 18, 1943.

Coca-Cola Co. *Facts, Figures, and Features*. Atlanta, Ga.: Consumer Information Center, Coca-Cola Co., 1992.

Coca-Cola Company. In, *International Directory of Company Histories*, ed. Paula Kepos. Detroit: St. James Press, 1990–92.

Petretti, Allan. *Petretti's Coca-Cola Collectibles Price Guide*. Radnor, Penn.: Wallace-Homestead, 1989.

64

Uneeda Bakers overlay and box, ca. 1920–25 (See plate 26)

National Biscuit Co., New York, N.Y.
Paperboard, chrome, glass
H. 11¾ in., W. 10½ in., D. 10½ in.
Museum purchase

The Abbotts' "Little Corner Store" utilized 16 dispensers of this kind, arranged in two racks to the right side of the front door. The reusable glass and metal overlay, hinged at the left, fits snugly over the square cardboard box below. When the box was empty, it was simply removed and a fresh one put in its place. The glass lid permits viewing of the biscuits, crackers, cookies, or even marshmallows underneath. The products within were arranged in decorative patterns, with the layers separated by cardboard inserts. The boxes were produced in several different heights, and they were placed on the shelves of the rack at a slight upward angle to facilitate opening.

In this example, the lid bears the Uneeda Bakers name and text indicating that the design was patented March 13, 1923. The box now associated with the lid bears red-and-white applied stickers indicating that it held 6¼ pounds of Nabisco Cartwheels ("crisp and satisfying cookies with a molasses flavor"). The bottom of the box is stamped "PAT / SEPT 21, [19]20."

The National Biscuit Company (N.B.C.) was a pioneer in the marketing of packaged baked goods. Dispensers such as this replaced the cracker barrels that were a familiar component of stores in the late 19th and early 20th centuries, as well as N.B.C.'s own In-Er-Seal packages introduced in 1900. Although this overlay bears a patent date from the early 1920s, the design and function of these dispensers remained basically unchanged through the end of World War II. The metal overlays are stamped as the property of N.B.C., and they were probably provided to the grocer as a service. The museum collection includes boxes used for N.B.C.'s Fruited Ovals, Wafer Squares, Soda Crackers, Kennedy's Special Commons, Butter Crisps, and Raspberry Creams, and Sunshine Biscuit's Plain Vanilla cookies, as well as a Uneeda display rack (see PLATE 26).

The National Biscuit Company began abbreviating its name to Nabisco, rather than N.B.C., in 1941, to avoid confusion with the National Broadcasting System. Nabisco, however, did not become the company's official name until 1971. Nabisco merged with Standard Brands in 1981 to become Nabisco Brands, and Nabisco Brands was taken over by R. J. Reynolds, now R.J.R. Nabisco, in 1985.   GWRW

SOURCES:

Cahn, William. *Out of the Cracker Barrel: The Nabisco Story from Animal Crackers to ZuZu's.* New York: Simon and Schuster, 1969.

Grayson, Melvin J. *42 Million a Day: The Story of Nabisco Brands.* East Hanover, N.J.: Nabisco Brands, Inc., 1986.

Nabisco Brands, Inc. In, *International Directory of Company Histories,* ed. Paula Kepos. Detroit, Mich.: St. James Press, 1990–92.

Raycraft, Don, and Carol Raycraft. *Collector's Guide to Country Store Antiques.* Paducah, Ky.: Collector Books, 1987.

Strasser, Susan. *Satisfaction Guaranteed: The Making of the American Mass Market.* New York: Pantheon Books, 1989.

65

Telephone, ca. 1904

American Telephone and Telegraph Co., Western Electric
  Co., New York, N.Y.
Metal, bakelite
H. 12 in., Diam. (base) 5¼ in.
Gift of Charles E. Burden

Until its breakup in 1984, The American Telephone and Telegraph Company (AT&T) was one of the largest corporations in the world. Alexander Graham Bell established AT&T in 1885 to operate as the Bell System's long-distance subsidiary. The company continued to grow rapidly, but business fell off dramatically during the first few years after the stock market crash of 1929. By 1933, telephone use was on the rise again, and sales quickly exceeded pre-crash levels. The long-distance telephone industry grew tremendously during World War II, with 1.4 million new telephones being installed in 1941 alone.

Western Electric and Bell Labs were heavily involved in military work from 1942–1945, filling government contracts and making technological innovations to fulfill war needs. The most important innovation to emerge from this research was the development of microwave radio relays for transmitting long-distance telephone and television signals.

During the war, Bell System advertisements stressed the importance of long-distance communication lines by urging customers to keep the lines free and clear for emergencies. A *Better Homes and Gardens* magazine ad explained to consumers:

WAR NEEDS THE WIRES Telephone lines
are the life-lines of an army. Bell System
men and materials are helping to keep those
lines unbroken on many battlefronts. So if a
Long Distance call gets delayed once in
awhile, you know there's a good reason. The
additional equipment that could be used
here is serving the soldiers over there.

The stand-up desk set, also referred to as a candlestick telephone, was first introduced in 1879. This black, straight shaft model was the most popular and widely used telephone throughout the 1920s, and was the type used by the Abbotts until after the war. Although dial instruments were developed before 1900, it wasn't until the late 1920s that they became common.   KEC

SOURCES:

American Telephone and Telegraph Co. In, *International Directory of Company Histories*, ed. Paula Kepos. Detroit, Mich.: St. James Press, 1990–92.
Bell System advertisement. *Better Homes & Gardens*, January 1944.

66

Servel Electrolux Gas Refrigerator, ca.
1937 (See plate 6)

Servel Inc., Evansville, Ind.
H. 62½ in., W. 28½ in., D. 25¼ in.
Enamel covered metal, metal, rubber
Museum Purchase

In 1937, a new model of the popular Servel Electrolux gas refrigerator was introduced to the market. It was simple, noise free, and saved on upkeep as well as food bills. Advertisements boasted that "it saves silently because it freezes with no moving parts." This lack of moving parts was what separated Servel refrigerators from other gas refrigerators on the market. A tiny gas flame circulated the refrigerant—silently, and without friction or wear.

Servel Incorporated had its beginnings in 1902, when founder Col. William McCurdy moved the Brighton Buggy Company from Cincinnati, Ohio,

to Evansville, Indiana, and changed the name of the company to the Hercules Buggy Works. Hercules manufactured buggies, wagons, surreys, road carts, pony carts, and farm wagons. Most of its products were sold to the Sears-Roebuck Company and what Sears did not buy was sold primarily in the southern and southwestern United States. McCurdy's connection with Sears-Roebuck sparked his interest in the gas engine business, and he bought the Sparta Gas Engine Company from Sears, renaming it the Hercules Gas Engine Company. Over the years the company expanded, manufacturing gas engines, truck bodies, farm tractors, and eventually, their best-known product, the Servel gas refrigerator.

In 1922, three engineers from Detroit designed an automatic refrigeration unit, later called the Servel, a name shortened from "serve electrically." By 1926, the Hercules Company was reorganized as Servel Incorporated. In addition to the gas refrigerator, Servel also manufactured commercial refrigeration and air conditioning equipment.

Automatic refrigeration soon caught on with the public, and by 1930 the number of refrigerators produced exceeded the production of ice boxes. By the late 1930s, Servel employed about 5000 people and produced more than 1200 refrigerators a day. Prices fell steadily and, by 1941, more than 3.5 million Americans owned refrigerators.

When refrigerator production was halted by the government during World War II, Servel produced wings for the Republic P-47 Thunderbolt. To keep its name before the public Servel continued to advertise its refrigerators during the war and to promote a number of wartime conservation measures, including the "Servel Nutrition In Industry Plan," which appeared in *Better Homes & Gardens* in 1942. The four-step plan to keep war workers healthy involved:

1) Putting up posters in war plants to tell your Jim or Joe the right foods to eat . . . and why.
2) Cooperating with plant cafeterias in suggesting Victory Lunches—in featuring energy-rich foods.
3) Encouraging neighborhood restaurants to serve balanced meals and the recommended Victory Lunch.
4) Helping YOU pack health-building lunches . . . prepare delicious meals at home.

At the bottom of the advertisement there is a note about the company's dedication to the war effort, it reads: "The Advertising and Promotion Department as well as the entire plant of Servel, Inc., peacetime manufacturers of the gas refrigerator, is today completely converted to the war program."

Gas refrigeration, as well as gas heat and gas

air conditioning were marketed as the wave of the future in the 1940s. The American Gas Association promised, in an advertisement in *Good Housekeeping*, that natural gas was "The magic flame that will brighten your future" and "The wonder flame that cools as well as heats." This and other ads focused on the ease with which the American housewife would live her life once gas appliances were available again. Images of women wearing crowns, floating in the sky, and relaxing in a bubble bath with tiny cherubs flying above, were accompanied by messages such as "live like a princess in a house that runs like magic. . . ." Gas companies promoted postwar "New Freedom Gas Kitchens" as "economical, trouble-free, and completely modern." Servel promised that

> When peace returns—and Servel is "mustered out" of total war work—millions more will be able to enjoy not only this modern convenience, but new ones made possible by the magic of the flame.

Employment at Servel's production plant reached an all-time high during the war, but quickly dropped back to pre-war levels when refrigerator manufacture resumed, only to climb back up to wartime levels in the early 1950s. Evansville, which also was home to the Sunbeam Electric Company (now Whirlpool), became the refrigerator capital of the world. Competition with Whirlpool ultimately proved disastrous for Servel, which shut down its operations in 1957.

KEC & GWRW

SOURCES:

American Gas Association advertisements. *Good Housekeeping*, June 1944, March 1945.

American Gas Association advertisement. *American Home*, March 1945.

Celehar, Jane H. *Kitchens & Kitchenware*. Lombard, Ill.: Wallace Homestead, 1985.

Giedion, Siegfried. *Mechanization Takes Command*. New York: W. W. Norton, 1975.

Meikle, Jeffrey. *Twentieth Century Limited: Industrial Design in America, 1925–1939*. Philadelphia: Temple University Press, 1979.

Murlock, James E. *The Evansville Story*. Evansville, Ind.: Creative Press of Evansville, 1956.

Schleper, Anne. "Evansville Recalls the Days." *The Evansville Courier*, September 7, 1992.

Servel Incorporated advertisement. *Better Homes & Gardens*, November 1942.

67

Cathedral Radio, ca. 1934 (See plate 2)

Philadelphia Storage Battery Co.,
    Philadelphia, Penn.
Wood, nylon, metal, glass
H. 14³/₁₆ in., W. 12 in., D. 8 in.
Gift of Charles E. Burden

The Philco Corporation had its beginnings in 1892, when its predecessor, Helios Electric Company, began manufacturing carbon arc lamps. In 1929, the firm's name was changed to the Philadelphia Storage Battery Company. The trademark name "PHILCO" first appeared in 1919 on the Diamond Grid Battery, but did not become a part of the company's official name until 1940. From 1940 to 1961 Philco was a publicly owned company; it then became a wholly owned subsidiary of Ford Motor Company.

The company experienced tremendous growth in the 1920s, as the popularity of the radio constantly increased. The invention of radio loudspeakers in 1921 enabled the whole family to listen to the radio together. Radio broadcasting became particularly important during World War II, when thousands of people around the world were dependent on radio for the latest war news. Radio was also an important vehicle for disseminating information useful to citizens on the home front. Portsmouth's radio station, WHEB, frequently broadcast speeches on the need for food conservation, how to cook point-wise meals, and other timely programs. In addition, propaganda broadcast in the language of the enemy became an effective weapon of war. The famous voice of Japanese broadcasts aimed at Allied forces in the Pacific, "Tokyo Rose," became synonymous with enemy efforts to undermine military morale.

During the war, the War Production Board ordered radio companies to cease making consumer products and retool their factories for war production work. On February 13, 1942, the headlines of an article issued by the Associated Press read: "ALL RADIO PLANTS ORDERED TO DO WAR WORK ONLY: Factories not Converted in four Months will be Taken over by U.S." As a result, American families continued to rely on pre-war radios throughout the conflict. Bertha Abbott owned a Philco model 84B like this one, and kept it in her kitchen, adjacent to the store, where she could keep abreast of war news and listen to her favorite programs throughout the day.

KEC & GWRW

SOURCES:

Johnson, David, and Betty Johnson. *Guide to Old Radios*. Radnor, Penn.: Wallace-Homestead, 1979.

News Dept., Philco Corporation. "Historical Sketch: Philco Corporation. A Subsidiary of Ford Motor Company." Philadelphia, Penn.: Philco Corp., n.d. Courtesy of George Brightville, Urban Archives, Temple University, Philadelphia, Penn.

Ward, Gerald W. R. *American Case Furniture in the Mabel Brady Garvan and Other Collections at Yale University* (New Haven, Conn.: Yale University Press, 1988).

68

Side Chair, ca. 1920–29 (See plates 2 and 3)

Smith, Day and Co., Indianapolis, Ind.
Oak, leather
OH. 38¼ in., H. (seat) 17½ in., W. 16⅞ in.
Museum Purchase

69

Dining Table, ca. 1920–40

(See plates 2 and 3)

Unidentified Maker, American
Oak
H. 29 in., Diam. (closed) 43 in.
Museum Purchase

During the 1920s and 1930s the dining set consisting of a round oak dining table and square T-back leather-seat side chairs was one of the most popular ones on the consumer market. This side chair, made by Smith, Day and Company, is of solid oak with a full, box-type, removable slip seat. Chairs of this design were also available in fumed oak and/or pad seats. Advertised in period mail-order catalogues, such as Montgomery Ward and Sears and Roebuck, as "Master-Made Dining Chairs—All Extra Values," and "Dining Chairs Low In Price—High In Value," they were easily affordable for most consumers. A chair like this one ranged in price from $1.95 to $3.85.

Smith, Day and Company began operations in Baldwinsville, Massachusetts, in 1871. Within the next two decades, the company opened up offices and factories in Detroit, Michigan, and Indianapolis, Indiana. The business was sold in 1929 and became the Bourn, Hadley, Fairbanks Company, which continued to manufacture chairs until 1946.

Dining tables of this type, often referred to as "extension tables," were available in "select" oak in a choice of golden or fumed finish. The tables were generally 42 inches in diameter, and consumers could choose from two extension sizes—six feet or eight feet. The table top of this example rests on an eight-inch turned column with four scrolled legs, sometimes called "colonial" legs. Tables of this type were sold by Montgomery Ward and Sears-Roebuck and ranged in price from $12.85 to $21.95.   KEC

SOURCES:

Cohen, Hal L., ed. *1922 Montgomery Ward Catalogue, Reprinted in its Original Form*. New York: HC Publishers, Inc., 1969.

Hyman, Max R. *The Journal Handbook of Indianapolis*. Indianapolis, Ind.: Indiana Journal Newspaper Co., 1902.

Lord, Elizabeth. *The Story of Templeton*. Templeton, Mass.: The Narragansett Historical Society Inc., 1940.

Mirken, Alan, ed. *1927 Edition of the Sears, Roebuck Catalogue*. New York: Crown Publishers, 1970.

"Smith, Day & Co." *Cottage and Ready Record* [Baldwinsville, Mass.], December 15, 1891.

70

Walker Coal bag, ca. 1930–50 (See plate 9)

Charles E. Walker and Co., Portsmouth, N.H.
Printed paper
H. 23¼ in., W. 7½ in.
Gift of Cameron Russell Holt-Corti

The two most common types of coal sold for residential and commercial purposes are anthracite and bituminous. Anthracite coal is a hard shiny substance that, when burned, emits fewer pollutants than the softer bituminous coal. Anthracite was the coal recommended by the United States government for residential use. It was brought to New Hampshire from Pennsylvania and West Virginia by train or barge and delivered to other parts of the state via rail.

In 1868, Portsmouth-native Charles E. Walker (1835–1908) established his business on Pier Wharf, at the corner of State and Water (now Marcy) streets in the area of Portsmouth known as Puddle Dock. Walker and Company acted as importers and dealers in coal, lime, and cement, but it was the wholesale and retail sale of anthracite coal that brought the company its prominence. When Charles E. Walker died, his son Charles H. Walker took control of the company. Charles H. expanded the business in the 1920s by purchasing the lumber mill wharves of John H. Broughton, which were located next to the Walker wharves at the end of State Street (fig. 88). In June of 1951, C. E. Walker and Company was nearly destroyed by a devastating fire that burned buildings, coal piles, and trucks. Although Charles H. Walker rebuilt the wharves and buildings, the declining need for coal coupled with the cost of rebuilding after the fire, kept Walker and Company from regaining its previous success. In 1964, the City of Portsmouth, acting on behalf of the Prescott Fund, purchased the Walker property from Charles H. Walker for $80,000, and the old wharves and coal yard became part of what is now Prescott Park.

In 1943 a heating fuel shortage led to a request by New Hampshire state officials for consumers to convert from oil to coal. As the war progressed, fuel consumption became controlled by War Production Board allotments and Office of Price Administration rationing. In 1944, the United States Department of the Interior set up the Solid Fuels Administration for War (SFAW). Representatives were appointed from various states including New Hampshire and Vermont. These state representatives were to make sure that coal dealers received a minimum of 80% of their quota during a coal year, April 1 to March 31. It was also the job of the state representatives to see to it that the coal suppliers and dealers adhered to SFAW regulations. Both the Federal Fuels Administration and the State Fuels Administration worked to ensure that consumers received the quantities of fuel to which they were entitled. However, in order to stock up, many consumers had registered with several dealers at a time, thus threatening a coal shortage in the East at the beginning of 1945. State and Federal officials implemented restrictions on consumers that required them to register with one coal dealer only. Area directors were appointed to keep state officials informed of local shortages and current conditions. These area directors were also responsible for discouraging consumers from converting back to oil. The "Coal Watch" lasted until the end of the war, when the SFAW and its state and local sister agencies disbanded in the latter part of 1945.   TEA

Fig. 88. *Walker Coal Yard, Portsmouth, N.H., ca. 1920, by an unidentified photographer. Historic Photograph Collection.*

SOURCES:

Ray A. Brighton. *The Prescott Story*. New Castle, N.H.: Portsmouth Marine Society, 1982.

_____. *They Came to Fish*. Portsmouth, N.H.: Portsmouth 350, Inc., 1973.

Gallen, Hugh J. *The Rock That Burns*. Concord, N.H.: Governor's Council on Energy, 1982.

Guyol, Philip N. *Democracy Fights: A History of New Hampshire in World War II*. Hanover, N.H.: Dartmouth Publications, 1951.

Leading Business Men of Portsmouth, Exeter and Newmarket. Portsmouth, N.H.: Portsmouth Athenaeum, 1870.

"Walker Coal Wharf Destroyed by Blaze In Loss of $200,000." *The Portsmouth Herald*, June 9, 1951, p. 1.

Questions and Answers for the Coal Fireman. U.S. Dept. of Interior, 1941.

Smith, Herman L. "Excerpts from 'History of War Price and Rationing Board 1–14–8'" (1946). Portsmouth War Records Committee Files, Portsmouth Public Library, Portsmouth, N.H.

Paul S. Boyer et al. *The Enduring Vision: A History of the American People*. Vol. 2, *From 1865*. Lexington, Mass: D.C. Heath, 1990.

71

Cookstove, ca. 1915–20 (See plate 2)

Somersworth Foundry Co., Salmon Falls, N.H.
Cast iron, nickel-plated chrome
H. 54 in., W. 28½ in., D. 48 in.
Museum Purchase

This cast-iron cookstove was manufactured by the Somersworth Foundry Company of Salmon Falls (now part of Rollinsford), New Hampshire. Organized in 1900, the Somersworth Foundry Company replaced the Somersworth Machine Company (1848–1900) on the site of William Henry Griffin's early 19th-century latch factory.

The Somersworth Foundry Company was involved in the

> manufacturing of stoves, ranges, heating and cooking apparatus and castings. The manufacturing of machines made in whole or in part of iron; the buying and selling of iron, or its products, made in whole or in part of iron.

The corporation manufactured "Standard" stoves until 1942, at which time the factory closed down, probably because of the strict cut-backs on stove production mandated by the federal government during World War II. The Somersworth Foundry site continued in use, under the management of several different firms, for ten more years; it was destroyed by fire in 1952.

This stove, the "Standard G" brand, was probably made between 1915 and 1920. It is a six-burner type cookstove with a side shelf at the left and a backplate with two shelves for the cook's convenience. The bake oven is on the right side, and there is a temperature gauge at the center of the door. The fire box is on the left side and the ash pit extends from the box. This plain stove, with cabriole legs and a straight skirt, was very affordable when new and is similar to the one owned by Walter and Bertha Abbott. The Abbotts probably acquired their stove shortly after they purchased their house in 1918. This stove has been converted, as was the Abbotts' stove, so that it can utilize kerosene. Bertha Abbott cooked on her iron stove in the winter, to supplement the oil furnace, and cooked on her more modern gas range during the summer months.   KEC

SOURCE:

Catalfo, Alfred, Jr. "Revised from the History of Rollinsford." M.A. Thesis, Dept. of History, University of New Hampshire, Durham, N.H., 1952.

72

Blackout Candles and box, ca. 1941–45

(See plate 9)

Will and Baumer Candle Co., Inc., Syracuse, N.Y.
Paperboard, wax
H. 2½ in., W. 6¹¹⁄₁₆ in., D. 5¼ in.
Gift of Charles E. Burden

Cities along the East Coast and West Coast of the United States endured "dim-out" hours every day, as well as periodic blackouts. Citizens were asked to take special precautions so that, in the event of an emergency, they could darken their homes and businesses to make them invisible to enemy aircraft. Blackouts were announced in the media one or two days beforehand, and neighborhood wardens patrolled cities to make sure that people observed blackout regulations. In a city like Portsmouth, which was home to a major military installation and war production plant—the Portsmouth Naval Shipyard—the observance of blackout hours was particularly important, and early in the war air-raids were considered to be a real threat.

On January 27, 1942, Louise Grant, a Portsmouth schoolteacher, recorded ordering material and making blackout curtains in her diary:

> Ma and I tacked up a piece of curtain on kitchen window to make it all right for a black out. Now we have to do the rest.

She also recorded ordering special blackout candles:

> The stearic acid candles came from Paine's. Each candle is supposed to burn 6 hr. Hope we never need them, for war purposes I mean. . . .

The Will and Baumer Company introduced these specially designed Blackout Candles in early 1942. As soon as the candles went on the market, orders began to pour in. Considerable quantities of candles were produced for the Army and Navy, in addition to the quantities sold to civilians. The candles, which burned for up to six hours, could be purchased by the dozen in a black-and-white cardboard box, and were designed "to eliminate the risk of burning from lighted matches." Images of the various uses of the candles are depicted on the sides of the box, and the text on the top is printed within a gray or pink explosive cloud. The candles have a pedestal base which allows them to stand alone, without a holder of any kind.

KEC & BMW

SOURCES:

Guyol, Philip N. *Democracy Fights: A History of New Hampshire in World War II*. Hanover, N.H.: Dartmouth Publications, 1951.

Newspaper clipping from *The Syracuse Post Standard*, January 22, 1942. Courtesy of the Onondaga Historical Association, Syracuse, N.Y.

Portsmouth, N.H. Strawbery Banke Museum. S. Louise Grant Papers. Louise Grant Diary.

Index

NOTE: Italic numerals refer to illustrations and their captions.

A&P, Portsmouth, 26, 107, 117, 140; national 118
Abbott, Bertha (nee Hiltz), 11, *21*, birth of, 21; children of, 22, 26; and Clough, Leslie, 29, 150; death of, 32; early life, 22; family furnishings, 152, 153, 157; grandchildren, 14, 26, 29, 150; grocer, 25–26, 28–30, 62, 117–118, 125, 126, 129, 130, 134, 140, 157; landlady, 64; parents of, 21; purchase and alteration of Marden House, 22, 24–25, 151; retirement, 32
Abbott, Inez. *See* Hoyt, Inez
Abbott, Mabel. *See* Holt, Mabel
Abbott, Walter, 11, *20, 21, 23*; birth of, 21; Boston and Maine Railroad laborer, 22; children of, 22, 26; death of, 27; grandchildren, 14, 26, 29, 150; grocer, *20, 23*, 25–27; Inspector of Petroleum, 27; parents of, 21; purchase and alteration of Marden House, 22, 24–25, 151; Sealer of Weights and Measures, 26, 27; sister (Edith Abbott O'Hara), *25*; State Legislator, 27
advertising industry during WWII, 42–43, 123–128
African-Americans and WWII, 50–52
Aircraft Warning Service (AWS), 180
Air Raid Wardens, 61
Allen, Ida Bailey: cookbook, 106, 109
American Can Co., 194
American Cigarette and Cigar Co., 220
American Gas Assoc. advertising, 231
American Telephone and Telegraph Co. (AT&T), 229
Anderson, Harry (illustrator), 218
Anthony, Cora, 110
Armour Co. advertising, 125
Armour's Star Vienna Sausage, *166*
Armsden, Douglas (photographer), *63*
Arney, Dr. Jonathan, 167
Artists for Victory, 174
Aunt Jemima Pancake Mix packaging, 162
Auxiliary Firemen, 61
Auxiliary Policemen, 61
Ayer, N.W. Collection, National Museum of American History, 154

B & M Beans packaging, 188
Badger Farms Creameries, 205; products, 205, 206
Barclay, McClelland: poster designs, 176
Bayer Aspirin packaging, 219
Bean, Ruth: cooking seminar, 69
Bell Laboratories, 229
Best Foods Inc., The, 208
Bisquick packaging, 162
Black, Jeannette (Portsmouth grocer), 129
Black's Market, Portsmouth: population served, 32

black market, 40, 43, 86, 184
Blais, Rudolph (Portsmouth grocer), 125
Block, The, 21, 22, 63
Boraxo packaging, 94
Bolster candy bar, *203*, 224
Boston Woven Hose and Rubber Co., 185
Bourne, Hadley, Fairbanks Co., 233
Bowles, Chester (OPA administrator), 90
Boy Scouts of America, 71–72
Brewster, Edith (Portsmouth YWCA house director), 71
Brighton Buggy Co., 230
Broughton, John H.: lumber mill, 234
Brown and Williamson Tobacco Corp., 221
Bull Dog Jar Rubbers, 112, 185
Burnham and Morril Co., 188, 189
Burden, Charles E., 5, 12, 149, 154

Cadarette, Roland, 75
Cain's Mayonnaise advertising, 42
California Fruit Canning Assoc. (CFCA), 187
California Packing Corp. (Calpak), 187, 188
Campbell's Soup, *168*
Camp Langdon, 62
Can Manufacturers Inst. of New York, *93*, 194
Canada Dry Pale Ginger Ale, 225
candles, black out, 237
Cashmere Bouquet packaging, 39, 217
celebrities and the war effort, 44, 47, 107
Cellophane, 126–127, 220
chain grocery stores, 26, 62, 85, 89, 118, *125*, 140
Cheese Industry of Amer. advertising, *120*
Chef Boy-ar-dee spaghetti, 109
children and WWII, 44, *45*, 47, 49, 71–72, 132, 133, 134, 179–180
Civilian Defense Organizations, 124, 181
Clough, Leslie, 5, *30*; Bertha Abbott's accounting system, 156; Bertha Abbott's assistant, 29, 126, 129, 157; Bertha Abbott's kitchen, 152; business during 1940s, 32; gas rationing, 128; Mom & Pop vs. chain stores, 117–118; neighborhood loyalty, 130–131; restoration help, 149–150
Coca-Cola, 166, 226–227
Colgate Co., 217
Colgate-Palmolive-Peet, 217
Committee to Defend America by Aiding the Allies, 69
Continental Shoe, Portsmouth, 62
Controlled Materials Plan, 91
convenience stores, Portsmouth, present day, 141
cooking advice, *70*, 106, 108, 109, 111, 112, *185*
Cooperative Extension Service, 106, 107
Copyright Office, 154
CPC International, 208
Crisco packaging, 94, 213–214

Dale, Charles: Prescott Park, 27
Davis, Brigadier General Benjamin O., 51
Decatur, Stephen, 28
Defense Homes Corp., 65–66, 99
de Graff, Robert: Pocket Books, 178
Del Monte Foods, 121–122, 124, 131, 187–188; packaging, 187–188
De Molay fraternal organization, 70
Department of Agriculture, U.S., 111, 112–113, *114*, 177
Department of Commerce, U.S., 134
Diggins, John Patrick (historian), 76
Dill's Best Smoking Tobacco, *81*
displays and packaging, 92, 94, 132, *135–136*, 154, *168*, 217
Dogs for Defense program, 72
Dondero, Mary C. (Mayor of Portsmouth), *76*, 77
Drisco House, 142
DuBois, W.E.B.: WWI, 50
DuPont Co., 52, 126–127, 194
Duraglas, 194, 206
Durkee-Mowers, Inc.: Marshmallow Fluff, *167*

Easy Washing Machine Co., 42
Economic Stabilization Act, 98
Elastic Starch packaging, 162
Emergency Price Control Act, 81, 95–96
Executive Order 8734, 81
Executive Order 8802, 51

Family Welfare Assoc., 71
Farm Security Admin., 154
Farrington, Dr. William (dentist), 72
Federal Bureau of Investigation (FBI), 46
Federal Food Admin., 119
Federal Fuels Admin., 234
Federal Housing Authority, 74–75
Fels-Naphtha soap, 214–215
Field Ration Bar, 223
First National Stores, Portsmouth, 26, 62, 89, 107, 117, 118
Flagg, James Montgomery, 175
Fleishman's Yeast: seminars, 195
Food Fights for Freedom campaign, 173
Force Foods Co., 208
Force Toasted Whole Wheat Flakes, *201*, 208
Ford, Henry: Willow Run factory, 38
Ford Motor Co., 38; purchase of Philco, 231
Friend's Baked Beans, 189
Frigidaire advertising, *108*

Gamble, James: Proctor & Gamble Co., 213
Garland, Martha, 111
General Electric advertising, 43
General Foods Corp., 124, 194, 209, 210, 212

General Maximum Price Regulation (GMPR), 96–97
General Mills, Inc., 207
Girl Scouts of America, 71
Good Luck Jar Rubbers, 185
Gould, Georgea ("Georgie") (nee Powell), 22, 62, 129
Gould, Melvin, 22
Gould's Market, 31, 32, 129, *130*
Gourmet Society (New York City), 111
Grant, Louise, *107*, blackouts, 237; canning, 111–112; distributing ration coupons, 84; food shopping, 107; food shortages, 91; home life, 105; substituting for rationed foods, 108, 109, 115, 192, 206; Victory Garden, 110
Grape Nuts Flakes packaging, 209
Grocery Store (government publication), 134–135
Gross National Product (1939–1944), 38
Grover, Norad (mariner), 24
Guyol, Philip (historian), 84

Hamming-Whitman Pub. Co., 179
Hansen, Adam, 167
Hart, Leo Co., Inc., 180
Health and Welfare Survey, Portsmouth War Records, 49–50, 57–58, 64, 76
Health for Victory Campaign, 184, 206
Health for Victory *Meal Planning Guide*, 184, 206
Hecker Products, 208
Heinz, H. J.: Heinz Co., *166*, 186
Heinz Tomato Ketchup packaging, *166*, 186
Helios Electric Co.: and Philco, 213
Hercules Gas Engine Co., 230
Hersey, Frank (photographer), 58, 125
Hersey, William: Puddle Dock, 75–76
Hershey Chocolate Corp., 223
Hershey's Kisses: war shortage, 223
Hershey's Milk Chocolate bar, 223
Hesler, Harriet H.: cookbook, 106
H-O Cereals, 208
Holt, Dorothy Grace. *See* Ober, Dorothy Grace
Holt, Herbert, 14, 29, 150
Holt, Mabel (nee Abbott), 22
Holt, Walter, 29
Home Canners Text Book, 185
home canning, 111–113, 185
Home Front Pledge Campaign, 173
Hooz, Sam: scrapyard, 30, *31*
Hormel Co., 211
How You Can Defend Your Home, 181
Howells, John Mead, 28
Hoyt, Arthur, 14, 16, 18, 21, 26, 29, 150, 152
Hoyt, Eugene, 26
Hoyt, Inez (nee Abbott), 22, 26, 32
Hoyt, Joseph, 14, 16, 18, 21, 23, 26, 29, 150, 152
Hubinger Co., 164

Imperial Co.: sewing table, 152

Jackson, Kenneth (historian), 75
Japanese-Americans and WWII, 53
Jell-O Co.: and Postum Co., 212
Jell-O Gelatin, *203*, 212

Jewish community, Portsmouth, 31–32
Johnston and Murphy Shoes, 43
Jolaine Pubs., 181
Jones, Etta May, 22
Junior Aircraft Warning Service Kit, 180

Kaiser, Henry J.: shipyards, 38
Kiene, Julia, 184
Kleenex Tissues advertisement, 42
Knight, George P., 22
Knox, Charles B.: gelatin, 193
Koerner, H.: Artists for Victory, 174
Kool-Aid packaging, *154*
Kraft Foods, 192
Krug, J. A. (chairman, WPB), 91

Lamour, Dorothy, 44; visit to Portsmouth, *44*
Latinos and WWII, 52–53
Libby, McNeill and Libby, 121, 133
Liberson's Market, 31
Library of Congress, photos from, 154
Little Corner Store, *2, 6, 20, 23*, 25–27, 29–30, *118*, 124, 135, *146, 147, 148, 149*, 150, *156*; closing, 32; children and, 157; displays, 197, 228; extending credit, 129; furnishings, 154–157, 204; gas rationing and, 41, 128; population served, 31, 32; profitability, 32; rationing and price controls and, 32, 39; restoration, 9, 11, 12, 142, 144, 157–158; sign, *156*; social function of, 130, 156–157
Little Golden Books, 179
Lucky Strike cigarettes, 42

M & M Bakeries, 195–196
M & M bread, 195–196, *201*
M & M candies, 222
M and M cream doughnuts, *195*
Manchester, New Hampshire, 60, 65
Mansfield, Harvey C. (historian), 82
Manwarring, T. E., 95
Marcus, Stanley (fashion retailer), 40
Marden, James (mastmaker), 24, 150–151
Marden-Abbott House, 2, 22, 23, 24, 25, 32, 144, *145, 149*
Marden Mast Yard, 24
Marquette, Joseph: M & M Bakeries, 195
Mars, Inc., 222
Marshmallow Fluff, 167
mass media: government cooperation, 67
Maxwell House Coffee, 194, 210
May, Ralph (historian), 69
Mayo, Capt. Chester G., 28
McCurdy, Col. William, 230
McIntosh, Jim: reproduction boxes, 155
McLaughlin, J. J.: Canada Dry, 225
McManus, Patrick H.: M & M Bakeries, 195
Milky Way candy bar packaging, 222
minorities and WWII, 50–53
Minute Plain Unflavored Gelatin, 193
Minute Tapioca Co., 193
Model Tobacco, 166
Montgomery Ward Catalogue, 222, 223
Morley, —.: poster design, 177
Morley Company, 59, *60*, 91–92

Morse, Elizabeth, 159, 160, 161, 165
Mott's Prune Juice: radio show, 121
movie industry and WWII, 46, 174
Moxie sign, 166
Mueller's macaroni, *168*
music and WWII, 43, 46, 47, 48, 49, 113–114

NAACP, 50
Natl. Archives photo collection, 154
Natl. Assoc. of Retail Grocers, 134
Natl. Biscuit Co. (Nabisco), 228
Natl. Cash Register Co.: cash register, *153*
Natl. Defense Advisory Comm. (NDAC), 81
Natl. Gypsum Co., 59
Natl. Nutrition Conference for Defense, 113
Natl. War Labor Board (NWLB), 37, 39
New England Confectionery Co. (NECCO), 224
New Hampshire Retail Grocers' Assoc., 154
New Hampshire Society for the Prevention of Cruelty to Animals, 72
New Hampshire State Council of Defense, 57, 67, 174
New Hampshire State Planning and Development Commission, 49
99th Pursuit Squadron, 51
novels, WWII, 47, 178
Nutting, Wallace: photographs by, 151
Nylander, Jane, 12, 13, 147, 149

Ober, Dorothy Grace (nee Holt), 14, 16, 18, 29, 150
Office of Civilian Defense, 67, 181
Office of Censorship, 46
Office of Economic Stabilization (OES) posters, *175, 198*
Office of Price Administration (OPA): education, 90, 91, 106, 120; establishment of, 81; food availability, *89*, 112–113, 119, 188, 213; price controls, 37, 39, *40, 96*, 96–98, 99, 100; rationing, 39, 83–84, *85*, 86, 88, 234
Office of Scientific Research and Development (OSRD), 45
Office of War Information (OWI): education, 120; films, 46; and the media, 46, 123–124, packaging photos, 154; posters, *41, 80, 83, 104, 173, 174, 182, 199*; publications, 89
Oh Henry! candy bar packaging, *168*
Old Colony Black Pepper Substitute, 190
Old Colony Packing Co., 190
Old Dutch Cleanser, 163, 167
Overseer of the Poor, Portsmouth, 26–27, 76
Owens-Illinois, 194, 206
Oxford Paper Co., 219
Oxydol detergent, 160, 216

P and G Soap, 214, 215
Pacific Coast Borax Co., *160, 164*
Pall Mall cigarettes, *202*, 220
Palmolive Bath Beads, 162
Pannaway Manor, Portsmouth, 48, 75, 99
Parkay margarine, 192
Patch, Garland, 61
Pemberton, Dr. John Styth, 226
Pento's Market, Portsmouth, 32

People's Market, Portsmouth, 85, 125
Pepperidge Farms, 110
Perkins Products Co.: Kool-Aid, *154*
Petroleum Administration, 81
Philadelphia Storage Battery Co., 231
Philco Corp., 231
Pierce, Ike, *62*
Planning Dept., Portsmouth, 65, 66, 76
Portsmouth, New Hampshire: aerial view, *59*;
    civic organizations, 70–72; development and
    growth, 23–24, 27, 30; ethnic neighborhoods,
    31–32; housing problems, 60, 65–66, 74–75;
    maps, *22, 24, 28, 65*; religious organizations,
    73–74; street views, 27, 30, 31; transporta-
    tion problems, 41–42, 66; wartime
    production in, 38, 58–60; wartime volun-
    teers, 60–61, 67–69
Portsmouth Chamber of Commerce, 44, 54, 72
Portsmouth Council of Defense, 61, 62–63, 66,
    67–70
Portsmouth Herald, The (newspaper), 47, 49,
    68, 69, 76, 84, 85, 88, 98, 190
Portsmouth Naval Shipyard: employment at,
    39, 41, 58, 99; impact on Puddle Dock, 23,
    30–31, 62, 64; visit by FDR, 57; prison, 196;
    war production, 31, 38
Pocket Books, 178
Post, Charles W.: Post Products, 209–210
Post, Marjorie Merriweather, 210
Post Office, U.S., 72–73, 182
Postum Cereal Beverage, 209, *210*
Prem luncheon meat, 94
Prescott, Josephine: Prescott Park, 27
Prescott, Mary: Prescott Park, 27
Prescott Park, 27
President's Comm. on Fair Employment
    Practices (FEPC), 51
price controls, *40*, 95–100
Price Control Board, Portsmouth, 83, 84, 98, 99
Pridham, Joe, *62*
Pridham, Zeke, *62*
print media and WWII, 41, 42, 47, 109, 130, 224
Procter, Willliam, 213
Procter and Gamble Co., 94, 213, 214, 215, 216
Puddle Dock, 21, *22,* 23, *24,* 27–28; businesses,
    23, 24, 27, 30, 31; demographics, 31, 62, *63,*
    75–76; gardens, 27–28; housing values, 64;
    neighborhood grocers, 31–32, 86, 128, 142;
    salvage business, 23, 30; V-mail to, 182; and
    WWII, 30, 32, 60–62, 64, 134

Quick Elastic Starch, *164*

radio and WWII, 47, 69, 113, 115, 216
Ration Board, Portsmouth, 83
ration books and coupons, 83–87, *88, 127*
rationing, 39–41, 82–87, 88–91, 107, 120–121,
    128, 189
reconversion, 99–100
Red Cross, 51, *73*
Redden, Alvin F., 82
Republic P-47 Thunderbolt aircraft, 230
Reston, James B., 178
Revenue Act of 1942, 44
Richardson's Supermarket, Portsmouth, 140

R. J. Reynolds Co.: and Nabisco, 228
Rochester Inst. of Technology, Center for Imag-
    ing Science, 167
Rockwell, Norman, 115, 125, 126
Roosevelt, Eleanor, 181; margarine tax, 109
Roosevelt, Pres. Franklin D., 37, 57, *58,* 80, 81,
    113, 115, 174
Rowe, Stewart (Mayor of Portsmouth), 69
Rudkin, Henry, 110
Rudkin, Margaret: Pepperidge Farm, 110
Runyon, Everett: Del Monte Foods, 131

Schlaiki, —: poster design, 180
Seacoast Defense Area, 59–60
Sears-Roebuck Co., 230, 232–233
7-Eleven, 132–133
Seven Keys to Victory Campaign, 175
761st Tank Battalion, 51
Servel Electrolux Gas Refrigerator, 230
Servel Inc., 230, 231
Sheaffer Pen Co., 183
Simon and Schuster: Pocket Books, 178
Skilton, Louisa Pryor, cookbook, 106, 114–115
Skrip Ink, 183, *200*
Smart, Ethel (Portsmouth grocer), 31, 62, *131*
Smart's Market, Portsmouth, 31, 32, 131
Smith, Herman L., 82, 98
Smith-Connelly Labor Act, 39
Smith, Day and Co., 232, 233
Snickers candy bar packaging, 222
Solid Fuels Admin. for War (SFAW), 234
Somersworth Foundry Co., 236
Somersworth Machine Co., 236
Sonoco Products, 217
Spam luncheon meat, 211
Sparta Gas Engine Co., 230
Spry packaging, *92,* 94
Standard Brands: seminars, 195
State Defense Councils, 82
State Fuels Admin., 234
Stetson Hat Co. advertisement, 42
Stickney and Poor's spices, 39
Stock, Frederic W., 195
Strawbery Banke, Inc., 8–9, 144, 149, *150, 161*
Supermarket Game, 133
Swift and Co., 36, 94, 191–192
Swift's Allsweet Vegetable Oleomargarine, 191
Swift's Brookfield Butter, 191
Swift's brands of beef, *36*

Tillman and Bendel Co., 187
Thurber, Bernice: Marden House, 32
Thurber, Morris: Marden House, 32
Treasury Dept., U.S., posters, 174
Treet luncheon meat, 211
Tropical Bar (Hershey), 223
Troy, William A: package design, 217
Truman, Pres. Harry S., 74, 100
Twenty Mule Team Borax packaging, 159,
    160, 164

Uneeda Bakers display, *204,* 228
USO, 51, 59, 70
Utility Repair Squad, 61

V-Black Ink, 183
Vance, Ethel, 178
Vick Chemical Co., 218
Vicks Vapo Rub, *200,* 218
Vicks Va-tro-nol, *200,* 218
Victory Brand Imitation Chocolate Concen-
    trated Extract, 190
Victory Extract Manufacturing Co., 190
Victory Gardens, *29,* 43–44, 79, 110; govern-
    ment program, 88, 90, 124, 177
V-Mail, 73, 182

Wait, Pearl B.: Jell-O Co., 212
Walden, Keith: window displays, 132
Walker and Co., 234
Walker Coal bag, *234*
Walker Coal Yard, *235*
War Advertising Council, 123–124
war bonds, 44, 45
War Food Admin., 81; education, 124, 173, 177,
    198; and grocers, 119; restrictions, 93, 214
War Manpower Comm. (WMC), 37
War Production Board (WPB), 37, 81; educa-
    tion, 174, 176, *199*; packaging restrictions,
    91–95, 99, 217, 232; and rationing, 42–43,
    188, 194, 213, 234
Ware, Caroline F., 96–97
Warshaw Collection, National Museum of
    American History, 154
Washburn Crosby Co., 207
Weir, Walter: advertising, 123
Wentworth Acres, Portsmouth, 48, 65–66, 99
Wessel, Stanley and Co., 182
Western Electric: military contracts, 229
Western Publishing Co., 179
Westinghouse Electric and Manufacturing Co.,
    108, 184, 226
Wheaties, 207
WHEB (Portsmouth radio station), 69, 231
Whitman Publishing Co., 179
Wickard, Claude R., 84
Widtsoe, Leah: cookbook, 190
Will and Baumer Co., 237
William Walthe Co., 216
Winebaum's News Shop, *100*
Wings Cigarettes, *202,* 221
women and WWII, 36, 43, 48–50, 60–61
Women's Christian Temperance Union, 71
Woodward, Orator Francis, 212
World War II, U.S. mobilization, 37, 38; con-
    sumerism and, 40; employment and, 38–39,
    48–49; industry and, 38; medical community
    and, 72; minorities and, 50–53; rationing
    and, 39–41, 43; shortages, 40–41, social
    problems, 48–49; transportation problems,
    41–42; women and, 48–50
Wyeth Inc. advertisement, 218

Young Americans Paint Book, 179
YMCA war effort, 71, 72
YWCA war effort, 70–71

Zeidman's Scrap Yard, Portsmouth, 30